SOVIET DISSIDENTS

Their Struggle for Human Rights

by

JOSHUA RUBENSTEIN

WILDWOOD HOUSE
LONDON

ISBN 0 7045 3062 7

Printed and bound in The United States of America

First published in Great Britain 1981

Wildwood House Limited
1 Prince of Wales Passage
117 Hampstead Road
London NW1 3EE

Published in arrangement with Beacon Press,
Boston, Massachusetts

(hardcover) 9 8 7 6 5 4 3 2 1

Portions of this book first appeared in *Canto*, Volume 1, Number 4 (1977-78), reprinted by permission of the publisher, Realforms Co., Inc.; the *Columbia Journalism Review*, Volume XVII, Number 3, September/October 1978; and *Moment Magazine*, Volume 1, Number 3, September 1975.

Grateful acknowledgment is made for permission to quote from: *To Build a Castle: My Life as a Dissenter* by Vladimir Bukovsky, copyright © 1978 by Novelpress S.a.r.l., English translation copyright © 1978 by Viking Penguin Inc., reprinted by permission of Viking Penguin Inc.; *Russia's Underground Poets*, selected and translated by Keith Bosley, with Dimitry Pospielovsky and Janits Sapiets, © 1968 Possev-Verlag, V. Gorachek KG, English translation © 1968 Keith Bosley, Dimitry Pospielovsky, reprinted by permission of Holt, Rinehart and Winston and Longmans, Green & Co., Ltd.; *Selected Poems by Yevgeny Yevtushenko*, translated by Robin Milner-Gulland and Peter Levi, copyright, ©, 1961, by Robin Milner-Gulland and Peter Levi, reprinted by permission of E. P. Dutton; *The Current Digest of the Soviet Press* for the quotation from "The Heirs of Stalin" by Yevgeny Yevtushenko; *In Quest of Justice*, edited by Abraham Brumberg, © 1970 by Praeger Publishers, Inc., reprinted by permission of Holt, Rinehart and Winston and Pall Mall Press; *Uncensored Russia* by Peter Reddaway, copyright © 1972 by Peter Reddaway, used with the permission of the author and McGraw-Hill Book Company; *Red Square at Noon* by Natalia Gorbanevskaya, 1972, translated by Alexander Lieven, with an introduction by Harrison Salisbury, copyright © 1970 by Edition Robert Laffont S.A., copyright © 1972 by Andrei Deutsch Limited, reprinted by permission of Holt, Rinehart and Winston Publishers; Random House for quotations from *To Defend These Rights* by Valery Chalidze, translated by Guy Daniels, 1974; Rose Styron from her adaptation of "Babi Yar" by Yevgeny Yevtushenko, from *Poets on Street Corners*, edited by Olga Carlisle, Random House, Inc., 1968; Universe Books for quotations from *The Last Exodus* by Leonard Schroeter, 1974; copyright © 1973 Original Russian, Les Editeurs Réunis, Paris, copyright © English translation by Vallentine, Mitchell & Co., Ltd., from the book *Prison Diaries* by Edward Kuznetsov, translated by Howard Spier, reprinted with permission of Stein and Day Publishers and Vallentine, Mitchell & Co., Ltd., London; and the poem by Bella Akhmadulina about Andrei Sakharov, © 1980 by The New York Times Company, reprinted by permission.

For my friends, my family and my colleagues
in Amnesty International

ACKNOWLEDGMENTS

MANY PEOPLE helped and encouraged me to complete this book. In particular, I would like to thank: Lyuda Alexeeva, Ed Kline, Mark Kuchment, and Shomer Zwelling for reading the manuscript and offering invaluable suggestions; Tom Walter, my editor at Beacon Press, for his confidence in the project; and Susan Jo Gardos, the librarian of the Russian Research Center at Harvard University, for her patient assistance.

Finally, I could not have conceived or completed this book without the love and encouragement of my friends. Their contribution has been the most telling of all.

FOREWORD

Numbers do not count. If the strength of the Soviet dissident movement were measured by census figures these lines would not be written; this book would not be published; the KGB would be dozing comfortably, secure in knowledge that all was safe within the realm.

No one has attempted to compile an accurate estimate of how many amongst the 260,000,000 citizens of the U.S.S.R. consider themselves or are considered by the authorities to be "dissidents." In fact, the term dissident is not included in Soviet police statistics. Oh, they know a dissident when they see one; or read his mail or search his rooms. They simply do not use that term nor recognize that category in the criminal code.

But to put it another way: were there only *one* dissident in the Soviet Union that would be too many according to the concept under which the country is governed and ruled by the Communist party. In this, the sixty-fifth year since Vladimir Lenin carried out his coup d'état on November 7, 1917, which put his Bolsheviks in power in Russia, the existence of one dissident constitutes an affront to the state ideology, for the received doctrine is that the Soviet Union is a paradise created by the workers in the image of the dreams of Marx and Lenin. To dissent from that can be an act only of insanity or treason.

This is the iron maiden which crushes Moscow between its rigid ideal and the real world in which people hate their government, find Soviet society oppressive, and wish to change it — or at least speak their minds.

That is why dissent in the Soviet Union is not going away, is not going to vanish, is there to stay and will persist whether it speaks with one voice or a thousand. There is no cure for it except in the unlovely words of Nikita Khrushchev, spoken to the sculptor Ernst Neizvestny during a famous confrontation at an exhibition of young artists at the Manège hall. Neizvestny's war wounds left him slightly hunched. "As the saying goes," observed Khrushchev, "only the grave will cure the hunchback."

Yevgeny Yevtushenko sprang to the defense of Neizvestny, but Khrushchev's words still dangle as a metaphor of the only way in which dissent can be suppressed in the Soviet Union, that is, in Stalin's way, by death, by prison, by the forced labor camp.

In the 25 years in which Stalin ruled Russia there was no effective dissent against the regime. No one raised his voice. If a poet like Osip Mandelstam did dare to write that Stalin's "fingers [are] fat as grubs," Stalin might toy with him for a year or two but eventually Mandelstam died in the frigid prisoner land of the east and was buried in an unmarked grave. If an old friend or a relative of Stalin's expressed a timid dissent, he vanished into the Lubyanka cellars, never to emerge. The lines were precise, clear, finite. Once, walking away from Dynamo stadium after a football match, I saw people suddenly start to scurry down the street. They were hurrying to get out of earshot of a drunken fan, rolling down the way, cursing Stalin in a loud voice. People didn't even want to *hear* dissent. That alone might cost them their lives or their careers.

One must match today's Russia against yesterday's, the Russia of Khrushchev and Brezhnev against Stalin's, to get the full force and flavor of the meaning of dissent. The fact that it is even possible now to lift your voice in the Soviet Union is a great advance. The fact that there is, relatively, so little dissent and that it is repressed so rigorously is a measure of the enormous distance yet to be traveled.

Joshua Rubenstein emphasizes the role of writers and poets in the early manifestations of dissent. That is right and proper. It is always the poets with their sensitivity who speak first. Every revolution has been heralded by the poets, even the American, which may have been the least poetic of uprisings. Surely the poets of Russia's 20th Century were the harbingers of the events consummated in 1905 and 1917. Andrei Bely prefigured the Russian Revolution as surely as Yeats the Irish. It was the poets, the old surviving poets like Pasternak and Ehrenburg and Berggolts, who prefigured the post-Stalin thaw. And it was the glorious new poets, the Yevtushenkos, the Bella Akhmadulinas, the Andrei Voznesenskys, and the Joseph Brodskys, who picked up the call and carried it to the new generations. None of this could have happened under Stalin. The survival of men like Pasternak and Ehrenburg into the next era was, as Ehrenburg once said, merely the luck of the draw.

The post-literary development is one to which we devote our current attention, the rise of the movement which is symbolized by such diverse men as Andrei Sakharov and Aleksandr Solzhenitsyn, by younger figures like Valery Chalidze, Pavel Litvinov, Alexander Ginzburg, the remarkable Natalya Gorbanevskaya, Yuri Galanskov, Benjamin Levich, Father Gleb Yakunin, and too many others to list.

Each of these men and women is an individual. Each dissents from a different social, political, and moral vision. There is no real "dissident movement" and that is its strength and its weakness. The dissidents come together from a hundred directions, the religious, the legalists, the ethnic spokesmen, the writers, the scientists, the poets, the workers, the housewives, the Balts, the Georgians, the Crimean Tartars, the Ukrainians, the Kazakhs. They are young and old; they represent Moscow and Leningrad and unknown villages in the Urals. If they could be gathered in one room they would create a shouting match such as has never been heard before. They disagree among themselves on everything except for the right to be heard freely in their homeland.

Some wish to leave the Soviet. Some can only be moved out by force, like Solzhenitsyn and Brodsky. Some wish to reform the system, like Zhores Medvedev and his brother, Roy. Some, like the Medvedevs, take Vladimir Lenin as their icon and trace Russia's trouble to deviations from his ideals. Others, like Solzhenitsyn, see Lenin as the source of the evil.

They are a diverse and unruly band, the dissidents. Time and again the police have thought they had put them down. They have shipped a hundred, two hundred, three hundred activists out of the country and sent even more to the labor camps. They have permitted hundreds of thousands of Jews (whom they regard, a priori, as a class, as dissenters or potential dissenters) to leave the Soviet Union. Several tens of thousands of ethnic Germans have been repatriated to West Germany. Armenians have gotten permission to leave.

The greatest names in dissent have been dealt with. That is, Solzhenitsyn was compelled to go abroad where from his Vermont home he continues to write and speak with devastating impact on the rulers of his homeland. The remarkable physicist Andrei Sakharov has been exiled to the Volga river city of Gorky. Every kind of difficulty is put in the way of his continuing to play a public role. Yet through the courage and faith of his wife, family, and friends, his clear voice continues to be heard by the people of his country and of the West.

The lesson is plain. Russia is suffering from a disease for which her rulers have no cure. It is a disease called lack of freedom, and 64 years of propaganda, prison, regimentation, exhortation, pressure, and censorship have not cured it.

There can be no more joyful tidings for America. The Soviet experience has proved once again what the faint-hearted so long have doubted. The instinct for liberty and freedom, for truth and justice, is far more strongly rooted in humanity than dictators and the "engineers of human souls" have recognized. Its outward manifestations can be suppressed by terror, as Stalin suppressed them in Russia, as Hitler suppressed them in Germany, as lesser authoritarian and militaristic rulers manage to do. But the spirit survives. At the slightest chance it pushes through the pavement like new grass in spring. The doomsayers who tell us that democracy cannot stand up to the challenge of dictatorship possess blinkered eyes. Russia's dissidents tell us that hope cannot be quenched while man lives. It is a lesson we should engrave in our hearts.

HARRISON E. SALISBURY

INTRODUCTION

INDIVIDUALS make history. Under dictatorships, they choose to conform or to rebel, sometimes through overt acts of violence. Under Joseph Stalin, official terror in the Soviet Union reached such massive and arbitrary dimensions that few people dared to express—even to family and close friends—their disbelief in and hatred for the Supreme Leader. After Stalin's death, his heirs reduced the level of repression. Independent voices emerged, like grass growing through the cracks in cement.

This book is about those blades of grass.

Individuals chose to defend friends, values, and ideas. Under Khrushchev, several writers asserted that artists should have greater creative independence. Under Brezhnev, an increasing number of people objected to the regime's abuse of human rights. These people were called dissidents in the West. Though they faced a common enemy, the dissidents themselves represented a broad range of interests and conflicts within Soviet society.

This book does not attempt to describe all the significant groups of dissenters that coalesced during Brezhnev's rule. *Soviet Dissidents* focuses on events and personalities of the democratic movement in Moscow. Petitions and demonstrations there served as an example for numerous other groups—Lithuanian Catholics, Ukrainian nationalists, Crimean Tatars,

Georgians, Armenians, ordinary workers, Baptists, and Pentecostals — whose struggles are barely touched on in this book. The scope and purpose of my research could not permit inquiry into all the expressions of dissent just mentioned. The Jewish emigration movement also was inspired, in large part, by the activity of the dissidents in Moscow. Because of close personal links between Zionists and democrats, the availability of first-hand testimony and evidence, and my own personal interest, *Soviet Dissidents* also describes the relationship between these two movements.

My approach has been to explore the origins and development of dissent through the lives of important activists. Most of the information assembled in this book came from interviews with dissidents who have immigrated to Europe, Israel, and the United States, and from *samizdat* material, especially the *Chronicle of Current Events*. Based on this information, I chose personalities, events, and themes that appeared essential for understanding how the dissidents work and what they hope to achieve. My hardest task has been to decide which trial, appeal, or demonstration to include and which ones did not fit into my narrative.

I also tried to approach the dissidents as individuals. The human rights movement in general does not attract ordinary, cautious citizens. Given its obvious risks, it is not surprising that the movement includes people with eccentric qualities. Dissidents are also vulnerable to personality traits common to their society. Life in the Soviet Union breeds suspicion, even paranoia. For the dissidents, everyday problems are compounded by KGB harassment. (Vladimir Bukovsky used to walk about Moscow and, looking at the faces of other pedestrians, wonder how they would behave under interrogation.) Almost always deprived of their professional work, dissidents must still support themselves and their children. They find menial jobs or free-lance work as typists, translators, or bookbinders. They shop like ordinary citizens, standing in line for hours to buy necessities. Only afterward is there time to type *samizdat*, collect signatures, meet journalists, or visit the families of political prisoners. Emigration, for many, is not only a means of escape from a regime but an alternative to their difficult, exhausting life.

I hope that my book does justice to their struggle and their sacrifice.

JOSHUA RUBENSTEIN
CAMBRIDGE, MASSACHUSETTS
JANUARY 1980

CONTENTS

1

REFREEZING THE THAW

THE PASSING of a dictator marks the end of one era and the onset of another. Nothing can remain completely the same, even when the regime survives. For Soviet leaders, the death of Joseph Stalin on March 5, 1953, immediately generated a dilemma they have yet to resolve: how to place Stalin himself in Soviet history.

Stalin maintained total control of the Soviet regime for nearly twenty-five years. His opponents, both real and imagined, were destroyed. Not only intellectuals and so called kulaks (a large group among the peasants who owned a bit more land and livestock than their neighbors; they were suppressed during the period of forced collectivization between 1929 and 1932, resulting in the death of nearly five million people) but several ethnic minorities, large numbers of workers, religious believers, and a significant portion of the Communist party itself were decimated. In *The Gulag Archipelago*, Alexander Solzhenitsyn recounts innumerable episodes of arrests. The police in some cities were obliged to fulfill a quota and often rounded up groups of people arbitrarily. Solzhenitsyn describes the labor camps as a "sewage disposal system" whose pipes sometimes strained to near bursting. At Stalin's death, millions of people were still detained in prisons and labor camps. Their fate, too, had to be decided.

Although Stalin wreaked havoc on the population, one of the most perplexing aspects of his regime was the popularity and overwhelming awe he commanded. In his memoir, *To Build a Castle*, Vladimir Bukovsky, one of the most active dissidents in the 1960s, recalls how "enormous unorganized crowds streamed through the streets to the Hall of Columns, where Stalin lay in state. There was something awe-inspiring about these immense, silent, gloomy masses of people. The authorities hesitated to try to curb them and simply blocked off some of the side streets with buses and trucks, while the waves of people rolled endlessly on. . . . This vast procession continued for several days." As a boy of ten, Bukovsky mourned Stalin's death as "something terrible and irreparable." When life returned to normal, when adults went to work and children to school, he felt bewildered. "Hadn't God died, without whom *nothing* was supposed to take place?"

Under Stalin, dissent could not be expressed publicly. But as we know now from those who survived his labor camps, myriad groups of people — students, Marxists, Party members — shared their thoughts with one another, were betrayed, and then imprisoned. The classics of nineteenth-century Russian literature provoked a moral awakening in many people. Even the works of Marx and Lenin, which everyone was encouraged to read, can bring the realization that Stalin's or his successors' speeches did not conform with the reality of Soviet life.

Shortly after the war, in 1946, a student named Victor Krasin — who later became an important figure among the activist intellectuals in Moscow — began to meet with a group of his friends once a week to discuss literature and philosophy. One member of the group had lost his parents. He lived alone in a room, an unusual circumstance, for at that time

Moscow was experiencing a severe housing shortage. It was common for whole families to share a room similar to the one he had to himself.

The young people discussed what they were learning in school. They also scoured used-book stores that were stocked with libraries people had sold during the war. Krasin bought a complete set of Friedrich Nietzsche, in Russian, that had been published before the Revolution. Old editions of Dostoevsky were available too, although he was not studied in school and was referred to only as a reactionary writer. Krasin and his friends also came across copies of the New Testament, works by Schopenhauer and of Indian philosophy, and other books that rarely, if ever, appear in the Soviet Union.

It was a paradoxical situation. In the country at large there was a growing terror, first against leading cultural figures and then against the Jews. The writers Anna Akhmatova and Mikhail Zoshchenko were denounced in the press, then expelled from the Writers' Union. During this same period Krasin and his friends maintained a free discussion group. Artists talked about their work, poets read their verse. They were young and naïve, still teenagers, not at all suspicious of the occasional stranger who joined them.

At the beginning of 1948, the secret police learned of the group's activities and sent an informer to gather information. He was older than the members of the group, a war veteran who had fought the Germans. For nearly a year, he supplied information to the secret police, reporting on the group's discussions of philosophy and art. Gradually, though, he grew ashamed of his work and one day revealed himself to two of the young people; he wanted to discontinue his activities and sought their advice. They suggested he write a letter to his superiors, declaring that all his previous reports were false. Ten days later, seven of the young people were arrested. Victor Krasin and the informer were among them.

At the time of his arrest, in January 1949, Krasin was

nineteen years old, a student of philosophy at Moscow State University. He was kept in jail during the investigation. The long hours of interrogation always began at night and lasted until the morning. During the day the prisoners were not allowed to sleep. If a prisoner dozed off, a guard immediately woke him. If he dozed a second time, he was taken to solitary confinement. Tired and disoriented, often beaten, many prisoners broke down and offered confessions. No one was ever acquitted. Krasin received eight years in the labor camps.

He was sent to a place near Bratsk, in Siberia, where prisoners worked on construction sites. He tried to escape in a group of five prisoners, but soldiers caught up with them in the taiga. Ten years were added to Krasin's sentence, and he was transferred to Kolyma, in the far northeast part of the country near the Arctic Circle.

He spent four years in Kolyma.* At the time, about half a million prisoners inhabited a region that covered thousands of kilometers. Most of them worked in gold mines or at other forms of hard labor. No exact figures are available, but in Kolyma, during the years of Stalin's rule, about three million prisoners perished, mostly from the freezing temperatures, the work, and the lack of nourishment. But Krasin and his friends were lucky. They survived and later were released.

Stalin's death brought immediate changes. Within months of his passing, articles began appearing that raised long-suppressed ideas about art and culture. By allowing the articles to be published, the regime hoped to reassure the country's intellectuals that Stalin's successors would not continue his strict regulation of the arts. The new leaders also had to assert their own legitimacy and needed the coopera-

---

*See Robert Conquest, *Kolyma: The Arctic Death Camps* (Viking, New York, 1978). Through reports of former prisoners and other useful sources, Conquest is able to estimate the number of prisoners who passed through the region and to document the horror they experienced.

tion of writers to promote the regime's policies. So there was a relaxation in the control of literature.

The poet Olga Berggolts defended lyrical poetry, insisting on the poet's right to strike an individual and personal mood. Ilya Ehrenburg, one of the country's most prominent writers at home and abroad, suggested that creative artists be allowed greater freedom and that passion and spontaneity be encouraged. Ehrenburg's essay "On the Role of the Writer" defended the autonomy of the artist:

> An author is not a piece of machinery. An author writes a book not because he knows how to write, not because he is a member of the Union of Soviet Writers and may be asked why he has published nothing for so long. An author writes a book because he must tell people something of himself, because he is "sick" with his book, because he has seen people, things and emotions that he cannot help describing.

Soon after, the critic Vladimir Pomerantsev challenged the monopoly of the Writers' Union. Although not directly attacking the tenets of "socialist realism," Pomerantsev pleaded for "sincerity in literature" and blamed the official, cultural bureaucracy for stifling genuine talent. As Pomerantsev observed, "I have heard that Shakespeare was not a member of a union at all, yet he did not write badly."

The regime tolerated this discussion for a time, especially during the months following Stalin's death, when articles in many journals criticized Party attitudes toward culture. Most of the liberal writers contributed to *Novy Mir* (New World), a monthly literary magazine whose editor, Alexander Tvardovsky, sympathized with their views. This period became known as "the thaw," after Ehrenburg's novel of the same name.

It was to be short-lived. By January 1954, the regime and its conservative spokesmen took the offensive. Pomerantsev was criticized for turning "the reader's attention to consideration chiefly of the dark, unwelcome sides of our reality." Several poets, like Olga Berggolts and Margarita Aliger, were censured for emphasizing the virtues of personal, subjective feelings. Finally, *Novy Mir*, too, came under pressure. Editor in chief Alexander Tvardovsky was dismissed and replaced by Konstantin Simonov, a popular Soviet novelist.

A makeshift pattern was established that would last throughout Nikita Khrushchev's years in power. Unwilling to invoke Stalin's methods of control, Khrushchev tolerated a certain degree of discussion until pleas for greater freedom of expression overstepped the boundaries and led inevitably to areas reserved for official comment. Sometimes liberals would be heartened by the publication of their articles, but then the conservatives would take the initiative. Both liberals and conservatives vied for control of the artists' unions. Although each group gained small successes, ultimate control never extended far from Khrushchev himself.

Nonetheless, under Nikita Khrushchev the regime took an enormously significant and irreversible step: it began to release political prisoners. From 1954 to 1959, between seven and eight million people returned from labor camps, prisons, and Siberian exile, with stories of torture and slave labor. Many were now angry, determined opponents of the regime. Some who had been staunch Marxists retained faith in the Revolution and the Communist party, holding Stalin responsible for their personal misfortune and the betrayal of what they understood to be Lenin's ideals.

Khrushchev realized the government had to respond to the new mood of the country. People expected a more secure and prosperous life. They needed assurance that brutality and arbitrary terror would not be applied again by their rulers. For Khrushchev there seemed no better way to gain the confidence of the population than by dissociating himself and the Party from Stalin.

Khrushchev denounced the "cult of personality" at the Twentieth Party Congress in February 1956. He spoke for more than five hours to a closed session of Party members, concentrating on the arrest and murder of loyal Communists and ignoring the suffering of the general population. He recounted how even members of the Politburo feared for their lives. There was no reference to the human cost of forced collectivization or mention of Stalin's anti-Semitism. Khrushchev made it seem as if the Party was more to be pitied for what it had endured than condemned for what it had permitted and supported.

The regime could not control the discussion Khrushchev himself had begun. Too many questions begged for answers, too many answers could not be given. One anecdote involving Khrushchev is often told; the incident probably did not actually occur, but it still reflects the predominant attitude of that period. While he was on the dais at a Party meeting, someone sent a note up to him. "Where were you when all this was going on?" the message asked. Khrushchev read the note aloud and asked who wrote it. Nobody, of course, responded. "All right," said Khrushchev, "I was where you are now."

"Many people liked that answer," Vladimir Bukovsky recalls in his memoir,

> but I despised both Khrushchev and the author of the note. They both knew the truth; yet neither had the guts to say so openly. And neither of them was obliged to be in a public position where guts were needed; no one had forced them to be in that hall, so close to power.
>   How could it happen that people were still afraid to stand up? How could one man, or say ten men, seize power and keep all the rest in fear and ignorance? When did it all begin? Khrushchev seemed to think that he had explained everything, that he had given answers to all the questions. According to Khrushchev they had

got to the bottom of it, released the innocent, spoken well of the dead, and life could go on. But for us, and especially for my generation, the questions were only just beginning. We had just had time to be taught that communism was the world's most progressive doctrine and Stalin the incarnation of its ideas when presto, Stalin turned out to be a murderer and a tyrant, a terrible degenerate no better than Hitler! So what was the nature of the ideas that had produced a Stalin? What was the nature of a Party that, once having brought him to power, could no longer stop him? What difference did it make now whether they had been afraid or simply ignorant? After all, even now, when all had been revealed, they were still frightened to stand up and be counted.

Khrushchev's speech brought unrest particularly among Party members and cultural figures. Alexander Fadeyev, who had served as general secretary of the Union of Soviet Writers from 1946 to 1953, shot himself. As a union official and earlier, in the 1930s, he had approved the arrest warrants for many of his colleagues. Fadeyev himself was a complex, not wholly unsympathetic figure. He was much more than a cultural bureaucrat who proved useful to the regime. He had a genuine taste and love for literature. Ilya Ehrenburg once recalled how, after a meeting chaired by Fadeyev during which Boris Pasternak was condemned, Fadeyev invited Ehrenburg for a drink and then recited Pasternak's poetry by heart for two hours.

Fadeyev, however, loved the exercise of power. He may not have taken the initiative to condemn the writers whose arrest warrants he signed, but he signed them nonetheless. No one knows the exact reason for his suicide. Yuri Kratkov, a Soviet journalist who defected to the West in the 1960s, reported that after Stalin's death one imprisoned writer returned to Moscow. This writer, whose identity Kratkov withheld, denounced Fadeyev and then hanged himself. Kratkov believes this suicide contributed to Fadeyev's own. Other people in Moscow believe that Khrushchev's speech against Stalin frightened Fadeyev. He feared an investigation that might implicate him in Stalin's crimes. Overwhelmed with shame and fear, according to these reports, he took his own life.

Other writers took courage from Khrushchev's speech. New stories, poems, and novels appeared by writers determined to confront the reality of Soviet life.

Not by Bread Alone, a novel by Vladimir Dudintsev, became the focus of the literary struggle. (In the West it generated so much attention that it appeared in eighteen translations.) Dudintsev tells the story of a quixotic engineer, Lopatkin, who designs a machine for casting iron pipes. He works virtually alone, outside the approved and conventional framework of a collective. His machine promises to be far more efficient than one designed by a recognized authority. For years, however, his plans are denigrated while attempts are made to steal his ideas. He is even sent to a labor camp. In the end, Lopatkin survives to see his machine built and acclaimed.

Not by Bread Alone is not an elegantly written novel. The characterizations are crude, and the story takes predictable and not wholly convincing turns. But in the course of the novel Dudintsev describes a bureaucracy of total corruption, where fawning lackeys advance and honest people and genuine talent are excluded.

The novel provoked intense debate. Its literary merits and weaknesses were of little importance next to the picture of life that readers recognized. At universities and Komsomol (Young Communist League) meetings, people fiercely defended *Not by Bread Alone*, using Dudintsev's work as a means to criticize the corruption and economic backwardness of the country.

Not by Bread Alone is associated with what is remembered as the "second thaw," the period following Khrushchev's speech, when a spate of writers grasped the opportunity to extend the limits of artistic expression. Yevgeny Yevtushenko, among others, began his remarkable career at that time. His poem "Zima Station" castigated established writers for the role they had assumed.

> What is he now, a writer?
> He's not an influence, he's a custodian
> as if his thoughts were public monuments.
> Oh there are changes: but behind the speeches.
> Elsewhere from what was publicly spoken
> this nebulous exercise takes place:
> this rumination of yesterday's silence,
> and silence smothering yesterday's events.

Khrushchev's speech and the publications of the second thaw stirred excitement and hope. Russians have always used art and literature as a barometer to gauge the limits of their freedom. As the regime seemed to grow more candid about its own failings, writers felt encouraged to explore themes that, in earlier times, were strictly off limits. This second thaw, however, was also short-lived, for the Soviet occupation of Hungary in October and November of 1956 brought harsher internal measures. At the same time, many people were dismayed by their government's action. (Their anger would be far more profound and dispirited twelve years later over the invasion of Czechoslovakia.) Reports emerged of student protests in Leningrad and Moscow. Thousands of high school students were said to have been expelled.

A year later, the intellectual community was shaken by another event, the publication of Boris Pasternak's *Doctor Zhivago*. For decades, Pasternak had served as a symbol of quiet defiance to the regime. He had managed to maintain his integrity and survive, while other writers, less fortunate or less steadfast than he, were either compromised or destroyed (and sometimes both) by Stalin. But he did not survive unscathed. After the war, during the virulent attack on the arts led by Andrei Zhdanov, a close associate of Stalin who acted as his lieutenant in cultural matters, Pasternak was censured by the Writers' Union. His companion, Olga Ivinskaya, was arrested and tortured; the regime wanted her to confess that she and Pasternak were "agents of Western imperialism." The authorities knew about the novel well before publication. For some time, Pasternak had read chapters to friends and openly discussed the book and its relation to his own life. Ivinskaya's interrogator wanted her to attest that *Doctor Zhivago* was the work of a British spy. She resisted successfully but was sent to a labor camp and was not released until after Stalin's death four years later.

Ten poems from *Doctor Zhivago* appeared during the first thaw in 1954. The novel itself was completed in 1955 and circulated among numerous Soviet magazines and publishing houses. In the end none published it, although the editors of *Novy Mir* sent Pasternak a long letter, explaining why the book was unsuitable for publication. There are reports that the authorities considered publishing an abridged and censored version — which Pasternak might have accepted and which would have prevented the subsequent scandal — but nothing more definite emerged.

Pasternak also sent a copy of the manuscript to Italy, where Giangiacomo Feltrinelli, a member of the Italian Communist party and a prominent publisher, arranged for it to appear in several Western translations. Frantic efforts were made to prevent publication: Pasternak's life was said to be in danger; telegrams arrived over his signature asking that publication be stopped; Soviet and Italian Communist party leaders asked Feltrinelli to postpone releasing the novel. He refused.

Doctor Zhivago appeared in Italy on November 15, 1957. Critical reaction was varied. There was much praise, but critics raised serious reservations about its plot development and about lifeless, didactic episodes. The reviews also noted that the novel prompted important questions about Soviet life and history.

At first there was little comment in the Soviet press. Then, on October 23, 1958, the Swedish Academy awarded Boris Pasternak the Nobel Prize for literature. Two days later, Pasternak cabled his acceptance. The regime could not control its anger. Articles dubbed him "an infuriated moral freak" and "a malicious literary snob." He pointedly was advised to reject the award. The Writers' Union then expelled him. That same week, at a public gathering of fourteen thousand people in a Moscow sports stadium, with Nikita Khrushchev and other Party leaders present, the head of the Komsomol compared Pasternak to a pig "who fouled the spot where he ate and cast filth on those by whose labor he lives and breathes." The speaker added that if the writer wished to depart for "a capitalist paradise" he was free to go.

Pasternak intended to withstand this pressure. He regarded *Doctor Zhivago* as the fullest expression of his artistic and spiritual beliefs. The regime, however, threatened Olga Ivinskaya too; she lost all her work as a translator. Pasternak could not let her suffer once more on his account. On the day of the public rally, he sent a telegram to the Swedish Academy renouncing the Nobel Prize. Still, attacks on him continued. On November 1 Pasternak wrote to Khrushchev, apologizing that his book had been used for political purposes in the West. He also pleaded that he not be forced to emigrate. Four days later he abased himself further, writing in *Pravda*, the Party newspaper, that he had rejected the prize on his own initiative when he realized the award was politically motivated.

The attack on Pasternak aroused significant attention. Western intellectuals, like Graham Greene and Bertrand Russell, appealed on his behalf, as did several Communist writers, such as the Brazilian novelist Jorge Amado and the Nobel laureate from Iceland, Halldór Laxness. Inside the Soviet Union, too, several of Pasternak's colleagues objected to the regime's campaign. At the Writers' Union, some members vigorously protested his expulsion and had to be removed from the meeting. One man, who had written a calumnious article against Pasternak, was slapped in public by an outraged colleague. The cellist Mstislav Rostropovich refused to attend a public meeting where he was expected to condemn Pasternak.

By sending his novel abroad before it had been rejected by Soviet publishers, Pasternak violated an explicit taboo imposed by the regime: that the government alone has the right to cultivate contact with the West. At that time, in 1957, Russians had hardly emerged from the isolation of the Stalin years. The International Youth Festival in 1957, the first to be held in Moscow, brought thousands of young Europeans to the city. Boris Shragin, a former dissident who now lives in New York, remembers following a group of young Scandinavians about the city. He never spoke to them, but by their clothes and demeanor he recognized a sense of personal freedom and nonchalance that his own generation, born after the Revolution, lacked completely.

Russians have nurtured both envy and hostility of the West for centuries. The decades under Stalin reinforced these emotions. Russian intellectuals have always held an envious fascination for the personal and artistic freedom of the West, together with a defensive insistence on Russia's unique role in history. The regime knows how to manipulate this ambivalence. One of the privileges cultural figures receive is the occasional opportunity to travel to the West, attend conferences, perform concerts, or give poetry readings. The government can also withdraw this privilege, in response to a lack of cooperation or a loss of confidence. When Pasternak sent his book abroad, many of his colleagues were still caught in the web of this psychology. They regarded it as something vaguely unseemly, even unpatriotic, an admission that a Western audience was a legitimate alternative to the inability to publish freely in one's own country. In 1957, many Russians were not ready to accept the idea that an artist had the right to circumvent the regime's internal censorship. Within a decade, the human rights movement would completely reverse this attitude.

The government, of course, reacted even more strongly to Pasternak's defiance. For the authorities, a writer has no more right to arrange publication of his book abroad than a factory manager has to export shoes on his own initiative. After Stalin's death, numerous books and articles had appeared that raised delicate issues about life under his rule. But these were all published with the regime's permission, within a framework it hoped to control. *Doctor Zhivago* embodied an independent voice and one that provoked fundamental objections to the course of the entire Revolution. The lyrical and religious aspects of Pasternak's work also deeply affected people; among many intellectuals, interest in religion increased enormously as *Doctor Zhivago* circulated in Moscow and other big cities.

Today, however, *Doctor Zhivago* seems restrained compared to the explosive character of Solzhenitsyn's novels or the extravagant satire of Vladimir Voinovich. Khruschchev claimed in his memoirs that he was deceived by Pasternak's literary rivals into believing that *Doctor Zhivago* was a counterrevolutionary, anti-Soviet novel. Once he had a chance to read it, so the story goes, Khrushchev thought it was not so dangerous and that it should have been published, if only to avert a self-defeating scandal.

Khrushchev's effort at hindsight too strongly resembles conventional Soviet attempts to rewrite history. Zhivago's experiences during the civil war, his lack of ideological commitment, and his devotion to poetry stimulated thinking about an individual's place in society. As Zhivago states in the novel:

> The great majority of us are required to live a life of constant, systematic duplicity. Your health is bound to be affected, if, day after day, you say the opposite of what you feel, if you grovel before what you dislike and rejoice at what brings you nothing but misfortune.

In the same conversation he concluded that "men who are not free always idealize their bondage." Such sentiments did not endear the book to those who controlled literature in the Soviet Union.

The rejection letter to Pasternak from the editors of *Novy Mir* was published in the midst of the campaign against him, in 1958, two years after it was originally sent. In explaining why they could not publish the novel, the editors defined the issues in *Doctor Zhivago* which the country's intellectuals were only just beginning to perceive and discuss, and which the regime was determined to suppress. As the editors wrote to Pasternak,

> The spirit of your novel is that of nonacceptance of the socialist revolution. The general tenor of your novel is that the October Revolution, the civil war and the social transformations involved did not give the people anything but suffering and destroyed the Russian intelligentsia, either physically or morally. . . . This watershed — the year 1917 — is a dividing line between the awaited and the accomplished. Before it, your heroes were waiting for something different from what actually occurred, and beyond it came what they had not expected and did not want and what, as you depict it, led them to physical or moral death.

Only Pasternak, until then, had dared raise these issues publicly. He could not be forgiven. Just a few years after Stalin's death, the new leaders were trying to assert their legitimacy. They knew how they had come to power, and they recognized (or at least Khrushchev did) that they had to reassure the population that they were different from the tyrant they had served. *Doctor Zhivago*, they believed, sought to undermine the legitimacy of the Revolution itself and not simply point out abuses the Party ostensibly could prevent.

Gradually, the attacks on him abated. The drama, however, was not quite over. On May 30, 1960, Pasternak succumbed to cancer of the stomach. Although many members of the Party and the Writers' Union were given special assignments to keep them occupied, over a thousand people attended his burial at Peredelkino, the writers' colony outside of Moscow. His funeral was a quiet public display of reverence and defiance. The pianist Sviatoslav Richter accompanied the procession as Pasternak's coffin was carried out of his house by his sons and two young writers, Andrei Sinyavsky and Yuli Daniel. Over his open grave the mourners recited his poems as a final tribute.

Pasternak was hounded to death, but even so, the example of his courage and genius would not be forgotten. The balladeer Alexander Galich added a touch of irony to his voice when he sang of Pasternak, "We are proud that he died in his bed." For Soviet intellectuals, that was a victory in itself.

While the efforts of writers like Ilya Ehrenburg and Boris Pasternak to challenge the conventional control of literature gained considerable attention and support, there were also spontaneous attempts, primarily by young people, to create opportunities for artistic expression. The most important episode began in Mayakovsky Square in Moscow. On July 29, 1958, a statue of the poet Vladimir Mayakovsky was unveiled. After the usual speeches, several poets read their verse to the crowd, concluding the official ceremonies. Then a group of poets in the audience began reading their poetry too. The crowd reacted with enthusiasm and, as twilight approached, the group agreed to meet at the statue again.

A month later, an official newspaper announced "to the young people of Moscow" that lovers of poetry were invited to gather at Mayakovsky Square for public readings once a month. These meetings soon took place more often. Poets read their own work as well as the verse of Mayakovsky, Esenin, Yevtushenko, the martyred Gumilev, Akhmatova, and Pasternak, who was not yet under attack. After the readings, people lingered in the square, discussing what they had heard. Their talk naturally led to other topics. They spoke of philosophy, of literature and censorship; they even discussed politics. The authorities did not tolerate this open-air club for long. After several months, crowds were no longer permitted to assemble.

Other projects continued. Alexander Ginzburg knew the organizers of the Mayakovsky Square readings. Born in 1936, Ginzburg grew up under Stalin. His father was an ethnic Russian who died while Alexander was still a child. At the height of Stalin's anti-Semitic campaign, he took his mother's family name, Ginzburg, as a gesture of defiance, although to this day he is a practicing member of the Russian Orthodox church. As a teenager, he showed particular interest in poetry and the theater. He was also an accomplished athlete; in 1954, he placed first in the All-Union Youth competition in the kayak and canoe events. He also took evening courses in journalism at Moscow University. In 1957, he served on the preparatory committee for the Sixth International Youth and Student Festival and helped produce films about it. The following year, he found a job as an actor in a small theater outside of Moscow, where he worked for almost two years.

In addition, Ginzburg was interested in "unofficial" art. By the late 1950s, numerous artists in Moscow were pursuing experiments in painting. Although there was little, if any, political content to their work, the authorities were annoyed by their abstract designs. The painters themselves were isolated, and there was no place to meet or exhibit their work. Ginzburg tried to help them. He organized several exhibitions of young artists in private apartments and also began publishing a typewritten magazine, *Syntax*. This became the first *samizdat* (or self-published) journal of the post-Stalin period.

Ginzburg managed to compile three issues of *Syntax* before he was arrested. The magazine printed only verse, some by poets who already were or would become well known, among them Bulat Okudzhava, Bella Akhmadulina, and Joseph Brodsky. In general, *Syntax* expressed a pessimistic, disheartened mood. One poem by Pavel Antokolsky had been written in 1956, after Khrushchev's revelations about Stalin. Its bitterness reflects the profound disillusionment of Ginzburg's generation.

All we who in his name
Have won renown
And passed in peace the time
That now is gone
    All we, his fellows, who
    Kept silence while
    Out of our silence grew
    The greatest ill
Who of nights could not sleep
And locked our doors
When he from our own group
Made murderers
    We who dispensed sweet reason
    Bear the bloodshed
    Of jails, the trials for treason
    Upon our head.

Let our contemptuous
Sons cast the same
Stigma on each of us:
Ours is the shame.
> Those truths need not be weighed
> In any balance.
> We hate him who has died
> Less than our silence.

Ginzburg was expelled from the university in 1960, arrested, and kept in Lubyanka prison while the authorities initiated an investigation under article 70 of the Russian criminal code, which forbids "agitation or propaganda carried on for the purpose of subverting or weakening the Soviet regime." The KGB (secret police) interrogated over a hundred people but could not construct a convincing case against him. An alternative was discovered. Shortly before his arrest, he had taken an examination for a friend, switching photographs on his identity card for this purpose. Article 70 was dropped. Instead, Ginzburg was convicted for forging documents and received the maximum two-year sentence. Pavel Litvinov, a friend of Ginzburg's, has explained that friends often take examinations for each other in Moscow. Litvinov does not mean to condone this behavior, but usually, when such cases are discovered, the examination results are annulled and the offending students are embarrassed publicly, then expelled. Ginzburg, however, was sent to a labor camp.

Alexander Ginzburg was not the only compiler of unofficial verse collections. Other young people more closely connected to the readings in Mayakovsky Square were hoping to circulate new poetry magazines; Vladimir Osipov edited one issue of *Boomerang*, while Yuri Galanskov put together *Phoenix-61*. Galanskov and Osipov had come to know a wide array of people in Mayakovsky Square. Not only young poets, but scholars and artists had joined the crowds. Osipov and his friends also liked to attend official lectures and discussions and raise troublesome questions.

Soon their circle was joined by another student named Vladimir Bukovsky, who already had caught the attention of the authorities. As teenagers, he and some friends wrote satirical stories and read them aloud in school. Before long they were all punished. Bukovsky was even brought before the Moscow City Committee of the Party, reprimanded, and removed from his school. They wanted him to work in a factory—to "temper him"—but he contrived a means to enter the university. There he met new friends and together, in September 1960, they decided to start anew the readings in Mayakovsky Square. Almost immediately, large crowds gathered each weekend.

For months, the authorities tried to stop the readings. Students identified in the Square were warned or expelled from the university. Searches were conducted; *samizdat* material was confiscated. The press maligned the organizers as parasites who did not work. But this only gave the readings more publicity and the crowds grew larger.

The organizers planned an ambitious reading for April 14, 1961, the anniversary of Mayakovsky's suicide. But two days before, Yuri Gagarin made his space flight. Bukovsky, Osipov, and the others wondered whether they should go ahead with the reading, for they did not want to strike a discordant note when the streets were full of people celebrating Gagarin's achievement. Too many of their friends had been contacted, however, for them to postpone the reading. That night, an immense crowd gathered. The police also were ready. As the poet Anatoly Shchukin began to read they rushed and dragged him and Osipov to a nearby vehicle. The crowd reacted angrily, almost overturning the car. Shchukin got fifteen days "for reading anti-Soviet verses" while Osipov received ten days "for disturbing the peace and using obscene language."

Bukovsky, too, was receiving more attention. He was forced out of the university. Then, one night after a reading, he was picked up by the KGB and beaten. They warned him to stay out of Mayakovsky Square or they would kill him.

The readings became increasingly difficult to arrange. People were reluctant to come regularly; snow plows were sent into the square and let loose on the crowd. Several of the principal organizers, like Vladimir Osipov, Ilya Bakstein, and Edward Kuznetsov, were already under arrest; Bukovsky, Yuri Galanskov, Victor Khaustov, and about twenty others were interrogated on a regular basis. The readings could no longer continue and were soon officially banned.

Among the many people Bukovsky came to know during this period was the mathematician Alexander Esenin-Volpin, whom Bukovsky first met in Mayakovsky Square. The son of the poet Sergei Esenin, Volpin is often referred to as "the father of the human rights movement." By the time the two met, Volpin had been arrested several times. Under Stalin, he spent a year in a psychiatric hospital for reading a group of poems to his friends, and then he was exiled to Karaganda, in Siberia, returning to Moscow after Stalin's death three years later. During the Youth Festival in 1957 Volpin was held in a hospital for three weeks to ensure that he did not meet foreign tourists. Two years later, he sent a collection of his verse and a philosophical essay to the West with an American tourist. The book was published under the title *A Leaf of Spring*. The essay, especially, was important to him, for he was determined to explain his opposition to dialectical materialism. Again he was arrested and sent to a mental hospital, where he was diagnosed as a schizophrenic. The doctors wanted him to admit that their behavior was proper, warning him that he might have to stay a long time. Volpin refused to answer their questions. He adopted a procedural defense, insisting that the doctors (and the KGB) were violating the law by holding him. He was released after a year and returned to Moscow in February 1961.

By this time, Volpin was convinced of the need to nurture

and to demand respect for the law. After Stalin's death, his successors abolished the "special commissions," three-man tribunals that had processed millions of prisoners. Instead, the new leaders proclaimed, trials would be held in accordance with "socialist legality." Volpin, however, wondered if the trials would be genuinely open to the public. Otherwise, he feared, the reform would not provide adequate protection for the defendants.

At first, Bukovsky saw little practical use for Volpin's insistence on respect for the law. In February 1962, Ilya Bakstein, Edward Kuznetsov, and Vladimir Osipov were tried and convicted for "anti-Soviet agitation and propaganda," that is, for the readings and discussions in Mayakovsky Square. Formally, the trial was open to the public, but neither relatives nor friends were allowed into the courtroom. But Volpin was not daunted. On the day the sentences were pronounced, he showed a copy of the criminal code to the guards, convincing them that the public must be allowed to enter. Bukovsky was amazed. "Little did we realize," he would write years later, "that this absurd incident, with the comical Alik Volpin brandishing his Criminal Code like a magic wand to melt the doors of the court, was the beginning of our civil-rights movement and the movement for human rights in the USSR."

Bukovsky himself expected to be arrested at any time. KGB agents openly followed him about the city. Once he organized an exhibition for two nonconformist artists, but it lasted only ten days because the KGB pressured the apartment's tenant to close it. Bukovsky soon grew tired of waiting for his own arrest. One day he eluded the agents and boarded a train for Siberia. In Novosibirsk some friends arranged for him to join a geological expedition. He wandered over Siberia for six months, getting as far as the Chinese border.

Bukovsky returned to Moscow resigned to imprisonment. However, he remained at large for seven months, until the wife of an American correspondent lent him a copy of Milovan Djilas's *The New Class*. Rather than read it quickly, Bukovsky decided to photocopy the book and then return it. The KGB came the next morning, knowing exactly what to find. Bukovsky was not brought to trial but was kept in a mental hospital until February 26, 1965, when he was discharged to the care of his mother.

While the activity of Bukovsky and his friends at Mayakovsky Square provided contacts and experience that would later prove immensely important, there were other events within the framework of public life that also moved the country further away from its Stalinist past. In 1958 and again in 1960, the regime introduced reforms in the fields of criminal law and judicial procedure. The changes in many respects were specifically directed against the abuses that marked Stalin's rule. The death penalty was no longer the sole punishment for many crimes; it was to be used as an alternative sentence, to be applied at the discretion of the court. The maximum punishment was reduced for many crimes, and the KGB's power to carry out investigations and administrative punishment was curtailed. A new and fundamental legal principle also assured people that "justice in criminal cases shall be administered only by courts. No one may be deemed guilty of committing a crime or subjected to criminal punishment except by judgment of a court." Previous legislation, as well as the Soviet constitution of 1936, stated that justice shall be administered by the courts, but the word *only* was not included.

These legal reforms encouraged the country's writers to further expose the crimes of Stalin. In 1960, *Novy Mir* began publishing Ilya Ehrenburg's memoirs, *People, Years, Life*, providing the younger generation with an evocative account of Soviet cultural history. While the memoirs were incomplete, they still managed to raise fundamental questions about Stalinism. A year later, in September 1961, Yevgeny Yevtushenko caused a literary and political sensation with his poem "Babi Yar." Although it focused on the Nazi massacre of the Jews of Kiev, Yevtushenko complained in the opening verse that "There are no monuments on Babi Yar / A steep ravine is all, a rough memorial." The poem was a direct indictment of Soviet anti-Semitism. At poetry readings audiences recited the stanzas in unison, forcing Yevtushenko to repeat them again and again. In reaction, the Party severely rebuked the young poet, terming his politics "crudely adolescent." Khrushchev himself angrily denounced "Babi Yar," insisting that anti-Semitism had been abolished under communism.

A month later, at the Twenty-second Party Congress, Khrushchev renewed his attack on Stalin, providing new disclosures of the dictator's cruelty. During one session he even quoted a letter written by Lenin in 1922 to a forthcoming party congress, warning that "Stalin is too harsh" and should be removed from the position of general secretary. Soon after, Stalin's embalmed corpse was taken from the Lenin Mausoleum and placed beneath a concrete slab near the Kremlin wall.

Khrushchev may well have used these revelations to shore up his declining popularity and undermine his rivals for power in the Politburo. A year later, in November 1962, he took an even bolder step, personally approving the publication of Alexander Solzhenitsyn's *One Day in the Life of Ivan Denisovich* in *Novy Mir*. Solzhenitsyn's career was launched. His short novel proved to be the most explosive literary work permitted to appear in the post-Stalin period. It depicted the grim life of Soviet concentration camps and the extent of injustice in the country. Solzhenitsyn succeeded in making the labor camp system — the Gulag Archipelago, as he would later call it — represent life under Stalin, for prisoners and for those at large.

The reaction to his work was overwhelming. Hundreds of thousands of people rushed the bookstores for copies. The official press praised him. Konstantin Simonov, writing in *Izvestia*, called Solzhenitsyn "a true assistant to the Party in the sacred and necessary cause of combatting the cult of the individual and its consequences." The novel provoked a widespread longing for further disclosure. Khrushchev admitted the following year that "it is said that periodicals and publishing houses are being flooded with manuscripts about the life of people in deportation, prisons, and camps. This is a very dangerous theme." He might have added that it would no longer be tolerated.

Just a month after Solzhenitsyn's novel appeared, the Party called a meeting of four hundred writers, artists, and intellectuals. Khrushchev introduced them to Solzhenitsyn, and then Leonid Ilyichev, chairman of the Ideological Commission of the Central Committee, harangued the group for nearly ten hours. Recently published books had strained the permitted framework for public discussion. Ilyichev intended to warn the creative intellectuals and not allow them to assume that "since an end has been put to arbitrariness in our country and people are not arrested for political dissent, this means that everything is allowed and there are no restrictions on what one wishes."

At this time, there was still opportunity for genuine exchanges between the authorities and the recalcitrant writers who formed the "cultural opposition." Their discussions had a human, spontaneous dimension and were not yet the vicious circle of censorship, protest, and arrest that would characterize their relationship under Brezhnev.

One incident, in particular, will always be remembered. After Ilyichev's tirade, Yevgeny Yevtushenko defended the painters and sculptors who pursued experiments in abstract art. He assured the leadership that "formalist tendencies in their work will be straightened out in time."

Khrushchev's reply stunned the assembly. "As they say, only the grave straightens out the hunchbacked."

"I hope, Comrade Khrushchev," Yevtushenko answered, "we have outlived the time when the grave was used as a means of correction."

As the audience applauded the poet's remark, Khrushchev, too, sheepishly joined in.

Throughout the winter, the confrontation between conservative and liberal writers in Moscow continued. In February 1963, Ilya Ehrenburg was rebuked for admitting in his memoirs that while he knew many of Stalin's victims were innocent, he was compelled to be silent out of fear for his own life. The implication was clear. If Ehrenburg knew, then the country's present leaders must also have known. The issue was too delicate to be explored. Ehrenburg's accuser, Vladimir Yermilov, declared that other leaders did not know of Stalin's crimes, so they could not protest. Ehrenburg's admission, he implied, made him an accomplice.

For a time, the assault on liberal writers and the defense of the regime's cultural controls did not lead to arrests. Several writers, like the novelist Victor Nekrasov and Yevgeny Yevtushenko, were upbraided for their conduct and their work. Nekrasov was even threatened with expulsion from the Party. There was a famous incident between Khrushchev and a group of artists whose modernist paintings were on exhibit at the Manège museum in Moscow. On viewing their work, Khrushchev denounced it with the most vulgar language. In front of one he asked, "What's this one all about? It looks like the work of a child who soiled himself while his mother was out of the room and then spread it all on the floor." Turning to another painting, Khrushchev wondered whether it was not the work of a donkey who accidentally dipped its tail into a can of paint.

Far more symptomatic of the changing mood, however, was the arrest of the young poet Joseph Brodsky in December 1963. Brodsky was then twenty-three years old but already well known to the country's foremost poets for his verse and his translations. He had left secondary school and on his own learned Polish and English. He was drawn to the metaphysical poets, and today his translations of the work of John Donne are especially prized. But in 1963, Brodsky was arrested as a "parasite" and brought to trial in Leningrad.

More than two years before, in May 1961, the Supreme Soviet had issued a decree "concerning the intensification of the struggle against individuals who evade socially useful work and lead an anti-social and parasitic life." On the face of it, the decree referred to the numerous idlers who practiced petty theft and drank conspicuously on the streets. But there was an ulterior motive for the law too. The government could deprive someone with unorthodox ideas of his work and then use his lack of employment as a pretext to send him into exile.

Brodsky's supporters understood the regime's intentions and tried to help him. Efim Etkind, a teacher and anthologist of poetry, and Frida Vigdorova, a Moscow journalist, were especially active. She had numerous contacts in the country's cultural establishment. Through her efforts, three Lenin Prize winners came to Brodsky's defense: the composer Dmitri Shostakovich and the writers Samuil Marshak and Kornei Chukovsky. Letters protesting his arrest were sent to Khrushchev. Although they did not prevent his conviction, they were a novel gesture of defiance that had never been attempted under Stalin.

The trial itself proved to be an embarrassment for the regime. Near the courtroom a notice announced "The Trial of the Parasite Brodsky." The judge was hostile and condescending. To her questions, Brodsky consistently replied, "But I did work. I wrote poetry."

"But there are people who manage to work in a factory and still write poetry. Why didn't you do that?" the judge asked him.

"But people aren't made the same way. Even the color of their hair and their facial expressions are different," he replied.

"We don't need you to tell us that. You'd do better to explain to us how we should assess your contribution to the great onward march to communism."

Another time she asked him, "And who declared you to be a poet? Who put you on the list of poets?"

Brodsky answered, "No one. Who put me on the list of human beings?"

Brodsky was convicted and sent to Archangelsk, in the Arctic north, for five years. His trial, however, generated much attention and support. The letters to Khrushchev on his behalf were unprecedented. Outside the courtroom, large crowds, mostly of young people, stood in the corridor and on the staircase. The judge expressed surprise when she saw them. Someone answered: "It's not every day they try a poet." Finally, the transcript compiled by Frida Vigdorova reached the West and parts appeared in *The New Leader*. The regime relented. After more than two years of hauling manure in the far north, Brodsky was permitted to return to Leningrad.

By that time, Nikita Khrushchev was no longer in power. For several years his conduct of foreign affairs and agricultural development produced difficulties and disappointments. He inherited vast economic problems from Stalin, then tried to resolve them too quickly.

Under Khrushchev, too, segments of the population had violently resisted some of his measures. The government announced drastic increases in the price of butter and meat in 1962; on the same day, in one factory in Novocherkassk, piece rates were lowered by as much as 30 percent. The workers soon called a strike, leading to the stationing of army units in the city. But the strikers were not intimidated; about three hundred, including women and children, began a procession, carrying portraits of Lenin into the center of town. An order was given to fire on the marchers, but one army captain shot himself in front of his men rather than pass it on. Other soldiers opened fire. That day more than seventy people were killed.

The Soviet Union also suffered difficulties in foreign affairs. Soviet troops had to intervene in Hungary. Other Communist-bloc countries, like China and Albania, grew hostile to Soviet intentions. In Cuba, Khrushchev compromised Soviet prestige, first installing missiles and then withdrawing them under American pressure.

Khrushchev, however, did accomplish certain reforms that his successors have not been able to reverse. He made sure the country would not soon again be overwhelmed by police terror. He released millions of political prisoners, allowing them to return home and confirm the magnitude of Stalin's crimes. His successors have not displayed greater economic discernment, but what gave Khrushchev his unique stature may have insured his downfall in October 1964. No doubt his colleagues grew apprehensive that he was letting too much out of the bag.

The policies of the new regime, led by Leonid Brezhnev and Alexei Kosygin, seemed encouraging for a time. Peasants were allowed to expand their private plots. Scientists were heartened when the biologist Trofim Lysenko, whose absurd genetic theories had disrupted scientific life and agricultural research for a generation, was removed from his positions of power. The intellectual community was promised that censorship would not be tightened. A new editor in chief of *Pravda*, Alexei Rumyantsev, called for greater creative freedom and condemned Khrushchev's crude anti-intellectual prejudice.

Other developments, however, were more ominous. Solzhenitsyn's problems began to increase. The manuscript of his novel *The First Circle* was confiscated by the KGB, along with other parts of his personal archive. In the summer of 1965, a series of articles in *Pravda* criticized writers who focused on the negative aspects of Soviet life. Writers were called upon to reinforce the people's desire "to build communism" and not disorient Soviet youth about the country's past. Unfortunately, the campaign did not remain only polemical, for in September two Moscow writers, Andrei Sinyavsky and Yuli Daniel, were arrested. After a decade of struggle against censorship, the "cultural opposition" of the Khrushchev years came to an end. Now the liberal intellectuals would have to make the connection between civil rights and intellectual freedom.

2

THE AWAKENING

THE ARREST of Andrei Sinyavsky and Yuli Daniel began a crucial series of events. Under Stalin, a host of well-known cultural figures—such as the writers Isaac Babel and Boris Pilnyak, the actor Vsevolod Meyerhold, the geneticist Nikolai Vavilov, and an endless list of major and minor poets including Osip Mandelstam—simply disappeared. No one protested their fate, inside or outside the country. During Khrushchev's regime, numerous people were arrested for political crimes but no one was executed. An account of Joseph Brodsky's trial reached the West and so embarrassed the regime that he was allowed to return to Leningrad from Archangelsk well before the end of his exile.

Brodsky was not an established figure, but a vulnerable young poet. Andrei Sinyavsky, however, was the first prominent member of the Union of Soviet Writers to be arrested after Stalin's death. For his many friends and for other intellectuals, Sinyavsky's arrest marked an unmistakable challenge: they would have to protest and try to restrain the regime or face a possible return to outright Stalinist methods. Their response to the trial set a necessary precedent. As the writer Anatoly Yakobson remarked, it was the "start of people's *self-liberation* from the humiliation of fear, from connivance in evil."

At the time of his arrest, on September 8, 1965, Andrei Sinyavsky was a respected literary critic. Born in 1925, he graduated from Moscow University after World War II and became a senior staff member at the Gorki Institute of World Literature; he also taught courses at the university. In addition, he wrote essays on a wide variety of literary and artistic themes. His major work before his arrest had been *The Poetry of the Revolutionary Era*, which he wrote with another scholar. It was the first book on Soviet poetry that revived the names and reputations of many writers whose work (and who themselves) had been repressed under Stalin. Sinyavsky used to read verses of Osip Mandelstam and Pasternak to his students at a time when their work was virtually impossible to find; the students may not even have known Mandelstam's name. He gave many students their first opportunity to read these poets, as well as Western authors like Aldous Huxley, whose books he kept at home.

Sinyavsky was especially devoted to Pasternak and, at the request of the poet's wife and son, had been a pallbearer at Pasternak's funeral. Sinyavsky, in turn, asked his friend Yuli Daniel to help him. Sinyavsky attracted considerable attention for the first time in 1962 when he reviewed a slender volume of Pasternak's verse that had appeared the previous year. As often happens in the Soviet Union, once a writer of independent stature and talent dies, his work may be published, for the regime likes to exploit the veneration his name evokes. As Sinyavsky made clear in his review, the poems were not representative of Pasternak's work. Verses had been deleted from individual poems, others were changed, and in some cases the final lines were missing.

Sinyavsky continued his effort to protect the integrity of Pasternak's work. Barely three months before his arrest, the censors permitted another volume of Pasternak's poetry to appear, this time with a lengthy introduction by Sinyavsky. Many critics consider this essay the most perceptive explanation of Pasternak's verse.

Sinyavsky's association with the ideals and work of Pasternak led him to the most defiant period of his career. In the late 1940s, while studying at the university, he met and befriended Helène Peltier, the daughter of a French embassy official. As a diplomatic courtesy, she had been given permission to attend courses in Russian literature, a favor granted to a handful of Western residents. At the time, Sinyavsky maintained a naïve belief in communism. In 1951, however, his father was arrested on false charges and, though he was released after Stalin's death, he died shortly afterward.

This experience profoundly affected Sinyavsky. Although communism remained "a luminous aim" for him, he found, in the work and life of Pasternak, a more suitable guide for his own career. He also hoped that the process of de-Stalinization would return the country to the creative vigor of the revolutionary years. Sinyavsky read *Doctor Zhivago* at Pasternak's home and learned that the poet was arranging publication of the novel abroad. He decided to send his work to the West also. His old friend Helène Peltier used to visit Moscow frequently, and she agreed to help him.

Although his first pieces reached the West in 1956, they did not begin to appear until 1959. In all, Sinyavsky published one long essay, "On Socialist Realism," two novellas, *The Trial Begins* and *Lyubimov* (*The Makepeace Experiment* in English translation), a short book of aphorisms, *Unguarded Thoughts*, and the story "Pkhentz," which appeared a month after his trial. They were published under the pseudonym Abram Tertz. For a time, many people questioned the identity of Abram Tertz, regarding his work as too fanciful and sophisticated for a Soviet writer to produce in the literary and cultural isolation of Moscow. There was speculation that Tertz was really a Polish writer (some of his work originally appeared in a Polish journal in Paris) or an émigré. The Soviet press, in its few references to Tertz before the author's arrest, called him a "white émigré bandit of the pen." The regime might have believed that Tertz lived in the West, for Sinyavsky avoided the authorities for five years. During that time, he showed his stories to friends, risking the possibility that an informer might betray him.

The other defendant, Yuli Daniel, had no public reputation before his arrest. Like Sinyavsky, he was born in 1925. After finishing secondary school, he joined the army and was severely wounded at the front. Demobilized because of his injury, he received a pension as a war invalid. Later, he taught school before starting his career as a writer of verse translations from Caucasian, other Slavic languages, and Yiddish. His one attempt to publish an original work "legally" in the Soviet Union did not succeed. In the winter of 1960, Daniel asked Sinyavsky to help forward his work abroad. Under the pseudonym Nikolai Arzhak, Daniel published four stories: "This Is Moscow Speaking," "Hands," "The Man from Minap," and "Atonement."

Sinyavsky had suspected the KGB knew his identity, but he refused to discuss with friends how they should react to his and Daniel's arrests when they occurred. The two arrests brought no immediate public reaction, either among their supporters or in the official press, though Moscow's intellectual community was both confused and alarmed. Alexander Tvardovsky, who was again editor of *Novy Mir* and who had published many of Sinyavsky's essays, assured Sinyavsky's wife that he would be released, for no one thought him capable of writing such excellent work. Marya Sinyavsky replied that it would be proved her husband had written Tertz's books. (The September issue of *Novy Mir* was supposed to include an essay by Sinyavsky on the poetry of Yevgeny Yevtushenko. The issue, however, came out six weeks late, with the article removed.) Other writers were apprehensive because the opinions they had expressed when Khrushchev was in power might make them vulnerable to arrest under the new regime. There were rumors, too, of prepared lists of names—two thousand of them, some said—of people to be rounded up.

Two weeks after the arrest of Sinyavsky and Daniel, Alexander Esenin-Volpin visited Marya Sinyavsky. Volpin did not know Sinyavsky personally, although he did know Daniel. He intended to organize a demonstration in their behalf. Mrs. Sinyavsky was astonished by this proposal; she feared it would harm the defendants. That fall, Volpin discussed the demonstration with his friends. He had a number of concerns because of what had happened at other public protests in the country. A large group of students calling themselves SMOG (an acronym based on the Russian words for courage, thought, form, and depth) had organized a demonstration in April 1965. Demanding freedom of artistic expression and the right to circulate ideas, several hundred young people marched from Mayakovsky Square to the Union of Soviet Writers building where they presented a petition to a union official. On the way KGB agents and volunteers beat up and arrested many of the students and tore down their banners as well. Volpin also knew about the events in Novocherkassk, where striking workers were shot down by army troops. He intended to avoid a disorderly demonstration that might provoke either a violent response by the authorities or provocations designed to discredit their demands.

Volpin wanted the demonstration to be well defined. Because Sinyavsky and Daniel were already under arrest, he hoped to embarrass the regime by demanding a public trial, in conformity with provisions of the Soviet constitution. Volpin realized that he could not organize the protest by himself. He was regarded as an eccentric mathematician, with a permanently disheveled look and the appearance of total impracticality. By this time, however, Vladimir Bukovsky had returned to Moscow. Volpin knew he needed Bukovsky's help to make the demonstration effective because Bukovsky was known and respected for organizing the poetry readings in Mayakovsky Square. Several years before, Bukovsky had been skeptical of Volpin's advice, but his months in a mental hospital and the logic and example of Volpin's behavior convinced him of the need to adopt Volpin's strategy. Bukovsky comments in his memoir:

> Alik's idea was both inspired and insane. The suggestion was that citizens who were fed up with terror and coercion should simply refuse to acknowledge them. . . . The inspiration of this idea consisted in eliminating the split in our personalities by shattering the internal excuses with which we justified our complicity in all the crimes. It presupposed a small core of freedom in each individual, his "subjective sense of right," as Volpin put it. In other words, a consciousness of his personal responsibility. Which meant, in effect, inner freedom.

Volpin, in other words, encouraged his friends to act as free, responsible citizens. This behavior confounded the authorities, for the regime preferred to contend with genuine conspiracies and even violence, as if convinced that all its enemies were similar to itself. Soviet psychiatrists later ascribed the dissenters' tactics to mental illness. "You keep talking about the Constitution and the laws," the doctors would explain to Bukovsky, "but what normal man takes Soviet laws seriously? You are living in an unreal world of your own invention, you react inadequately to the world around you." As Bukovsky remarked, "We were born to make Kafka live."

Bukovsky did not remain at large long enough to attend the demonstration. Three days before it was to be held, he was arrested. Again there was no trial, just a perfunctory interview with a psychiatrist before he was taken to a mental hospital. Bukovsky's friends considered canceling the demonstration. It was unclear how many people would attend, if any, and how the authorities would react. Friends of Marya Sinyavsky took her out of Moscow to be sure she did not go. Volpin thought it was too late to call it off. Instead, he had another poster made, this one calling for the release of Bukovsky, too.

At six o'clock in the evening on December 5 — Soviet Constitution Day — about two hundred people gathered in Pushkin Square. Not everyone intended to participate. Victor Krasin and a friend who had also survived Stalin's camps walked on the periphery of the square, looking for buses that would take the protesters to prison. Another man carried a pair of skis over his shoulder, as if he happened upon the crowd only by chance, and then stopped out of curiosity. For a time people did not know what to do, but as the crowd grew larger and there was no reaction from the KGB plainclothesmen looking on, they moved closer to Pushkin's statue. Then Yuri Titov, an artist and friend of Bukovsky's, pulled several small posters from inside his coat and handed them to his companions. Volpin, too, held a sign that read, "Respect the Constitution." Within minutes the KGB reacted, pulling at the signs and detaining those who held them. At the police station, when they asked Volpin if his poster was addressed to government leaders, he replied characteristically, "If you feel they need the advice, let them have it." After two hours of interrogation, Volpin and the others were released.

The demonstration and numerous letters of protest compelled the regime to react. In January, *Izvestia* published the first of two articles that maligned both Sinyavsky and Daniel. The authorities hoped to exploit their use of pseudonyms, branding them as hypocrites and cowards.

The trial opened in Moscow on February 10, 1966, and lasted four days. Sinyavsky and Daniel were tried under article 70 of the criminal code, accused of "anti-Soviet agitation and propaganda." The regime may have wanted to try them formally for publishing their works abroad under assumed names, but no provision of Soviet law prohibits such behavior. (In a conversation with Professor Harold Berman of Harvard Law School, Lev Smirnov, the judge at their trial, claimed that the writers had committed blasphemy. When asked where the word *blasphemy* occurs in the Soviet criminal code, he had no reply.)

For the first time in Soviet history, the main evidence against the defendants was their published work. As the translator Max Hayward once remarked, "Many Soviet writers have been imprisoned, banished, executed, or driven into silence, but never before after a trial in which the principal evidence against them was their literary work." Three of Sinyavsky's works formed the basis of the charges against him; all four of Daniel's stories published abroad were used to incriminate him.

In his essay, "On Socialist Realism," Sinyavsky criticized the official literary dogma and encouraged writers not to feel constrained by the themes and styles "recommended" to them by the Party. He also made a direct attack on realism itself, speaking out against a revival of a naturalist school in Russian letters and for a replacement of "realistic descriptions of ordinary life" with a commitment to the "grotesque." Instead of the objective truths of realism, he wrote, literature should "teach us how to be truthful with the aid of the absurd and the fantastic." According to Sinyavsky, nineteenth-century realism was a literature of skepticism and irony and cannot serve as a model for modern writers in a society that claims to know where it is going. Neither in his essay nor in his courtroom testimony did Sinyavsky express disbelief in the goal of communism. He did mention, however, that the methods adopted in pursuit of communism have not advanced society toward this goal. In "On Socialist Realism" he wrote, "So that not one drop of blood should be shed, we killed and killed and killed." The prosecution jumped on this phrase, repeating it again and again in an attempt to demonstrate the "anti-Soviet nature" of Sinyavsky's work.

The prosecution also quoted from Sinyavsky's stories, imputing to him the attitudes and remarks of his characters. *The Trial Begins* takes place in the final years of Stalin's rule, when his campaign of anti-Semitism led to the Doctors' Plot. (A group of Jewish doctors was accused of trying to murder Soviet political leaders. The campaign was supposed to culminate in the deportation of Jews in the western part of the country to Siberia. Stalin died before his plan could be carried out.) Sinyavsky's characters, including an anti-Semitic prosecutor and a cynical lawyer, depict the corrupt bureaucrats who enjoyed power under Stalin. It is clear to any fair-minded reader that Sinyavsky has no sympathy for these characters, but his protests during the trial were useless.

Yuli Daniel did not fare much better. His stories, which were more pointed and bitter than Sinyavsky's, angered the prosecutor. In the story "This Is Moscow Speaking," Daniel describes an imaginary Public Murder Day, when the government urges citizens to kill one another. The prosecutor insisted that the story maligned the reality of Soviet life. As Daniel remarked in his defense, under Stalin "things happened that were far more terrible than what I wrote — mass purges and the deportation and annihilation of entire peoples. What I wrote was child's play by comparison."

A second story, "The Man from Minap," develops from a single comic idea: that the hero is able to predetermine the sex of his children by thinking during intercourse either of Karl Marx if he wishes a boy or of Klara Zetkin (a founder of the German Communist party) if he prefers a girl. Although the joke is clever enough, the story is not particularly well drawn, as Daniel acknowledged at the trial. Nonetheless, it did not appeal to the court's sense of humor or to most members of the hand-picked audience.

Under questioning and in their final pleas, both defendants denied their guilt and tried to answer the prosecution's charges with rational arguments. As Sinyavsky explained in his summation, "The arguments of the prosecution give one the feeling of being up against a blank wall, on which one batters one's head in vain, and through which one cannot penetrate in order to get to some kind of truth." Both he and Daniel were convicted. Sinyavsky received the maximum seven-year sentence in the camps; Daniel received "only" five years, perhaps because of his wartime injury.

The wives of the defendants, Marya Sinyavsky and Larisa Bogoraz-Daniel, sat in the courtroom for four days taking notes, recording the testimony of witnesses and the defendants, remarks by the judge and prosecutor, and reactions from the audience. Later, a partial transcript was assembled; the final pleas aroused particular interest as people made copies for their friends, who, in turn, passed additional copies along.

The trial of Sinyavsky and Daniel was meant to intimidate the intellectual community, but the government miscalculated. Since the death of Stalin, Soviet society had changed. A new generation had matured who did not remember Stalin's terror. Among the older generation of writers and intellectuals, too, there was a determination not to allow the regime to impose Stalin's methods again. It was a crucial moment. In response to the trial and to defamatory articles about the defendants, petitions and letters of protest descended on the regime. The government failed to retaliate, not even removing from their jobs those who had signed their names. In the West there was a significant reaction as well; the trial was even criticized by Western Communist party leaders.

The trial of Sinyavsky and Daniel provoked anxiety not only over the issue of artistic freedom, but about the place of Stalin in Soviet history. Official references to Stalin are a useful barometer by which to gauge the repressive attitude of the authorities. When criticism of Stalin's conduct of the war, for example, is allowed or even encouraged, then his entire method of ruling is indirectly challenged. When his reputation is protected or enhanced, though, by applauding his efforts to industrialize the country or by exaggerating his contribution to Marxist theories, then the regime is defending the Stalinist heritage and, perhaps, preparing for further arrests.

Yevgeny Yevtushenko spoke to this theme after Stalin's body was removed from Lenin's Tomb in Red Square. Yevtushenko's poem, "The Heirs of Stalin," appeared in *Pravda* itself, urging the government

> To double
> To triple
> The guard at this slab
> So that Stalin may not rise,
> And with Stalin
> The past . . .
> We rooted him
> Out of the Mausoleum
> But how to root Stalin
> Out of Stalin's heirs?

Brezhnev and Kosygin made several efforts to restore Stalin to a place of respectability within a year after Khrushchev's removal. In the spring of 1965, Marshals Konev and Bagramian, heroes of World War II, suggested it was time to reevaluate Stalin's wartime role. Under Khrushchev, Stalin had been severely criticized for failing to anticipate the Nazi invasion and for failing to prepare the country adequately for war. The historian Alexander Nekrich, in his book *June 22, 1941*, which appeared in the fall of 1965, emphasized the effects of Stalin's purge of the military, when he destroyed virtually the entire high command of the Red Army, including all division and brigade commanders.

Nekrich's book is an excellent example of the changes in scholarly life that occurred under Khrushchev. Writers could not say everything they believed, but at least they did not have to say what they did not believe. Writing about the period before the war, Nekrich introduced information and a critical point of view that are generally absent in Soviet accounts. His book, however, was published at an unfortunate time, when the authorities were developing an official Party line that falsified the historical record and granted Stalin an honorable role in the initial period of the war.

Two days after the trial of Sinyavsky and Daniel, on February 16, 1966, the authorities convened a public discussion of Nekrich's book at the Institute of Marxism-Leninism in Moscow. Undoubtedly, they had hoped to use the meeting as a forum to intimidate Nekrich, but so many prominent historians and military personnel showed up (who generally favored the book) that the meeting turned into a raucous denunciation of Stalin. Nekrich could not be forgiven. He was expelled from the Communist party in July 1967, and shortly thereafter his book was withdrawn from the country's libraries.

The trial of Sinyavsky and Daniel, the controversy over Nekrich's book, and the rumors of Stalin's rehabilitation at the forthcoming Party Congress overwhelmed the intellectual community with a sense of foreboding. Before the congress convened in March, three petitions were sent to the authorities. Two were signed by writers in Leningrad and Moscow —

among them Alexander Solzhenitsyn, Yevgeny Yevtushenko, and Andrei Voznesensky — and described how much harm the conviction of Sinyavsky and Daniel had done to Soviet prestige abroad and asked that their sentences be reduced.

The third petition was even more startling. A group of eminent scientists, artists, writers, and other intellectuals sent a petition directly to Brezhnev, voicing their opposition to Stalin's rehabilitation. (Among the signers were the physicists Igor Tamm, Pyotr Kapitsa, and Andrei Sakharov, the dancer Maya Plisetskaya, and the former diplomat Ivan Maisky. Tamm had received the Nobel Prize in physics; Kapitsa would receive the same recognition in 1978. Andrei Sakharov would receive the Nobel Prize for peace in 1975 in honor of his human rights activities. This petition, in 1966, was his first public expression of political dissent.) They warned the Party that neither the Soviet public nor Western Communist parties would support the rehabilitation of Stalin and that it "would be a great disaster."

A month later, in March, the Twenty-third Party Congress convened in Moscow. Although it did not explicitly retreat from the condemnation of Stalin made at the preceding Party Congress under Khrushchev in 1961, there were several ominous incidents. Reacting to protests against the trial of the two writers, Brezhnev condemned "hack artists who specialize in smearing our regime." The only writer allowed to address the congress was Mikhail Sholokhov, who had just received the Nobel Prize in literature. His speech expressed nostalgia for Stalin's summary methods. Bemoaning the leniency Sinyavsky and Daniel received, Sholokhov reminded his audience that "had these rascals with black consciences been caught in the memorable 1920s, when judgment was not by strictly defined articles of the Criminal Code but was guided by a revolutionary sense of justice, the punishment meted out to those turncoats would have been quite different."

Such warnings no longer silenced other intellectuals. In the first of her eloquent letters defending her colleagues, Lidia Chukovskaya, a well-known writer and daughter of the beloved critic and children's writer, Kornei Chukovsky, answered Sholokhov's remarks. "In the whole history of Russian culture," she wrote, "I know of no other case of a writer publicly expressing regret, as you have done, not at the harshness of a sentence but at its leniency." And she ended her letter with a now oft-quoted curse: "Your shameful speech will not be forgotten by history. And literature will avenge itself. . . . It will sentence you to the highest measure of punishment that exists for an artist — to artistic sterility. No honors, money, national or international prizes will avert this sentence from your head."

Still, the defiance of eminent scientists and writers did not deter the authorities. In May, the young writer Andrei Amalrik was sentenced to exile in Siberia for two and a half years. Like Joseph Brodsky, Amalrik was officially punished for "parasitism"; his nonconformist opinions and his contact with foreigners, including a *Newsweek* correspondent and an American embassy official, were the real reason for his punishment. Several years later, Amalrik published a fascinating account of his stay near a collective farm, *Involuntary Journey to Siberia.*

The regime took another fateful step in the fall of 1966. The trial of Sinyavsky and Daniel had aroused criticism within and outside the Soviet Union. Many commentators had questioned the applicability of article 70 to their case, which required proof of intent to subvert or weaken the Soviet regime by circulating false information. How was their anti-Soviet motivation to be determined? The defendants claimed to be loyal citizens who hoped to reinforce the Soviet system by eliminating vestiges of Stalinist abuse.

In September, the authorities responded to this judicial difficulty by quietly adding articles 190-1 and 190-3 to the criminal code. (The change was not mentioned in the press, but announced in the *Bulletin of the Supreme Soviet*, which has a narrow, restricted circulation.) Like article 70, article 190-1 made it possible to convict persons for circulating false statements about the regime, but it did not require an intent to weaken Soviet authority. Article 190-3 prohibits violation of public order by a group either in a gross manner or in disobedience of legitimate demands by representatives of authority. This provision was also a response to the Sinyavsky-Daniel case because their supporters had organized group demonstrations.

These changes in the criminal code did not go unnoticed. People regarded them as additional means to inhibit and punish dissent. Twenty-one figures in the arts and sciences sent a collective letter to the Supreme Soviet, declaring the new laws contradictory to "Leninist principles of socialist democracy." Among the signers were the physicists Andrei Sakharov and Igor Tamm, who had signed an earlier appeal against Stalin's rehabilitation; the composer Dmitri Shostakovich also affixed his name.

In some respects, there is little difference between article 70 and article 190-1. The regime found it just as easy to convict dissidents under either provision. And a theoretically complete defense for either article — that an accused believes a statement to be true and can verify it — has never been accepted by a Soviet court. Defendants have not even been given genuine opportunities to corroborate the statements for which they are accused by allowing them to present evidence or call witnesses. The only meaningful change for the dissidents is that article 190-1 calls for a sentence of up to three years of deprivation of freedom rather than the maximum of ten years, plus the five years of exile provided by article 70. In some cases, depending on the nature of a defendant's protest or the attention of the West, the regime may prosecute under the less severe law, making article 190-1 a seemingly liberal alternative. On the other hand, article 190-3 covering demonstrations was designed to retaliate against protesters in clear violation of article 125 of the Soviet constitution, which guarantees the right to demonstrate peacefully. These changes were not an empty exercise of arbitrary power; within a short time, the government would put them to use.

In the midst of events following the trial of Sinyavsky and Daniel, the Moscow activists were joined by Anatoly Marchenko, a man whose origins differed completely from their own. Marchenko was born in 1938 in Barabinsk, a small town in western Siberia. His parents still live in the region, employed as railroad workers; they are both illiterate. Marchenko left school after the eighth grade, two years short of a full secondary education, and went to work on the Novosibirsk hydroelectric station, and then on similar construction projects in Siberia and Kazakhstan. One job was on the Karaganda power station. It was there, in 1959, that he was first arrested. He and the other workers lived near a settlement of Chechens who had been exiled from the Caucasus during the war. Forced to live in Siberia, in an alien climate far from their ancestral home, the Chechens were terribly embittered; they and the workers constantly brawled. After one incident, the police arrested everyone they could find in the workers' hostel and, after a perfunctory trial, sent them to labor camps. Marchenko was among them.

Prior to his arrest, Marchenko had never thought about politics. Even when he worked alongside political prisoners on construction projects, he remained indifferent to their fate. "I used to get my pay, go to dances on my days off and never think a thing of it," he remarks in his book, *My Testimony*. But his arrest and trial provoked an intense reaction. He felt insulted and degraded. Although the court originally sentenced him to five years in a labor camp, the sentence was reduced to two years shortly after it began. Nonetheless, Marchenko was determined to escape not only the camp but the Soviet Union itself. He did succeed in leaving the camp. For a time he lived in Tashkent, getting by with false identity papers. But on October 29, 1960, he and a friend were caught near the Iranian border.

According to *My Testimony*, he was then kept in solitary confinement for five months and received no parcels or letters from his family. The KGB accused him of high treason. They cut up his boots "in their search for the plan of a Soviet factory." In return for worthwhile evidence and a confession, they promised him more food. Marchenko refused to cooperate.

His two-day trial began on March 2, 1961, before the Supreme Court of the Soviet Socialist Republic of Turkmenia. Almost immediately, Marchenko was betrayed by his codefendant, Anatoly Budrovsky, who "had yielded under pressure from the investigator" and gave testimony damaging to Marchenko. The next day, while Budrovsky was convicted of illegally attempting to cross the border and given two years in the camps, Marchenko was found guilty of high treason and sentenced to six years in the labor colonies for political prisoners. He was then twenty-three years old.

Marchenko spent the next six years in various labor camps and prisons, suffering irreparable damage to his health. But his contact with other prisoners, most notably with the writer Yuli Daniel, changed the direction of his life. Near the end of Marchenko's term in 1966, the trial of Sinyavsky and Daniel took place in Moscow. Reading *Pravda* and other official newspapers that denounced the two writers, Marchenko and his fellow prisoners at first believed it to be a show trial, with a pair of contrite defendants eager to denounce themselves. Otherwise, they figured, it would take place secretly, with no press coverage or denunciations. But the prisoners soon understood what even the Soviet press could not conceal: that Sinyavsky and Daniel behaved with dignity, that they did not confess, but insisted on their right to freedom of expression. After the trial, Daniel was sent to the same camp in Mordovia where Marchenko was serving the remainder of his term.

When Daniel arrived, Marchenko's work gang arranged for him to join their crew. They knew that Daniel was unaccustomed to hard physical labor, and soon learned that an old shoulder wound from the war had not healed properly, making it even harder for Daniel to work. Although Marchenko's crew unloaded timber, they assigned Daniel the easier tasks, like cleaning the woodshed or stacking small logs. Daniel, in turn, developed friendships with several prisoners, including Marchenko. They were both partially deaf and found it amusing to shout in each other's right ear. Daniel understood how Marchenko had matured in the camps, how he had changed from a simple, uncaring worker into a determined and well-informed individual. Daniel wrote to his wife, Larisa Bogoraz, about him, and before Marchenko left the camps, Daniel suggested that he visit her in Moscow.

Marchenko went immediately to the capital, where he met several of Daniel's friends at her apartment. To them he resembled a creature from an alien world. While they all knew people who had served terms in Stalin's time, they believed that under Khrushchev political prisoners had become scarce. And, surely, conditions in the camps must have improved! Marchenko, in fact, was the first person they had encountered from the camps of the post-Stalin era, and though as Moscow intellectuals they were conscientious seekers of news and information, they soon realized how profound their illusions were. One woman even came to the apartment with a tape recorder, hoping to collect the latest folk songs from the camps.

Marchenko was almost totally deaf, the result of an un-diagnosed and untreated severe middle-ear infection that had gotten steadily worse in the camps. They expected him to eat voraciously, but, as he explained, regardless of his constant hunger, he could eat very little food because his stomach had shrunk from lack of nourishment. Eventually, Marchenko asked for their help. He was determined to write a book about his experiences, to bear witness to the suffering he had seen and endured. They tried to dissuade him. It was im-mediately clear to his new friends that he had not seen the last of prison. And later, when his activities brought him further reprisals, the friends who helped him felt responsible for his fate.

The friends Marchenko made through Larisa Bogoraz were among those most deeply involved in the defense of Sinyav-sky and Daniel. Larisa Bogoraz herself had been a staunch defender of her husband, although by the time of his arrest their marriage had all but formally dissolved. As his wife, she was entitled to maintain personal contact with him while others, mere *friends*, were restricted from doing so. For two more years she wrote widely circulated appeals on behalf of arrested dissidents until, in August 1968, she was arrested in Red Square for demonstrating against the invasion of Czechoslovakia. Marchenko also met Alexander Esenin-Volpin, who for many was the father of the human rights movement.

By making their views known to the regime, Bogoraz, Volpin, and others effected a change in their own lives, which in turn transformed the moral climate of Moscow and Leningrad. For years they had practiced doublethink, professing patriotism while concealing their ideas on politics and culture from neighbors and colleagues at work. But once they signed appeals to the authorities and to the West, they no longer had something to conceal. Often, their letters and names were broadcast in Russian over Western radio stations, like the Voice of America, the BBC, or Radio Liberty. They overcame their fear and their isolation and became more open — with each other, with casual friends, even with strangers. At work, colleagues who supported them came forward. Others, who disagreed or feared contact with dissidents, broke off friendships. They even learned to speak openly with the KGB of their political and philosophical views. Suddenly, they had cracked the façade of unanimity that totalitarian governments impose. For the first time since the early 1930s, an independent, more natural social life began to evolve.

Marchenko flourished among these people. Everyone he met seemed to share his compassion and sense of outrage. His friends, though, had to restrain him. In the camps he had studied Lenin, copying passages into a notebook and then examining their significance in relation to Russia's present situation. Meeting sympathetic people in Moscow, he believed they ought to organize an underground party, secure mimeograph machines, conspire against the authorities.

His friends disabused him of these illusions. The labor camps contained many people who had tried to organize independent circles — study groups — to discuss Marxism and its relationship to Soviet society. Invariably, the regime feared the subversive potential of such activity and always imprisoned the participants. In addition, the KGB enjoyed investigating the smallest hints of clandestine activity, for it was psychologically easier to pursue someone who indeed had something to hide.

Marchenko's friends turned to more practical matters. Upon his release, Marchenko had been given a "minus 100," forbidding him to live within a hundred kilometers of certain major cities, including Moscow. So his friends helped him find a room in Alexandrov, well outside the capital; he then registered with the police there as he was required to do. He was also supposed to find work, but the authorities knew he was sick and did not pressure him to find employment. For long periods Marchenko simply vanished from their sight. Once his friends arranged a month-long stay in a Moscow hospital where his ears could be properly treated. At other times he stayed in cottages outside the city, writing his memoir and consulting with friends.

During this time Marchenko and Larisa Bogoraz became lovers. She was nearly ten years older than he, an intellectual with advanced degrees in linguistics. For more than a year before they met, she had been involved in political struggle, writing appeals and circulating petitions on behalf of defendants, most notably for her estranged husband, Yuli Daniel. She must have understood, as others did, what was in store for Marchenko and for herself. They would be married in 1971.

After Marchenko completed writing *My Testimony* in longhand, his friend Boris Shragin, who came to the West in 1974, volunteered to type it for him. With a secondhand typewriter bought especially for the project, Shragin retreated to his mother's apartment, in a secluded area, where his typing would neither disturb anyone nor arouse suspicion. As was usual for such manuscripts, he typed eight copies, pounding heavily on the keys to impress the letters through the layers of carbon paper. Later, the machine was passed on to other dissidents who used it to copy *samizdat* material, until finally the typewriter was confiscated during a search. But even in 1967 the machine was old and the keys worn down. Shragin bruised and cut his fingers so badly that, in the end, he could only copy the manuscript by wearing gloves.

My Testimony was the first account of life in the post-Stalin-era prisons and camps of the Soviet Union to circulate unofficially in Moscow. Other books, like Valentyn Moroz's *A Report from the Beria Reservation* and Edward Kuznetsov's *Prison Diaries*, have since confirmed the incredible, indeed grotesque, episodes Marchenko describes. The chapter headings themselves alert the reader: "Hunger," "Self-Mutilation," "The Man Who Hanged Himself." *My Testimony* makes us believe what we have known all along: that Soviet political prisoners endure systematic starvation; that medical care is perfunctory; that the entire procedure of corrective labor is designed to humiliate the prisoner, to ruin his health, to break his spirit.

As Marchenko remarks, in camp "you work like an elephant, get fed like a rabbit." The prisoners work long hours unloading timber, polishing furniture in the camp factory, handling lathes in crowded, noisy rooms. Always there are quotas to fill, punishments exacted, beatings, weeks in solitary confinement. While Marchenko provides sordid, degrading details of prison life, the description of the derelicts he encountered leaves the most lasting impression:

Operations for removing tattoos were also very common. I don't know how it is now, but from 1963 to 1965 these operations were fairly primitive: all they did was cut out the offending patch of skin, then draw the edges together and stitch them up. I remember one con who had been operated on three times in that way. The first time they had cut out a strip of skin from his forehead with the usual sort of inscription in such cases: "Khrushchev's Slave." The skin was then cobbled together with rough stitches. He was released and again tattooed his forehead: "Slave of the USSR." Again he was taken to hospital and operated on. And again, for a third time, he covered his whole forehead with "Slave of the CPSU." This tattoo was also cut out at the hospital and now, after three operations, the skin was so tightly stretched across his forehead that he could no longer close his eyes. We called him "The Stare."

Prisoners like this one are actually criminals from the lowest stratum of Soviet society. Initially imprisoned in camps for violent convicts, they prefer to be transferred to political camps, for they believe the rumors that conditions for "politicals" are better than for ordinary criminals. In fact, the conditions are far worse, so the criminal employs his own form of protest. Many disfigure their bodies with tattoos. Others rip open their stomachs, swallow sets of dominoes or chess pieces, even bits of glass and barbed wire. "If there had been a museum of objects taken out of stomachs," Marchenko suggests, "it would have been the most astonishing collection in the world."

Living among these criminals and political prisoners, Marchenko underwent a radical personal transformation. In contrast to other Soviet dissidents, who came to oppose the regime out of an intellectual commitment to truth and justice, Marchenko deliberately cultivated an understanding of the government only after he sensed his opposition to it. His reading of Lenin and Plekhanov in the camps led him to challenge the camps' "education officers," exposing their false logic and inconsistencies. Provoked by human suffering, he penetrated the façade of lies and hypocrisy that camouflage the Soviet government. *My Testimony* is not an optimistic book. The moral degradation of prisoner and keeper alike does not reinforce one's faith in human nature. Yet Marchenko survived. He did not leave the camps defeated.

Undoubtedly, other former prisoners also wrote about their experiences. Their manuscripts either disappeared or never were completed. But Marchenko had been released at a fortunate time. He found friends who were able to help him, and gradually he became a visible part of dissident activity. By 1967, a widespread network of *samizdat* readers extended beyond Moscow and Leningrad to provincial capitals and even to collective farms. Poems and other literary works still circulated, but documentary material, including letters of protest, transcripts of political trials, and memoirs of prison life claimed an ever-growing proportion of uncensored literature. In addition, several dissidents were in close contact with foreign journalists and others who could help transmit material to the West.

Prominent among this *samizdat* material was a collection of documents on the Sinyavsky-Daniel trial compiled by Alexander Ginzburg. He had returned to Moscow in 1962 after serving his term in a labor camp. At first he had difficulty getting permission to live in Moscow with his mother. No school would accept him and he had trouble finding employment. For four years he had a series of different jobs, from lathe operator to librarian in the Museum of Literature. Only in 1966 was he able to take an evening course at the Historical Archives Institute. During those years, too, Ginzburg continued to foster contact among young artists and writers. In 1963, he arranged to show French films about Picasso, Utrillo, and other artists in various Moscow apartments. Although some of these films later played in Soviet theaters, Ginzburg's copies were confiscated and *Izvestia* published a satirical article against him called "The Windbags Ask for Europe." A year later, he obtained books from the guides at the Exhibition of American Graphics in Moscow. When the KGB learned of this, they detained him and again accused him of circulating "anti-Soviet literature." Ginzburg spent several days in Lubyanka prison, but the investigation was eventually broken off.

Still, the pressure on Ginzburg continued. He was warned that he might be arrested or exiled from Moscow at any time unless he publicly renounced his activities. Finally, Ginzburg wrote a letter that was published in the newspaper *Evening Moscow* on June 3, 1965. In the letter, which the paper's editors expanded, Ginzburg admitted that his interest in literature and art and his naïve sense of politics made him vulnerable to exploitation by Western journalists. "An underground writer and public figure is unearthed," he wrote. "I obviously looked like an entirely suitable object to Western propagandists." He ended the letter by declaring that "the glory of the fighter for Western rottenness is the glory of the leper." This letter shocked Ginzburg's friends and caused him considerable anguish. In reaction, it became important for him to demonstrate to them and above all to himself that he retained his commitment to creative freedom.

As the case of Sinyavsky and Daniel unfolded, it became clear that numerous violations of Soviet law were taking place and that the newspapers were providing a highly distorted account of the proceedings. Ginzburg decided to assemble all the materials on the trial he could find, including the partial transcript written by the defendants' wives, and then present his findings to Soviet officials, hoping it would lead to a review of the case.

By November 1966, he managed to produce five typewritten copies of his collection. Ginzburg did not keep his project a secret. He submitted one copy to the KGB and hoped to give the others to members of the Supreme Soviet, the country's nominal legislature. By working openly, he was emphasizing the legitimate nature of his work and thereby hoping to avoid arrest. Unfortunately, the KGB was not so understanding. In December, they urged him to repudiate the collection, give them all the copies, and reveal the names of people who had helped him. Ginzburg refused and was informed that he would soon be arrested.

Despite the pressure on Ginzburg, dissidents in Moscow expanded their work. However they did not try to organize a political party or a web of conspiracies to disrupt the government. The regime retained a monopoly on power, but without the use of total, arbitrary terror the authorities could no longer intimidate the population into complete silence. Alexander Esenin-Volpin prepared a memorandum on the rights of people under interrogation. Other dissidents, like Pyotr Grigorenko and Alexei Kosterin, established contacts with the Crimean Tatars, a small ethnic minority who had been forcibly removed from their ancestral homeland in 1944 and sent to central Asia. The whole nationality had been accused of betraying the Soviet Union, and in a single day, more than 200,000 people were taken from their homes. Since 1964, the Crimean Tatars had maintained an unofficial delegation in Moscow who tried to obtain hearings with government and Party leaders in order to help their people return to the Crimea. They had limited success. In 1967, the regime officially cleared them of the charge of treason but would not permit large-scale return to their homeland. The precedent would be too troubling. Other nationalities, too, had been "resettled" by Stalin and might also insist on their right to return. But the Tatars persisted and their efforts frequently led to arrests and dismissals from work. Grigorenko and Kosterin, as well as other dissidents, supported the Crimean Tatars and made their concerns a part of the dissidents' struggle.

The Ukraine, too, had seen a roundup of intellectuals beginning in the fall of 1965 and continuing well into 1966. Twenty leading Ukrainian cultural figures — artists, scientists, and writers — were accused of "malicious defamation of the Soviet system." Like their counterparts in Moscow, these defendants had not organized active opposition to the government but had circulated essays calling for continued de-Stalinization. In addition, their own preoccupations included the regime's attempts to destroy Ukrainian culture, limit the use of the Ukrainian language, and generally pursue a policy of russification.

Their trials did not reach the attention of the Moscow activists for some time. A journalist named Vyacheslav

Chornovil was assigned to cover some of the court sessions. Rather than produce the usual distorted reports, Chornovil came to the defense of the prisoners. He petitioned the public prosecutor and the head of the KGB in the Ukraine, charging that persecution of people for their ideas was a violation of "socialist legality." Unable to keep silent, Chornovil reminded the authorities of their own proclaimed goal, "that Communism is the highest flowering of the spiritual world of each individual. . . . The greatest material saturation, without the unfettering of thought and will, is not Communism. It is merely a large prison with a higher ration for the prisoners."

Chornovil did not remain at large for long. In May 1966, he was sentenced to three years in the labor camps. But his collection of material — *The Chornovil Papers*, as they came to be called — reached other dissidents and the West by the end of 1967. In years to come, the efforts of Ukrainian activists for greater democracy and cultural autonomy would reinforce the activities of dissidents in other cities.

Among the people who were most active in Moscow at this time was Yuri Galanskov. In the late 1950s, he had helped Vladimir Bukovsky and Vladimir Osipov arrange poetry readings in Mayakovsky Square. He also compiled a literary journal, *Phoenix-61*. His own poetry, especially the "Manifesto of Man," was often read in the square and reprinted abroad.

Born in 1939, Galanskov grew up under harsh conditions. His father operated a lathe in a factory; his mother was an office cleaner. Galanskov worked as an electrician in various theaters while he finished secondary school. Later he had other odd jobs. He studied at Moscow University for two years before being expelled for his nonconformist activity.

Galanskov had an extremely sensitive and credulous nature. Known as the Prince Myshkin of the movement, after the protagonist in Dostoevsky's *The Idiot*, he felt a personal need to respond to injustice. He became preoccupied with social problems and believed that publicity against hunger, war, and social inequality could effect significant change. Since the regime controlled all means of mass communication, he felt morally obliged to act on his own.

After he issued *Phoenix-61*, the authorities took a pronounced interest in him. He was periodically confined to mental hospitals in order to intimidate him. In 1965, undaunted by harassment, he held a one-man demonstration in front of the American embassy in Moscow to protest U.S. intervention in the Dominican Republic. After the trial of Sinyavsky and Daniel, Galanskov decided to collect a variety of material — literary, religious, and political — that had been turned down by publishing houses or by the official censors and to publish it openly on his own. The collection, *Phoenix-66*, included his own long letter to Mikhail Sholokhov in which Galanskov castigated the writer for condemning members of his own profession. The collection was ready by the end of 1966.

The KGB knew about Galanskov's and Ginzburg's projects. Anxious to prevent circulation of their material, the authorities decided to arrest them, hoping to frighten others from similar activity. The regime, however, knew that the trial of Sinyavsky and Daniel had provoked a hostile reaction and that another trial of writers would easily be vulnerable to criticism. For this reason the government invented a plot in order to convict them as conspirators, and not as publicists.

On January 17, 1967, the KGB detained Vera Lashkova, who had typed sections of Ginzburg's and Galanskov's anthologies. On the same day, the secret police conducted searches at the apartments of the two writers, as well as at the home of Alexei Dobrovolsky, who had contributed an essay to *Phoenix-66*. Except for Ginzburg, they were all under arrest by January 21; he was picked up two days later.

In the meantime, news of the arrests swept through Moscow. A year before, when prominent writers had been the prisoners, the world's attention was aroused. Now it was up to the activists to generate publicity. Vladimir Bukovsky had returned to Moscow the previous summer from his stay in a mental hospital; again he took the initiative. With his friend Victor Khaustov, he found other people willing to hold a demonstration. They prepared cloth banners and even attached them to poles.

This time, they realized, they could all be arrested under the provisions of article 190-3, which had just been introduced. They tried to prepare themselves, intending to demonstrate peacefully and quietly return home if the police intervened. They chose to demonstrate in Pushkin Square where there was no chance of disrupting traffic. Still, Alexander Esenin-Volpin cautioned them. He wanted to write out instructions—how to behave under arrest, what rights to claim. But they were in too much of a hurry.

On the evening of January 22, at about six o'clock, the demonstrators converged on Pushkin Square from three different directions. They carried signs and banners under their overcoats. The weather was unusually bitter, about 30 degrees below zero. Behind Bukovsky and the others came KGB agents; they had been followed all day. About forty people huddled together and then held up their banners. There was no reaction, no interference. For a moment, Bukovsky feared they would all go home with their signs instead of being arrested. He did not want to be ignored.

Bukovsky need not have worried. Without identifying themselves, a group of men in civilian clothes shouted at them and tore the banners. Khaustov still held on to his while they struggled to take it from him. He had to be wrestled to the ground. That night Khaustov was arrested, along with Yevgeny Kushev. Three days later, the authorities arrested Vadim Delone; the day after that they took Bukovsky and the teacher Ilya Gabai. At the time of his arrest, Bukovsky's apartment was searched, as if he could hide a violation of public order in his desk or between the pages of a book.

The arrest of Ilya Gabai brought his wife Galya into the struggle. In subsequent years they would both assume active and responsible roles in the movement. Galya, though, had been especially naïve and uninformed. In 1966, reading about Sinyavsky and Daniel in the newspapers, she felt that it was hypocritical to publish abroad under pseudonyms and that it was proper to imprison the writers. Ilya argued with her; he never knew his wife thought this way. The newspaper articles were no proof of guilt, and the quotations from their stories were probably taken out of context. Still, it bothered her that they published their work secretly. "Like it or not," Ilya replied, "but it's not *criminal* to publish books."

She had never thought about such issues before. Later, when Yuli Daniel returned and they became friends, she wondered what he would think of her if he heard how she had reacted at the time of his trial.

A year later, in January 1967, Galya did not know that Ilya had gone to Pushkin Square; she did not even know about the demonstration. One day while he was at work she received a note from the authorities that he was being called as a witness. Galya accompanied him to the procuracy office, along with their friend Pyotr Yakir.

Ilya stayed for the interrogation while she went home. That evening he returned to their apartment with two men. Galya, not knowing who they were, thought they were friends of Ilya's; she began to prepare a meal for them all. But when she saw them looking through their drawers and furniture she realized who they were. At the time the family was moving to a different apartment, and their books were tied up on the floor. Copies of Ilya's poetry, which the investigators may have been looking for, were hidden between pages of the books. The investigators did not search thoroughly. They left empty-handed. Ilya promised to call his wife later that evening and told her nothing else.

Galya called Yakir to tell him about the search and that Ilya would call back. "Galichka," he told her, trying not to be cruel, "in a cell there are no phones."

Only then did she understand that Ilya was under arrest.

The next day Yakir explained how she must proceed, which offices to visit, whom to see. At the procuracy, she learned that Ilya was only "detained" but that within three days the authorities must either place him formally under arrest — which they did — or release him. She went back to Yakir for help. At his apartment she met Alexander Esenin-Volpin for the first time. He had a list of lawyers she could try to consult. Listening to her story and knowing that Ilya had been only peripherally involved, he predicted his eventual release. Volpin turned out to be correct.

Galya Gabai went to the city court on February 15 to learn when her husband's trial would be held, only to be told that no date had been fixed. A few hours later, her husband's court-appointed lawyer told her the trial would begin the next day but that she would not be permitted to attend. In a subsequent conversation, the lawyer admitted that she could be present but urged her not to bring anyone else.

The next morning, Galya entered the courtroom with her mother-in-law, but only after much difficulty. She saw how relatives and friends of the codefendant, Victor Khaustov, were prevented from entering while a group of young men whom no one recognized were promptly allowed in. To her surprise, Ilya's case was separated from Khaustov's at the start of the hearing. The prosecutor claimed knowledge of "evidence of equally serious offenses previously committed" and requested time for further investigation. Four months later, Ilya Gabai was released; he was never brought to trial. By then, Khaustov had been convicted of malicious hooliganism and of holding a disorderly demonstration. He received three years in the labor camps. At the end of August, Bukovsky, Delone, and Kushev went on trial. They, too, were convicted.

A year later, looking back on these events, Anatoly Yakobson, a literary critic who became a central figure in the movement, explained that "since the Sinyavsky-Daniel trial, since 1966, not a single arbitrary or violent act by the authorities has passed without a public protest, without censure. This is a valuable tradition, the start of people's *self-liberation* from the humiliation of fear, from connivance in evil." But the cycle of arrest, trial, protest, and further arrests was just beginning.

3

NEW TRIALS, NEW ARRESTS

GRADUALLY, as more people came forward, the nature of dissent began changing: "Professors, academicians, writers — not to be compared with us striplings of the early 1960s," Bukovsky recalls in his memoir. For the authorities, the trials were nothing more than crude reprisals; for the dissidents, they became opportunities to expose the nature of the regime and to devise further means of protest.

The trial of Victor Khaustov in February and of Bukovsky, Delone, and Kushev in August presented the government with an ironical dilemma. The defendants were on trial for organizing a demonstration, yet the prosecution could not make it seem as if the freedom to demonstrate did not exist in the Soviet Union; the constitution, after all, guaranteed it. Bukovsky understood the absurd dimensions of this judicial procedure. During the investigation, when he was held for seven months in solitary confinement, he insisted on his rights, making the prosecutors and plainclothesmen explain the law to him. As Bukovsky makes clear in his memoir, long before the trial the authorities were already tying themselves in knots over their own laws. "How do you explain that it is all right to demand the liberation of Greek political prisoners, but not of Soviet prisoners? And where, in what law, is it written that the May 1 demonstration in Red Square is not a breach of public order, while ours in Pushkin Square was?"*

Bukovsky asked for a copy of the criminal codes. At first his request was refused; the authorities claimed prisoners were not allowed to have it. But when he threatened a hunger strike, they relented; it took them two days to find a copy. A KGB colonel had to lend Bukovsky his own, which was personally inscribed by Semichastny, the head of the KGB. Another lieutenant colonel took four days to find a copy of the constitution. He ended up buying one for Bukovsky.

After a time, Bukovsky was no longer interrogated. His investigator started calling him in just to talk. To their surprise they had become friendly, and the investigator was eager to exchange ideas. He had worked in the provinces and could hope to read only what he found during the searches. He, too, was not allowed to read Djilas's book, *The New Class,* and asked Bukovsky about it.

While Bukovsky and his friends remained in jail, the investigation continued in Moscow. Over a hundred "witnesses" were questioned while many of them had their homes searched as well.

With all this effort, however, the authorities tried to avoid a second trial altogether. The fiftieth anniversary of the Revolution was approaching in November, and they wanted to avert inconvenient publicity. They proposed that Bu-

---

*An anecdote dissidents enjoy telling describes the relationship of Soviet law to Soviet society:

One day a Western tourist visits the Moscow zoo and stops in front of a caged gorilla. On the side of the cage a sign describes the gorilla's daily menu: 2 pounds of bananas, 3 pounds of apples, 3 pounds of lettuce, 4 pounds of celery, 2 pounds of sweet potatoes, 5 pounds of monkey chow. The visitor is amazed and asks the attendant, "Is that really what he eats?"

"Of course," the attendant replies. "But who's going to give it to him?"

kovsky apply for a psychiatric examination — he had already spent two terms in a mental hospital — then he could be released in an amnesty to mark the holiday. Bukovsky rejected their idea: "Amnesties were never extended to loonies."

The trial itself revealed how weak a case the regime had prepared. The volunteers who had broken up the demonstration admitted they had been hired by the KGB. One policeman testified there had been no disturbance. Numerous witnesses confirmed that Bukovsky had instructed the demonstrators to behave properly and obey the authorities. They also noted that Bukovsky had cautioned Khaustov not to resist. In his summation, the prosecutor claimed that "basically, public order was violated by the slogans."

The conduct of the prosecutor did little credit to Soviet justice. His first question to Kushev was "Do you believe in God?" Later, the prosecutor examined Kushev's mother about her attitude to religion. Bukovsky's mother was asked, "Why is your son so embittered against Soviet law?"

She replied: "What do you mean? Vladimir is terribly keen on law."

The prosecutor did not pursue this line of questioning.

Alexander Esenin-Volpin also testified about his friendship with Bukovsky. At one point the judge asked Volpin what linked him to these young people.

Volpin hesitated for a moment, then answered, "We are all human."

Bukovsky's friends, Vadim Delone and Yevgeny Kushev, admitted partial guilt and repented. Bukovsky, though, did not give in, adopting a candid and defiant attitude from the very beginning of the trial: "It was in 1961 that I first asked myself whether in fact the democratic liberties guaranteed by the Constitution are a reality in the Soviet Union ... ever since I have been opposed to the atmosphere of oppression and concealment which exists in our country."

In his final speech, too, Bukovsky raised issues no Soviet court had ever heard before. While his friends listened with fear, knowing how much worse he was making things for himself, Bukovsky spoke for nearly two hours and demolished the prosecution's case.

What is the use of freedom to demonstrate "for" if we can't demonstrate "against"? We know that protest demonstrations are a powerful weapon in the hands of the workers and that the right to hold them exists in every democracy. And where is this right denied? Here is *Pravda* of the 19th of August — a news item from Paris says that May Day demonstrators are being tried in Madrid. They were tried under a new law: it had recently been passed in Spain and it imposes terms of eighteen months to three years in prison for taking part in a demonstration. Note the touching unanimity of Fascist and Soviet law.

Judge: Accused Bukovsky, you are comparing two things which cannot possibly be compared — the actions of the Fascist Government of Spain and those of the Soviet State. That a comparison between Soviet policies and those of foreign bourgeois countries should be made in court is an outrage.

His defiance cost him dearly. While Delone and Kushev received suspended sentences and were released, Bukovsky was sent to the labor camps for three years. But the term would not end his dissident career.

The two trials — first of Khaustov and later of Bukovsky, Delone, and Kushev — were not held secretly. Galya Gabai attended Khaustov's trial, expecting her husband to be in the dock. Friends of the defendants testified in the second trial and were allowed to remain in the courtroom. Afterward, with the help of Pavel Litvinov, they assembled their notes into partial transcripts of both trials.

This was the beginning of Pavel Litvinov's activity in the

movement. Brought up in the privileged caste of Soviet society — his grandfather was Maxim Litvinov, foreign minister of the Soviet Union and later ambassador to the United States at the height of World War II — Pavel Litvinov shared the general awe and belief in Stalin. After Stalin's death, when other family members sat in the kitchen making fun of Stalin, Pavel rushed from the room in tears. He was then thirteen years old.

Litvinov met Alexander Ginzburg for the first time in 1960 at an exhibition of the nonconformist painter Oskar Rabin; Ginzburg had helped to arrange the exhibit in a private apartment. But while Ginzburg grew quite active in the movement Litvinov remained aloof. He completed his studies, then taught physics at an institute in Moscow. When Ginzburg was arrested in January 1967, however, Litvinov felt a personal need to respond.

Shortly after Bukovsky's trial, on September 4, 1967, *Evening Moscow* carried a short news article, claiming that all three defendants had pleaded guilty. Although several people, including Alexander Esenin-Volpin, responded with letters to the editor disputing the newspaper's account, none of them were published.

Still, the KGB worried that a truthful account of the trial would reach the public. Pavel Litvinov was summoned by the KGB on September 26. They knew he was compiling transcripts of both trials and warned him "to go home and destroy everything you have collected." Litvinov was not intimidated. A week later he sent records of the discussion to newspapers inside and outside the country. For a time there was no reaction; in Western Europe it seemed too incredible to have such a document from the grandson of Maxim Litvinov, a fact the KGB official himself referred to in his warning to Pavel. Only at the end of November was the conversation published for the first time, in Italy, and then broadcast over radio stations to the U.S.S.R.

The KGB officer, Gostev, warned Litvinov that he would

be held criminally responsible if the trial documents were circulated or reached the West. Litvinov objected, wondering "what kind of slander could there be in recording the hearing of a case before a Soviet court." He mentioned how *Evening Moscow* had distorted the facts of the case and how the government ought to be interested in clearing up false information. Gostev disagreed. "The account in *Evening Moscow,*" he claimed, "is perfectly truthful and gives all the information that Soviet citizens are supposed to have about this case." Their conversation continued:

> *Litvinov:* But I don't know of any law that makes it punishable to circulate a non-secret document, simply on the grounds that it could be used for this or that purpose. A lot of critical articles from the Soviet press could also be misused by someone.
> *Gostev:* You must know perfectly well what we are talking about. We are only warning you, but the court will prove you guilty.
> *Litvinov:* I have no doubt it will, that's clear, if only from the trial of Bukovsky. Besides, my friend Alexander Ginzburg is in prison for just the kind of thing you are warning me against.
> *Gostev:* When Ginzburg is brought to trial, you'll know what he did. If he is innocent he will be acquitted. Do you really think that today, when the Soviet regime is in its 50th year, a Soviet court would bring in a wrong verdict?

Pavel did not answer the question. The trials of Bukovsky and his friends had not led people to forget the reason for the demonstration in Pushkin Square. Galanskov, Ginzburg, Dobrovolsky, and Lashkova were still in prison, their cases "under investigation." The KGB carried out numerous searches at this time, confiscating letters of protest and descriptions of events surrounding recent trials and demonstrations.

Usually, when searches took place at the apartment of someone under investigation (or already under arrest), the presence of the KGB discouraged friends and neighbors from visiting the apartment. By law, the police could compel anyone to remain in the apartment for the duration of the search (which could take more than six hours), search them also, and include their names in the official protocol of the investigation. This procedure succeeded in isolating the families of dissidents. In 1967, however, the dissidents embarked on a new strategy to embarrass the KGB. When a search took place, friends alerted friends. Then individuals and groups of people would converge on the apartment, demonstrating their solidarity with the family involved.

On September 5, 1967, a search was conducted at the home of Lyudmilla Ginzburg, the mother of Alexander, who was then awaiting trial. Anatoly Marchenko and Larisa Bogoraz visited the apartment during the four-hour search and stayed until its conclusion. Their names and addresses were listed in the official report. In addition, Marchenko and Larisa Bogoraz signed one of the innumerable appeals that were circulating that fall and winter. Demanding an open process for Ginzburg and his colleagues, the appeals cited violations of law committed by the authorities during the investigation. While the four defendants had been arrested in January, they were not brought to trial within nine months, the period stipulated by the Code of Criminal Procedure.

By the winter of 1967–1968, Marchenko's book, *My Testimony*, was already being read in Moscow. Although the KGB must have learned about it they did not arrest Marchenko, probably because the impending trial of Alexander Ginzburg and Yuri Galanskov, who were both well-known publicists, was generating controversy; the atmosphere was not right for the arrest of another writer. Furthermore, Marchenko's detention would simply bring greater attention to his book. Knowing his character, the KGB realized he would provide another pretext, sooner or later, for his own arrest. They were not mistaken.

Meanwhile, there was much anxiety in Moscow over the forthcoming trial of Galanskov and Ginzburg. Already on November 30, 1967, a letter signed by 116 people was presented to the procurator general, protesting the procedures at recent hearings where "formally open trials have been turned into closed ones" by excluding friends and relatives of the defendants from the courtroom. The signers expressed interest in attending the trial of Galanskov, Ginzburg, and their codefendants.

Another letter, which also circulated before the trial and was addressed to Soviet leaders, denied that Alexander Ginzburg could have broken Soviet law by compiling material on the Sinyavsky-Daniel trial. His arrest "cannot help to clear the atmosphere of a society which not long ago witnessed mass rehabilitations of persons sentenced on false charges," the letter asserted. Thirty-one people affixed their names, including distinguished professors and members of the Writers' Union.

Such protests and the publicity surrounding the defendants abroad (Ginzburg's book on the Sinyavsky-Daniel trial had appeared in the West) may have persuaded the regime to focus attention on the trial rather than conduct it unobtrusively, as the earlier trials of the demonstrators had been. Furthermore, the authorities were preparing a complex indictment against the defendants, portraying them as conspirators in league with the NTS, a Russian émigré organization based in Frankfurt, whose initials stand for the Popular Labor Alliance of Russian Solidarists. Although the group is small, it maintains effective channels for bringing news and manuscripts out of the Soviet Union and subsequently publishes the material in its two journals, *Possev* and *Grani*. This activity, in particular, infuriates the KGB, and the authorities hoped to discredit the four defendants by linking them to NTS, which the prosecutor claimed during the trial advocated "terror, spying, and the creation of armed detachments." Early in January 1968, a week before the proceedings, *Izvestia* began printing articles about a certain Brox-Sokolov, an alleged courier for NTS who had been arrested ten days earlier. He eventually was called as a witness, and *Izvestia* exploited his links to NTS as a way to impugn the four defendants.

The trial finally began on January 8, 1968, and immediately confirmed the dissidents' worst fears. Accused of "anti-Soviet agitation and propaganda," the defendants were hardly able to defend themselves. Defense lawyers were harassed by the judge, and witnesses were not permitted to give testimony favorable to the defendants. A general atmosphere of intimidation reigned in the courtroom, reinforced by a select group of spectators who insulted and jeered defendants and witnesses alike.

Early in the investigation, it turned out, the KGB had succeeded in compromising Dobrovolsky, who then began denouncing his codefendants. From a psychiatric hospital in Moscow he was permitted to send a note to Galanskov, urging him to testify as well. Galanskov at first incriminated himself for much of Dobrovolsky's activity involving currency speculation and conspiracies with the NTS; he hoped to make things easier for Dobrovolsky because Dobrovolsky had a family and had already been imprisoned once before in the 1950s. In addition, Galanskov expected to be punished anyway for compiling *Phoenix-66*. But when he learned of Dobrovolsky's false testimony, which placed innocent people within a conspiracy, Galanskov tried to repudiate his own false admissions; at the trial the court would not accept his change of heart.

On the evening of January 10, after the third session of the trial, Larisa Bogoraz wrote an "Appeal to World Public Opinion" on the conduct of the trial. Her draft was edited by Pavel Litvinov. It was signed by Bogoraz and Litvinov, who also added their addresses, although they did not ask for or expect any direct response. Their colleague, Natalya Gorbanevskaya, typed a final draft and, in the morning, gave a copy to the Reuters correspondent in Moscow. Litvinov had intended to hold a press conference, but when foreign reporters learned that Reuters already had a copy of the appeal, they knew it would reach the West. The press conference was no longer necessary, so instead the reporters stood outside the courthouse with the defendants' supporters, who were not permitted to enter.

The trial lasted one more day. On the twelfth, the defendants were pronounced guilty and sentenced. Dobrovolsky had admitted his guilt and helped the prosecution; he received two years at hard labor. Lashkova admitted her guilt also but had been involved primarily as a typist, so her sentence was only one year. (She had been detained nearly a full year before the trial began. Because sentences commence from the initial time of detention, Lashkova was released just after the trial.) Ginzburg and Galanskov, however, disputed their guilt and the criminal nature of their activity. The court showed them no leniency. Ginzburg received five years in a labor camp. Although Galanskov's lawyer warned that he suffered from a severe ulcer, the judge sentenced Galanskov to seven years in a labor camp. He would not survive his term.

The trial gained considerable notice within the Soviet Union, not only because of the official articles condemning the defendants but also because the appeal by Bogoraz and Litvinov was broadcast in Russian by the BBC. For weeks, Litvinov received letters voicing support for his efforts and indignation over the trial's procedures. One letter came from twenty-four secondary school students who had heard the appeal over the radio. Their response embodied the calm defiance and solidarity that the human rights movement was able to generate:

Thank you and Larisa Daniel for your brave and honest letter. We are revolted to the depths of our souls by the trial, and we understand what general silence and apathy can lead to. When Sinyavsky and Daniel were convicted, we realized the crying injustice of our organs of power and the cruelty of individuals who mockingly trample upon the literary and human rights of people.

Our fathers and grandfathers were shot or died in camps; they knew all the horrors of Stalinist reaction. We can imagine how terrible it is to live surrounded by silence and fear. Therefore, the thinking generation of the 1960's calls upon all people of integrity to support these two courageous individuals by signing their names to our letter. He who keeps silent commits a crime against his conscience and against Russia. And Russia pays dearly for this with the blood of her most intelligent and talented people, from Osip Mandelstam to Alexander Ginzburg. We are for the publication of Brodsky's verses, Romisov's and Zamyatin's stories, the poetry of the late Mandelstam, and the prose of Pasternak. We are for the release of Sinyavsky and Daniel; we favor a re-examination of the case of the four writers by an international tribunal in accordance with international law; we favor a severe admonition to the courts to restore the norms of socialist legality. We despise Dobrovolsky's vile treachery; he is nothing other than a Smerdyakov. We who are just emerging into life are already fed up with hypocrisy and deceit — we want truth and justice.

Only united can we succeed in accomplishing something; otherwise worse will follow: terror, reaction, innocent sacrifice. For we are responsible for all that happened in the world — after all, we are taught this by the best works of our literature. We cannot resign ourselves to the narrow-minded interpretations of Tolstoy, Chekhov, Kuprin, Blok or to the exclusion of Dostoevsky, Bunin, Tsevetaeva, Pasternak and others from the school curriculum. Our schools have produced reliable watchmen — stupid crammers who study the history of the Party and the fundamentals of historical materialism. We cannot keep silent when demagogy, journalistic lies, and deceit are all around. We are only sorry for our parents. We request that this letter be circulated so that it may reach those who are our own age and think as we do, and so that the fate of these writers will be justly decided.

We hope that, despite everything, we are not alone and that we will hear the voices of upright people.

The regime was slow to react; at first it only blocked Litvinov's mail from abroad. In addition, the Moscow inquiry office informed curious citizens that neither Bogoraz nor Litvinov existed. (There are few telephone directories in the Soviet Union. In Moscow, people must stop at an inquiry office to find a number or an address. Litvinov once inquired about himself and received notification of his own nonexistence. The official slip was later confiscated during a search.) But visitors found them anyway. People came from the Baltic states and the Ukraine, anxious to tell their pathetic stories. They hoped that Litvinov, whose name carried authority, might be able to help them.

A Baptist came, telling of his family's persecution. Ukrainian nationalists brought stories of attacks on their culture and heritage. An old Jewish woman from one of the Baltic states knocked on his door. She wanted to go to Israel; she had once approached the Israeli embassy only to be stopped and beaten by the police. For Litvinov, her dream seemed absurd. Like most Moscow intellectuals, he admired Israel's determination to survive, especially during the Six

Day War. But emigration seemed too outlandish a hope. One visitor was Ivan Yakhimovich, the chairman of a collective farm in Latvia. Although trained as a philologist, Yakhimovich decided to work on a collective farm as an expression of his belief in communism. His honesty and genuine idealism endeared him to the peasants; he was one of the first collective farm chairmen to pay peasants for their labor with money. The farm prospered under his leadership; even the Soviet press wrote a great deal about his accomplishments. After hearing the appeal of Bogoraz and Litvinov on the BBC, Yakhimovich wrote a letter to the Central Committee, protesting the trial of Ginzburg and Galanskov. Copies of his letter circulated in Moscow and soon found their way abroad, where it, too, was read over the radio. The KGB invited Yakhimovich for a "chat" and explained to him that Litvinov and Bogoraz had not signed any appeal and that it was actually an invention of the BBC. Yakhimovich visited Moscow to learn if Bogoraz and Litvinov really existed.

In reaction to protests over the trial of Ginzburg and Galanskov, the KGB began to retaliate more harshly against the dissidents. Many lost their jobs; others lost their membership in the Communist party. The KGB also kept track of those who merited special attention, among them Anatoly Marchenko.

For nearly half a year, Marchenko endured continual harassment. In February 1968, Larisa Bogoraz complained to the authorities "about the grossly illegal methods of persecution practised in the case of former political prisoner Anatoly Marchenko." As she later explained in an open letter to the West, Marchenko's life was growing considerably more difficult:

His Book *[My Testimony]* . . . aroused such hatred for him in the KGB that they began to bait him like a hare: KGB agents followed on his heels for months on end — I've spotted them so often that I know many of them by sight. And not only in Moscow, where he worked, and Aleksandrov where he lived: he went to visit relatives in Ryazan but wasn't allowed to leave the train and had to return to Moscow. He was seized on the street almost as soon as he had been discharged from hospital; and they smashed his face in and shoved him into a car when he came to Moscow for a literary evening.

Despite such conditions, Marchenko increased his activities. In March 1968, Alexander Chakovsky, the editor of *Literaturnaya Gazeta*, wrote an article replying to numerous letters from readers (none of which were published in the journal) that criticized the regime's conduct of the Ginzburg-Galanskov trial. In the course of his reply, which has become a notorious example of official baiting, Chakovsky made his own suggestion for the defendants' fate: "Instead of giving such people food and drink at the nation's expense in prisons and corrective labor colonies, the responsibility for their keep should be shifted on to the American, English, or West German taxpayers."

Marchenko prepared a reply on the day Chakovsky's article appeared. Citing the work prisoners do and the meager rations they receive, Marchenko berated Chakovsky for deliberately obscuring the truth:

In your article you assume the pose of a man with a civic conscience, as though you were genuinely concerned about our country's fate and prestige. A man in such a public position cannot justify himself by saying that he was unaware of something or ill-informed. If, indeed, you did not know until now, then you could have, and that means you should have known exactly how convicts in corrective labor colonies are fed, and at whose expense.

> ... Maybe the lofty civic pathos of your article can be explained precisely by the fact that you get a bit more for it than just a bowl of gruel and a ration of black bread.

Several weeks later, on April 17, Marchenko wrote another letter on the labor camps, this time to the chairman of the Red Cross Society, the minister of health, and other government and cultural officials. Expressing his frustration over his inability to "make my book known to the public," he explained that they "through their social position are among those most responsible for the state of society and its level of humanity and legality." He then detailed conditions in the camps, appealing to these gentlemen to demand a public investigation into the plight of political prisoners. "It is our civic duty," he reminded them, "the duty of our human conscience, to put a stop to crimes against humanity. For crime begins not with the smoking chimneys of crematoria, nor with the steamers packed with prisoners bound for Magadan. Crime begins with civic indifference."

Marchenko received only one reply to this letter. On April 29, the deputy chairman of the Union of Red Cross and Red Crescent Societies answered:

> The committee ... considers it necessary to point out briefly that our legislation and our Soviet conception of law look upon people who have attacked the conquests of the October Revolution as having committed a most serious offence against their people and as deserving severe punishment rather than any kind of indulgence or forbearance.
>
> In the light of the foregoing the entirely groundless nature of all of your other assertions becomes obvious.

While Marchenko became increasingly involved with the defense of political prisoners, other events in the spring of

1968 also absorbed his attention. In Czechoslovakia, liberal Communists were attempting to establish "socialism with a human face." Marchenko, along with other dissidents, followed events in Czechoslovakia as closely as he could. But the Soviet press distorted the significance of the Prague Spring, alluding to "internal forces of reaction" and an "imperialist intrigue." Marchenko understood the warnings. On July 22, he wrote a letter to several newspapers in Prague and to Communist journals in Western Europe. As in *My Testimony* and his previous letters, he revealed an acute understanding of his government's behavior. He did not believe Alexander Dubček's experiment would be allowed to continue, especially because the Czech liberals seemed determined to expose the crimes of their own country's Stalinists. Marchenko concluded:

> It is understandable why our leaders hasten to intercede for the likes of Urvalek and Novotny: the precedent of making party and government leaders personally responsible before the people is a dangerous and contagious one. What if our own leaders should suddenly be required to account for deeds that have shamefully been termed "errors" and "excesses" or, even more weakly and obscurely, "difficulties experienced in the heroic past" (when it was a matter of millions of people being unjustly condemned and murdered, of torture in the KGB's dungeons, of entire peoples being declared enemies, of the collapse of the nation's agriculture, and similar trivia)?

For the KGB, this was the last straw. On July 28, Marchenko was arrested on the street, taken to Butyrka prison, and charged with infringement of identity card regulations. His friends tried to help him. Appeals were circulated, petitions drawn up. One woman, Irina Belogorodskaya, was arrested on the night of August 7 while carrying copies of a letter in defense of Marchenko. Irina knew Marchenko well. A cousin of Larisa Bogoraz's, she frequently saw Marchenko in Moscow and knew he had not violated internal passport regulations by staying in the capital for more than three days. She herself had not signed the letter she carried, which claimed that Marchenko was really under arrest for writing *My Testimony*. Irina wanted to be called as a witness at his trial; she feared that by signing the protest she would diminish her chances of being allowed to testify.

The letter, which was signed by eight of his friends, reminded people of the sole means of protest the dissidents had:

> Marchenko's enemies have many ways to sentence him to a new term under any false pretext. They can do this secretly or slander him in the newspapers. They can deprive him of defenders or intimidate them. We, his friends, have only one way of helping him: publicity. May as many people as possible know of his courageous struggle and his new arrest.

Irina was the first person to be arrested for distributing letters in defense of prisoners of conscience. It happened almost accidentally. With her husband, Ivan Rudakov, she had been traveling around the city by taxi with the KGB following closely behind. She was carrying eighty-eight copies of the letter and hoped to send them to prominent Soviet citizens.

At one point, they left the taxi to make a phone call. Only then did she realize that she had left her bag in the taxi which had then gone on. Irina and Ivan took a second taxi in hope of finding the first, but without success. The KGB meanwhile suspected what had happened. They waited for the cab driver to return to his garage and upon finding the letters arranged a charade to explain how they came into the possession of the authorities. According to testimony at

Belogorodskaya's trial, the dispatcher at the garage found the bag and inspected it, discovering anti-Soviet material and an internal passport. The dispatcher supposedly showed everything to the director of the taxi company, who only then called the security police.

Belogorodskaya's friends tried to help her. Those who had signed the letter insisted that they also be arrested. They asked to give testimony in her defense, in order to corroborate that the letter was not slanderous but based on true information. Neither request was accepted. On February 19, 1969, Irina Belogorodskaya was convicted of "an attempt, which failed for reasons beyond her control, to distribute deliberately misleading falsehoods defaming the Soviet social and political system" and sentenced to a year in a labor camp. No one who actually signed the letter was arrested or called to testify.

By 1968, a small community of activists in Moscow had developed the courage and the means to publicize and to protest each act of repression that came to their attention. For a time, the authorities did not respond with widespread reprisals, choosing to arrest only those people who took the initiative to organize a demonstration or who dared to compile transcripts of political trials. Silent demonstrations on December 5, Soviet Constitution Day, continued each year, a tradition begun in 1965 after the arrest of Sinyavsky and Daniel. Sometimes a hundred people, occasionally many more, would gather in Pushkin Square, and, at six o'clock in the evening, doff their hats and bow their heads. Often KGB agents would outnumber the demonstrators. At trials, too, people would stand outside the courthouse to show solidarity with defendants.

The growth of *samizdat* also presented a new challenge to the regime. For decades Russians had been compelled to retreat from one another, not knowing an honest person from one who would denounce a neighbor for a critical remark or an anecdote; under Stalin people disappeared for more trivial things. As poetry and stories circulated among the population and, later, as trial reports and letters of protest passed among friends and even reached the West, more and more people overcame their fear and shared their thinking with others.

A decade earlier, after Khrushchev's revelations about Stalin, the Party could not control the discussion its own leader had initiated. In a similar manner, the increasing amount of uncensored literature raised so many individual issues — violations of judicial procedure, censorship, anti-Semitism, the suppression of ethnic minorities, and then, in 1968, the attempted liberalization in Czechoslovakia — that it was only natural for more general criticism of the regime to emerge that would place all these problems in perspective and thereby question the competence and legitimacy of the Soviet political system itself.

The most startling and famous of these early critiques was Andrei Sakharov's first memorandum, "Progress, Coexistence, and Intellectual Freedom." It appeared in Moscow in May 1968 and soon reached the West, where it and its author aroused widespread interest and curiosity. Sakharov outlined his belief in the convergence of the Western and socialist systems of government. "Convergence" was not a new idea in the West, but Sakharov's essay was the first indication that Soviet scientists shared the notion that "the rapprochement of the socialist and capitalist systems, accompanied by democratization, demilitarization, and social and technological progress, is the only alternative to the ruin of mankind."

Andrei Sakharov was not a conventional Moscow dissident, an energetic, young writer, say, or an experienced mathematics teacher. He was born in 1921, and by the time

Sakharov reached Moscow University he was regarded by the physics faculty as its most brilliant student. Deferred from military duty because of his scientific talent, he worked as an engineer in a military factory until the end of the war. He then received a full professorship in physics for his research on cosmic-ray theory. (A full professorship in the U.S.S.R. is considered a more advanced degree than an American doctorate.) In addition, he published several scientific papers until suddenly, in 1948, Sakharov's name ceased to appear in print.

The explanation was simple enough: Sakharov was drafted into developing a Soviet hydrogen bomb. His life changed completely. Working in deepest secrecy, Sakharov and a team of distinguished physicists succeeded in designing a thermonuclear reaction, thereby breaking the United States' monopoly over nuclear weapons. For this work and his involvement in other, related projects, Sakharov eventually received — in secret — three Orders of Socialist Labor (the most distinguished civilian honor in the U.S.S.R.), the Stalin Prize and the Lenin Prize, and an exceptionally high salary of over $30,000 a year by current exchange rates. He also received special housing, chauffeurs, restricted consumer goods, and a bodyguard who even went swimming and skiing with him.

At the same time, Sakharov was totally isolated from ordinary Soviet citizens. Only his colleagues in the highest echelons of scientific research, leading figures in the government, and officials of the Soviet atomic energy agency knew of his importance to the country. In 1953, at the age of thirty-two, Sakharov was elected to full membership in the Soviet Academy of Sciences; he was the youngest scientist ever so honored.

After Stalin's death, Sakharov did not long remain aloof from broader social and scientific questions. In 1958, he tried to stop Soviet atmospheric tests of nuclear weapons.

Knowing how advanced Soviet weapons research had become — with the launching of sputnik and the building of Soviet ICBMs — Sakharov did not think atmospheric tests were scientifically necessary; he also feared they could aggravate the arms race and increase the dangers of nuclear fallout. Although he managed to relay his message to Khrushchev, the political leadership rejected Sakharov's advice and the testing continued.

Sakharov did not lose heart. In 1961 and again in 1962 he complained directly to Khrushchev, urging the regime not to continue a series of large-scale nuclear tests. Nothing came of his efforts. Years later, in a conversation with Hedrick Smith, a New York *Times* correspondent in Moscow, Sakharov recalled the importance of these events in his own life. "I could not," he told Smith, "stop something I knew was wrong and unnecessary. It was terrible. I had an awful sense of powerlessness. After that I was a different man. I broke with my surroundings. It was a basic break. . . . The atomic question was always half science, half politics. . . . It was a natural path into political issues. What matters is that I left conformism. It is not important on what question. After that first break, everything later was natural."

For a time, Sakharov's focus remained within the framework of Soviet science. He was heartened by his contribution to the nuclear test-ban treaty in 1963. When talks between the United States and the Soviet Union seemed to founder, Sakharov reminded Soviet officials of an American fall-back position put forward by President Eisenhower in 1959. The Soviets revived the proposal and the treaty, which halted tests in the atmosphere, in space, and under water, was concluded. In 1964, he helped defend the integrity of scientific research against Lysenkoism. The biologist Trofim Lysenko had dominated Soviet genetics under Stalin, driving talented colleagues into prison where several perished. Lysenko was a charlatan whose bizarre theories — he claimed he could transform one species into another, for example, changing rye into wheat by altering its environment — severely impaired the development of Soviet agriculture. During Khrushchev's rule, Lysenko and his supporters retained some influence. But by the 1960s, at the initiative of the biologist Zhores Medvedev, a group of Soviet scientists began to expose Lysenkoism and its disastrous effect on the country's agriculture.

Andrei Sakharov joined these efforts. In 1964 an associate of Lysenko's, Nikolai Nuzhdin, was nominated for full membership in the Academy of Sciences. During the debate over his nomination, Sakharov vigorously opposed Nuzhdin, urging "all those present to vote so that the only yeas will be by those who, together with Nuzhdin, together with Lysenko, bear the responsibility for the infamous, painful pages in the development of Soviet science, which fortunately are now coming to an end." Nuzhdin was overwhelmingly rejected, but Sakharov was not easily forgiven his speech. The president of the All-Union Academy of Agricultural Sciences, Mikhail Olshansky, attacked him by name in the magazine *Rural Life*. The article, "Against Misinformation and Slander," referred to Sakharov as an "engineer by specialty" and branded him as "incompetent and naive." Two months later, though, after Khrushchev's removal from power, the Central Committee of the Party, under its new collective leadership, praised Sakharov's forthright stand.

Sakharov's growing interest in politics brought him into contact with a broader circle of people. He began to meet members of the capital's intellectual community who shared his concerns and feared a resurgence of Stalinism in the country's life. In particular, he met the twin brothers Zhores and Roy Medvedev. A manuscript by Zhores on Lysenko, published in the West as *The Rise and Fall of T. D. Lysenko*, was the first *samizdat* work Sakharov read. A year later, he was among the first to read Roy Medvedev's massive study of

Stalin's reign, *Let History Judge.* Their acquaintance exerted a significant influence on Sakharov's public career as a dissident. And though in subsequent years he and Roy Medvedev disagreed on many issues, Sakharov himself has acknowledged Medvedev's role in his own development.

In Moscow, Sakharov not only broadened his contacts and his ability to exchange ideas with other independent-minded scientists; he also found the opportunity to express his views publicly for the first time in a manner the regime could not control. In 1966, he signed a collective letter to protest Stalin's possible rehabilitation. Several months later he signed another protest, this time against the introduction of articles 190-1 and 190-3 into the criminal code. In a letter to Brezhnev, he also protested the arrest of Alexander Ginzburg and Yuri Galanskov.

Sakharov began to write "Progress, Coexistence, and Intellectual Freedom" early in 1968. At a time when events in Czechoslovakia offered profound hope to people throughout Eastern Europe and the Soviet Union, Sakharov's essay reinforced the heady optimism of that spring. While he summarized his concern over the fundamental dilemmas of modern industrial society — military expenditures, environmental pollution, the role of scientific and technological progress — he also described the continuing legacy of Stalinist dictatorship in Soviet society.

In a letter to Sakharov, Alexander Solzhenitsyn expressed the enthusiasm that Sakharov's essay provoked. As we shall see, although Solzhenitsyn took exception to many of Sakharov's ideas, he still acknowledged the unique nature of his contribution.

We so rejoice in every little word of truth, so utterly suppressed until recent years, that we forgive those who first voice it for us all their near misses, all their inexactitudes, even a portion of error greater than the portion of truth, simply because "something at least, something at last has been said!"

All this we experienced as we read Academician Sakharov's article and listened to comments on it at home and from abroad. Our hearts beat faster as we realized that at last someone had broken out of the deep, untroubled, cozy torpor in which Soviet scientists get on with their scientific work, are rewarded with a life of plenty and pay for it by keeping their thoughts at the level of their test tubes.

Sakharov had circulated his essay hoping for discussion of his ideas. But while "Progress, Coexistence, and Intellectual Freedom" was widely reprinted in the West, where it provoked intense speculation, especially because of Sakharov's standing as a scientist, the only public comments in the Soviet Union distorted and misrepresented his thinking. Activists read and copied the memorandum, students at Moscow University left copies in their desks for those in subsequent classes to read. Sakharov's colleagues knew of the manuscript — he began the essay by remarking that his views "were formed in the milieu of the scientific and scientific-technical intelligentsia" — yet the regime never officially responded.

The invasion of Czechoslovakia by Warsaw Pact troops in August 1968 foreclosed any possibility that Sakharov's ideas on liberalization would be taken seriously within the Eastern bloc. In the attendant atmosphere of disappointment and repression, Sakharov's life, too, abruptly changed. When he arrived one morning at his laboratory in his chauffeur-driven car, the guard would not allow him to pass, telling him that his security clearance was no longer in effect. Only later was he informed that he had lost his job. A year passed before he was employed again, this time as a senior researcher at the Lebedev Institute, where he had begun his career.

For the active dissidents and their supporters the invasion of Czechoslovakia became a turning point in their struggle. It marked the end of any illusions that moral protest could effectively improve the internal situation. The idea of immigration to Israel or to the West in general became a more widespread hope. The invasion also marked a new level in the regime's stepped-up campaign against nonconformist activity.

Since the trial of Ginzburg and Galanskov in January 1968, the government had begun to retaliate against those who had signed petitions or letters of protest. Party members were expelled, people lost their jobs. Anatoly Marchenko was harassed and then arrested for writing *My Testimony*. Irina Belogorodskaya was picked up for distributing letters in his defense. The regime could not allow the attempted liberalization in Prague or the unprecedented acts of protest in Moscow to be taken as evidence of its own weakness. The suppression of one necessitated the suppression of the other.

On August 21, 1968, the same day Warsaw Pact troops invaded Czechoslovakia, Marchenko was tried and convicted for violating internal-passport regulations. The trial held no surprises except one — all of Marchenko's friends were permitted to enter the courtroom. The authorities probably were afraid that if his friends were not admitted but forced to stand outside the courthouse, they would become outraged, since the trial coincided with the invasion of Prague. So about seventy of Marchenko's supporters witnessed his one-day trial. At one point the judge's two assistants were given the following instructions: "They were told they were dealing with a criminal so cunning and insidious that he had not broken the law, and this article of the Criminal Code was the only way of getting him into jail," the *Chronicle of Current Events* reported.

Marchenko was still a sick man. He had contracted meningitis in the camps of Mordovia, which led to a recurring infection in his middle ear. After he arrived in Moscow in 1966 he had a trephining operation on his skull. He also suffered from severe internal bleeding in the stomach and a dangerous loss of hemoglobin. Only a series of blood transfusions saved him. The court had access to his medical reports. Nonetheless, the judge sentenced him to a year in the camps, the maximum penalty for the crime he allegedly committed.

His friends had little chance to react, for they were immediately preoccupied with the invasion of Prague. Although Soviet newspapers reported the "unanimous" support of the Soviet people, in reality there were incidents of protest throughout the country. Moscow University students were arrested for collecting signatures on a petition; another student was sent to a mental hospital for distributing poems against the invasion. In Leningrad, a young man was arrested for painting a slogan on a piece of sculpture; others threw protest leaflets out of cars, hoping passers-by would read them. In Novosibirsk, the authorities used dogs (unsuccessfully) to track down people who had painted slogans on public buildings. At meetings called to voice approval for the regime's action, members of numerous institutes refrained from voting or even voted against the resolutions; some were then removed from their jobs. In Moscow's October Square an individual shouted out a slogan against the invasion and then was beaten by men in plain clothes. Two of them took him away in a car; a third remained beside a second car, watching pedestrian traffic.

These isolated incidents were overshadowed by the most audacious protest, which took place in Red Square itself. From the moment news of Soviet aggression reached Moscow, individuals felt the need to respond. On Sunday, August 25, at the initiative of Pavel Litvinov and Larisa Bogoraz, seven demonstrators converged on Red Square from different directions. Many people regarded the demonstration as hopeless, so they stayed away. Others were outside the city on vacation. Some were too frightened to come. Pyotr Yakir was supposed to participate but told everyone that KGB agents stopped him on the way to the square; actually he had become frightened and gone home.

The demonstrators were careful to choose a spot away from the traffic lanes. As they prepared to begin, Vadim Delone joined them. He had come to Moscow that morning from the country and learned about the demonstration from a friend. A year before Delone had behaved badly, giving evidence to the investigators and repenting at his trial with Bukovsky. He received a conditional sentence and left the court, ashamed but at liberty. Now he would be a hero.

The following people took part in the demonstration: Konstantin Babitsky, a linguist; Larisa Bogoraz, a philologist; Vladimir Dremlyuga, a worker; Vadim Delone, a poet; Pavel Litvinov, a physicist; Victor Fainberg, a fine arts specialist; Tatyana Baeva, a student; and Natalya Gorbanevskaya, a poet and translator.

Gorbanevskaya came to Red Square wheeling her three-month-old-son in a carriage. Two banners and a Czech flag lay under the mattress. She handed the banners to her friends, giving Litvinov one that read, "For your freedom and ours." They both held great store by the slogan. It originated in the nineteenth century among Polish insurgents fighting to liberate their homeland from foreign aggressors, and primarily from Russia. It was also the slogan of those Russian democrats who understood that a nation that oppresses others cannot itself be free.

It took a moment to unfurl the banners, then they all sat down on the slightly raised parapet at Execution Place in front of St. Basil's Cathedral. In a letter to newspapers around the world, Natalya Gorbanevskaya described what happened:

> Almost at once a whistle blew and KGB agents in civilian clothes rushed up to us from all sides of the Square: they had been on duty in Red Square, waiting for the Czechoslovak delegation to leave the Kremlin. They shouted as they ran towards us: "They're all Jews! Beat up the anti-Soviets!" We sat quietly and offered no resistance. They tore the slogans from our hands, struck Victor Fainberg in the face until he bled, and knocked some of his teeth out. Pavel Litvinov was struck in the face with a heavy suitcase and they tore and broke a little Czechoslovak flag I was holding. They shouted: "Disperse you scum!" but we went on sitting. After a few minutes cars arrived and all, except for me, were pushed into them. I had my three-month-old son with me and was therefore not seized immediately; I sat at the Execution Ground for roughly another ten minutes. In the car, I was struck. Some members of the crowd who had expressed sympathy with us were also arrested — these were released late in the evening. That night, the homes of all those detained were searched, on being accused of "collective actions gravely violating public order."

Not all the demonstrators were brought to trial. At the first interrogation, Tatyana Baeva claimed she had been in Red Square by accident, although she voiced solidarity with her colleagues. Her home was searched and she was questioned many times, but while the others — except for Natalya Gorbanevskaya — remained in custody, Tatyana was allowed to go free. Still, she expected to face charges because it was her third demonstration. In the end, though, she was neither brought to trial nor allowed to testify as an eyewitness. She was only expelled from the institute where she was studying.

Victor Fainberg also was not brought to trial. It was considered too inconvenient to present him in court because he had been beaten so badly in Red Square. The prosecution after all intended to argue that it was the *demonstrators* who "disturbed public order." An alternative was devised for Fainberg. Psychiatrists were brought in to examine him. To no one's surprise they found him mentally incompetent and unfit for trial. The doctors' report speaks of "delusions of reform" and "residual symptoms of schizophrenia." In Leningrad, where he was treated, the doctors told him his diagnosis was "schizo-dissension." He would spend over four years in Leningrad Psychiatric Prison.

Natalya Gorbanevskaya remained free for more than a year, though she expected arrest at any time. She also felt guilty because her friends were in jail for a demonstration that, at the time, seemed utterly useless. But she did not waste her months at large. As we shall see, Natalya Gorbanevskaya was the editor of the *Chronicle of Current Events*, the unofficial journal of the human rights movement. At the same time she compiled material on the August demonstration and the trial of the participants. Her book, *Red Square at Noon*, would be completed just before her arrest in December 1969; she would be kept in a mental hospital for nearly two years.

The other demonstrators were handled in a more conventional manner. Their three-day trial opened on October 9, 1968, and offered few surprises. Except for a handful of relatives, it was closed to the public. The group of five men who had detained the protesters gave conflicting testimony. Another witness, an official at a notorious labor camp, claimed he had entered Red Square from the GUM department store, which, as everyone knew, is closed on Sundays, the day of the demonstration.

A local traffic policeman also was examined. On the day of the protest he had submitted a report to his superiors that did not mention any disruption of traffic. A week later he submitted a new report stating there had been a disruption. During the trial it was proved that he had been summoned by the KGB before changing his report.

The trial proceeded without unusual incident, while outside the building the regime created a mood of scarcely suppressed mob violence. People living nearby were told that currency speculators were on trial, an easy way to incite hostility against the accused and their friends. On the second day of the trial, drunks began appearing outside the courthouse. They tried to provoke fist fights with the defendants' supporters. It turned out that the authorities had set out vodka bottles for people in a neighboring courtyard.

Ilya Gabai described the scene in his essay "Before the Closed Doors of the Open Court":

> A hundred drunken women were brought. A thousand might have been. They confined themselves to jeering, but, given the order, they could have killed. . . . Many complained that they hadn't been allowed to shoot, or, at least, to run people down with a bulldozer. . . . People were showered with curses, of the choicest and foulest sort. The drunken women seemed to compete against each other in their filthiness and dirty threats. . . . "I'm a worker," cried one woman, "and if I'm drunk, then it's on my own money." An oldish man replied: "You're lying. You're not a worker. You've got no honor. You're simply a hired thug." . . . On those three days the cage doors were opened only a crack; the animals sitting inside merely showed their claws. One day the whole zoo might be unleashed onto the street.

For some people the hypocrisy of the trial was too crude to ignore. One woman, who had been brought from her place of work to sit in the courtroom, later described to Natalya Gorbanevskaya how she and her colleagues were instructed to behave. Sitting in the courtroom, where relatives of the accused "looked at us with dislike," she felt ashamed. Two journalists who attended the trial for Soviet papers were said to have refused to write the articles required of them.

Finally, in his closing remarks the prosecutor dwelled on events in Czechoslovakia, though the defendants were not permitted to refer to the invasion in order to explain their motives. The trial ended predictably. Convicted of holding "a disorderly assembly in Red Square for the propagation of their slanderous fabrications," the defendants were given the following sentences: Vladimir Dremlyuga, three years in a labor camp; Vadim Delone, two years and ten months in a labor camp, including a portion of the sentence not served because of his conditional release in 1967; Pavel Litvinov, five years of internal exile; Larisa Bogoraz, four years of internal exile; and Konstantin Babitsky, three years of internal exile.

After the trial, the judge called the defense lawyers into her chambers and congratulated them for preparing their cases well. One of the lawyers, Dina Kaminskaya, represented both Pavel Litvinov and Larisa Bogoraz. A year before she had represented Vladimir Bukovsky and in 1968 she defended Yuri Galanskov and then Anatoly Marchenko before taking on the case of the Red Square demonstration. Each time she argued, in vain, for her client's acquittal.

Kaminskaya understood that her participation as a defense attorney enhanced the regime's charade. The authorities could point to her efforts, her plea for acquittal, as evidence of a trial's fairness. Nonetheless, Kaminskaya and other honest and talented lawyers, like Sophie Kallistratova, Boris Zolotukhin, and Yuri Lurie, understood the importance of accepting political cases.

Only a lawyer can visit a defendant before the trial begins. During the pretrial investigation that can last many months and sometimes over a year (defendants are picked up near the outset of investigations), a prisoner is not allowed to see relatives or friends. Lawyers help defendants use the law more effectively to expose the nature of the trials themselves. The lawyer's questions often dismantle the prosecution's case. Later, when transcripts of a trial circulate in *samizdat*, the lawyer's questions and pleas for acquittal *on the basis of Soviet law and legal procedure* reinforce the dissidents' claim that political trials violate judicial guarantees.

The exile of Pavel Litvinov and Larisa Bogoraz was a particular loss to the Moscow activists. For more than a year Pavel's energy and gregarious nature had attracted numerous other dissidents, creating contacts among people who might otherwise not have known one another. Among his closest colleagues were Jews who hoped to emigrate, convinced Marxists who despised the regime, and liberal intellectuals who developed the strategy of challenging the authorities on constitutional grounds. Pavel's own compilations, *The Demonstration in Pushkin Square*, concerning the trials of Khaustov and Bukovsky, Delone, and Kushev, and the massively detailed *The Trial of the Four*, about the Ginzburg-Galanskov case, were models of meticulous, dispassionate reporting.

Larisa Bogoraz had been an activist in the movement since its initial stirrings. She had supported her husband, Yuli Daniel. Later, as her relationship with Anatoly Marchenko deepened, she grew increasingly distressed as the KGB revealed their hatred for him before finally arresting him. Then the arrest of her cousin Irina Belogorodskaya depressed her further. For months Larisa had appeared positively somber to her friends. The demonstration in Red Square provided an important psychological release. Afterward, in the police station, "she visibly brightened. We were light at heart," as Natalya Gorbanevskaya reports in *Red Square at Noon*.

Some activists, perhaps, saw their sacrifice as a useless one. Anatoly Yakobson, distraught about missing the demonstration because, like many Moscow residents in August, he was out of the city, understood its significance. "All those in our country who seek the truth," Yakobson wrote,

> have heard of the demonstration; so have the people of Czechoslovakia; so has humanity at large. By speaking from London a century ago in defence of Polish freedom and against its oppressors on behalf of a Great Power, Herzen redeemed the honor of Russian democracy single-handed. These seven demonstrators have undoubtedly saved the honor of the Soviet people. The importance of the demonstration on 25 August cannot be exaggerated.
>
> Many people with humane and progressive views, however, who admit that the demonstration was both courageous and high-minded, also assume that it was an act of despair and that a demonstration resulting in the inevitable and immediate arrest of its participants and retribution against them was unwise and ineffective. Even "self-immuration" has made its appearance as a new word to match "self-immolation."
>
> I believe, on the contrary, that even if the demonstrators had been unable to unfold their slogans and their demonstration had remained unknown to all, it would still have been a sensible and justifiable act. Actions of this kind cannot be measured by the yardstick of ordinary politics where every action must produce an immediate and substantial result, a material advantage. . . . One must begin by postulating that truth is needed for its own sake and for no other reason; that human dignity will not permit one to condone evil, even if one cannot avert it.

The exile of Pavel Litvinov and Larisa Bogoraz to far-off areas of Siberia deprived friends of their help and inspiration. The dissidents, however, were no longer an improvised collection of individuals whose arrests could cripple activity against the regime. By the fall of 1968, after three years of sustained protest, their movement had matured into an established pattern of moral struggle.

4

THE MOVEMENT MATURES

THE TRIAL of Galanskov, Ginzburg, Dobrovolsky, and Lashkova was the first concerted attempt to intimidate the nascent movement as a whole. By alleging contacts with "shady" émigré groups, the authorities hoped to discredit the defendants and their supporters as well.

The crude tactics of the regime, however, produced unintended results. More people than ever before signed petitions. The appeal of Larisa Bogoraz and Pavel Litvinov was broadcast in Russian by the BBC and aroused support for the defendants across the country. The letter from a group of high school students has already been noted. Ivan Yakhimovich, a collective farm chairman in Latvia, wrote to Mikhail Suslov, the principal theoretician on the Politburo. In his letter, Yakhimovich cautioned his fellow Communist that "ideas cannot be murdered with bullets, prisons and exile. . . . I live in the provinces, where for every house with electricity there are ten without, where in winter the buses cannot get through and the mail takes weeks to arrive. If information [on the trials] has reached us on the largest scale you can well imagine what you have done, what sort of seeds you have sown throughout the country. Have the courage to correct the mistakes that have been made before the workers and peasants take a hand in the affair."

Many other people wrote directly to Pavel Litvinov or managed to find him in Moscow. They brought word of their own difficulties and hoped he could help them. He took notes on each visitor, passed them on to friends, pondered over which story would appeal to a journalist. Although most of the information was hardly surprising, much was new and, in a way, startling, for it reflected a ferment in Soviet society that even Litvinov, a central and energetic figure among Moscow's nonconformist intellectuals, had not yet recognized.

More than a thousand people signed protests against the Galanskov-Ginzburg trial, among them Ivan Yakhimovich, who would soon be expelled from the Communist party and then relieved of his kolkhoz responsibility. Many more also faced harassment. Each incident deserved to be remembered. Expulsions from the Party, loss of employment—such reprisals were not always easy to arrange. One teacher, Valeria Gerlin, defended her right to appeal to Soviet authorities on behalf of Galanskov and Ginzburg; some of her colleagues came to her defense and tried to prevent her dismissal. Their efforts failed but a record of the trade-union meeting reached the West and provided a revealing glimpse of the regime's extrajudicial controls.

Soon Litvinov and his colleagues could not handle all this information. They were overwhelmed by the number of protests, the available facts surrounding each reprisal, and the surge of new reports reaching Moscow from outlying republics. For months, prominent figures among the dissidents had discussed issuing a regular human rights bulletin. Sometime that winter Natalya Gorbanevskaya decided to begin the *Chronicle of Current Events*.

Born in 1936, Gorbanevskaya attended Moscow University during the early years of Khrushchev's rule. Some of her friends produced a wall newspaper, which commented on literary and artistic issues such as Dudintsev's novel *Not by Bread Alone* and the Picasso exhibit in 1956. But the invasion of Hungary affected their hopes and activities. Her friends were expelled from the university for opposing the invasion. Two years later, other friends were caught circulating leaflets. For three days Gorbanevskaya was interrogated in Moscow's Lubyanka prison. At first she admitted nothing, but after a day, frightened by her interrogators, she gave some testimony on the anti-Soviet mood of the leaflets. Released from prison, expelled from the university, she considered herself an unreliable person, one who ought not to know information that might compromise others.

Tired of politics, she devoted herself to poetry. By the end of the 1950s, *samizdat* was beginning to circulate. At first it was mainly poetry, of Pasternak, Akhmatova, a few poems of Mandelstam and Tsvetaeva, not even reproduced with a typewriter but copied by hand from old books. There were poetry readings, too, at youth clubs and even at Komsomol meetings. At one reading, Komsomol members denounced the poetry as "nihilism" and "modernism." Surprisingly, a young man spoke in defense of the poets. It was Yuri Galanskov, whom Gorbanevskaya met that night. He eventually included some of her poems in the first issue of his anthology, *Phoenix-61*. By then he had also introduced her to his friend Alexander Ginzburg, who was preparing another collection of underground poetry to be called *Syntax*. Ginzburg had already compiled three issues of what is today acknowledged as the first *samizdat* journal. Gorbanevskaya was helping him with the fourth issue when Ginzburg was arrested for the first time in 1960.

Other incidents contributed to her involvement in the movement. In 1965, a former teacher of hers at Moscow University, Andrei Sinyavsky, was arrested. Alexander Ginzburg then compiled the transcript of the Sinyavsky-Daniel trial, together with articles from the Soviet press and letters of protest to the authorities. Gorbanevskaya herself copied their final speeches innumerable times. Just when she was preparing the first issue of the *Chronicle*, Pavel Litvinov was collecting a mass of material on Ginzburg's trial.

The first issue of the *Chronicle* reflected the straightforward, dispassionate approach that Ginzburg and Litvinov had developed for their reports of political trials. Dated April 30, 1968, the title page carried the heading "Human Rights Year in the Soviet Union." Elsewhere on that page, the editor quoted article 19 of the United Nations Universal Declaration of Human Rights, as if to claim protection under it: "Everyone has the right to freedom of opinion and expression; this right includes freedom to hold opinions without interference and to seek, receive, and impart information and ideas through any medium, regardless of frontiers."

The first issue concentrated on the aftermath of the Galanskov-Ginzburg trial. Gorbanevskaya worked with a pile of index cards; each one listed the name of a person who had signed an appeal, along with information about the regime's reprisals: "chats" with the KGB, dismissals from employment, expulsions from the Party. Gorbanevskaya also reported on how she and Esenin-Volpin were forcibly interned in psychiatric hospitals for their part in the protests.

At the time of the Galanskov-Ginzburg trial, Gorbanevskaya was more than five months pregnant. The day after she sent her protest to Soviet officials, she became ill and a gynecologist suggested she enter a hospital. Along with anemia, she faced the threat of a miscarriage.

In February 1968, Gorbanevskaya entered a maternity clinic. She grew depressed in the hospital, unable to sleep or find people to share her thoughts. She wanted to leave but the hospital officials kept finding excuses for not signing her out, all the time assuring her that she could leave "the next day." As Gorbanevskaya later reported in the first issue of the *Chronicle*, someone had other plans for her:

> Without any warning and without her relations' knowledge, Gorbanevskaya was transferred on February 15th from maternity clinic No. 27, where she was being kept with a threatened miscarriage, to ward 27 of the Kashchenko hospital. The decision to transfer her was taken in consultation with the duty psychiatrist of the Timiryazev district, and the transfer was said to have been motivated by the patient's requests to be discharged. On February 23rd, Gorbanevskaya was discharged from the Kashchenko hospital as the psychiatrists admitted she was not in need of treatment.

Esenin-Volpin faced a harsher reprisal. He was taken from his home and spent nearly three months in psychiatric hospitals. As the *Chronicle* reported, nearly a hundred of the country's most eminent mathematicians appealed on his behalf but succeeded in gaining only limited improvement in his situation. He was moved from a ward for petty criminals in a prison hospital to a quieter ward in a regular psychiatric hospital before finally being released.

The first issues of the *Chronicle* passed almost completely unnoticed. Its stories of arrests and dismissals were not new to most dissidents, especially in Moscow, where word of repression traveled quickly. The KGB paid it little attention. Moreover, that spring and summer there were too many fresh and important items in other *samizdat* publications for people to notice a collection of familiar stories. Accounts of labor camp life and reports from Czechoslovakia took priority. Then in June Andrei Sakharov's first memorandum, "Progress, Coexistence, and Intellectual Freedom," began to circulate.

For Sakharov and all the dissidents, the invasion of Czechoslovakia deflated their hopes for liberalization. For many, it marked the end of activity for internal reform, while the idea of emigration took on greater urgency. For Gorbanevskaya and a small group of her friends, the invasion could not continue without a public protest. They were all arrested in Red Square but Gorbanevskaya, the mother of two young children, was released within a day.

Still, she expected arrest. She also felt guilty, for her friends remained under arrest for a demonstration that, at the time, seemed to have been utterly useless. The third issue of the *Chronicle* was almost ready, but, afraid of a search, she gave the material to a friend who had agreed to prepare the final draft. Her arrest did not come for more than a year. During that time, she continued to produce the *Chronicle* every two months, as well as to compile material on the August demonstration and the trial of the participants.

By the end of 1968, the *Chronicle* was a central part of the dissidents' struggle. Its regular appearance and its uniquely dispassionate tone underlay its appeal. In addition, activists already understood the *Chronicle*'s usefulness as an archive of their struggle with the regime. Gorbanevskaya no longer worked on it alone. Her friends collected facts and passed them on to her. Pavel Litvinov traveled to Leningrad for information on a trial in June. She herself would go to Riga to learn about events in the Baltic states. Leonid Plyushch brought reports from Kiev. Regular channels of information were established between Novosibirsk, Obninsk, Leningrad, and the capital. Reproduced on typewriters, eight copies at a time, the *Chronicle of Current Events* increasingly spread throughout the country as friends supplied copies to friends. The anonymous editors had to issue these instructions:

> The *Chronicle* is in no sense an illegal publication, and the difficult conditions in which it is produced are

created by the peculiar notions about law and freedom of information which, in the course of long years, have become established in certain Soviet organizations. For this reason the *Chronicle* cannot, like any other journal, give its postal address on the last page. Nevertheless, anybody who is interested in seeing that the Soviet public is informed about what goes on in the country may easily pass on information to the editors of the *Chronicle*. Simply tell it to the person from whom you received the *Chronicle*, and he will tell the person from whom *he* received the *Chronicle*, and so on. But do not try to trace back the whole chain of communication yourself, or else you will be taken for a police informer.

The KGB was now anxious to stop the *Chronicle*. Under increasing pressure and threat of arrest, Gorbanevskaya looked for a new editor. Galya Gabai, a Moscow schoolteacher, seemed ready to help. She and her husband Ilya had already helped Gorbanevskaya compile and reproduce several issues. When her husband was arrested in May 1969, Galya followed him to Tashkent, where the investigation and trial took place. Her reports then appeared in several issues of the *Chronicle*. Because of Galya's experience, Gorbanevskaya asked her to put together forthcoming numbers.

By this time, Gorbanevskaya and her colleagues were relying on Pyotr Yakir to help them gather information. Yakir, the son of General Iona Yakir, who was killed in the army purges of 1937, was arrested then at the age of fourteen and spent seventeen years in prisons and labor camps. Released after Stalin's death, he made a career as an anti-Stalinist, delivering lectures at factories and institutes on the dictator's crimes. Well known, seemingly fearless, the son of a now-heroic army general, Yakir was a beloved figure among the dissidents. Visitors came to him day and night, picked up copies of the latest *Chronicle,* and left notes in his mailbox. At the same time, though, his weaknesses of character and temperament made him vulnerable and not altogether reliable. He drank excessively and greatly feared violent reprisals against himself and his family.

A number of Yakir's colleagues grew reluctant to share information with him. He talked too much on the telephone — about the *Chronicle,* about appeals, about proposed discussions. As Leonid Plyushch remarks in his memoir, *History's Carnival,* "Suspicion is immoral but so is lack of caution." In addition, while some dissidents did exert moral pressure on their friends to sign petitions (and thereby subject them to possible unpleasantness if they did sign), Yakir would overstep the bounds of discretion and endanger hitherto uninvolved people with suggestions that they sign intemperate appeals.

Gorbanevskaya warned Galya Gabai not to tell Yakir that she was to continue the *Chronicle.* However, Galya could not accept this advice because Yakir was an exemplary figure to her. Yet when she told him she also cautioned him that if anyone else learned of her activity she would stop her work on the *Chronicle.* Because her husband was in a labor camp, only she could visit him and bring food packages. Were she to be arrested, Ilya, too, would suffer.

Galya prepared the tenth issue of the *Chronicle* in the fall of 1969. But she did not feel secure. Once, on a bus, a person she scarcely knew handed her a small package of paper. "For the *Chronicle,*" he whispered. Immediately, Galya feared the KGB must know of her involvement. In December, agents visited her apartment while she was preparing dinner; material for the *Chronicle* was piled in her kitchen. When the agents knocked on her door, she threw the papers into the borscht. Throughout the search, a friend calmly stirred the soup.

Gorbanevskaya had to prepare number eleven from scratch. She was also anxious to find a replacement for Galya. Most people were afraid to take the *Chronicle* on themselves. One friend who did seem willing to help was to come one evening to talk with her. That afternoon, though, Gorbanevskaya was arrested. Several friends were with her in the apartment and saw her cast a glance at her winter overcoat. Gorbanevskaya left in a light jacket. In the pocket of her overcoat her friends found material on hunger strikes in the Mordovian camps. It had reached her the night before her arrest.

Gorbanevskaya's trial took place on July 7, 1970. She was not present in the courtroom and, at first, none of her friends were allowed to attend. But a small group of supporters demanded entry. When several approached the windows of the building a policeman assaulted them, throwing two women to the ground. Then the authorities announced that one of Gorbanevskaya's friends could enter. The group chose Valery Chalidze, a physicist and active legal scholar, and it was he who reported on the conduct of the trial.

Inside the courtroom the regime pursued an arbitrary course. Eleven days after the Red Square demonstration, Gorbanevskaya had been taken to the Serbsky Institute for an outpatient examination, where the doctors concluded she suffered from "deep psychopathy" with "the possibility of sluggish schizophrenia not excluded." Although they recommended compulsory treatment for her, the procurator let her go because of her "insanity" and because of her two young children. Gorbanevskaya was released under her mother's guardianship.

A year later, in November 1969, she was called for

another examination. To her surprise, the medical commission found no grounds for a diagnosis of schizophrenia and saw no need for hospitalization. Gorbanevskaya could not understand this episode. On the one hand, she thought the regime was planning to arrest her and send her to a labor camp, so she would need to be considered healthy. On the other hand, it was possible that Dr. Yanushevsky, who directed the examination, wanted to foil the KGB's plans. At that time Soviet psychiatric abuse was beginning to attract publicity, and he may have been trying to establish his own integrity.

Gorbanevskaya was arrested in December and brought to Serbsky again in April 1970. There, under the leadership of Daniil Lunts and Georgy Morozov, the doctors had no difficulty detecting her mental illness. At the trial, Lunts described his diagnosis of "sluggish schizophrenia." As the *Chronicle* reported, he claimed it was "not characterized by crude, well-defined psychotic phenomena such as delirium, hallucinations, etc. The illness takes its course without affecting fitness for work or one's former intellectual level and skills." Armed with this diagnosis, the doctors had no need to explain away their patient's productive life as a translator and poet.

Accused of compiling the *Chronicle*, Natalya Gorbanevskaya was convicted of "anti-Soviet agitation." Because of her mental illness, however, she was declared not responsible and committed to compulsory psychiatric treatment for an indefinite period. She would spend nearly two years in mental hospitals, subject to treatment with antipsychotic drugs whose side effects prevented her from reading or writing coherently.

The KGB thought it had stopped the *Chronicle* with her hospitalization. It had not. The *Chronicle* was now in other hands.

It managed to appear every two months for two more

years. Each issue reflected the growth of the human rights movement as a whole and its ability to collect information and attract the attention of groups in outlying republics. With its numerous sources of information, the *Chronicle* reflected a far more complex and intriguing society than the contented, bland monolith depicted in the official press. (Even a high Soviet official once complained in the Party magazine *Kommunist* about the dullness of the country's papers, writing: "Before me are issues of several provincial papers published on the same day. . . . If it were not for the masthead . . . any one of the papers could be substituted for another and neither the reader nor the staffs themselves would notice.")

For years the Crimean Tatars had agitated for the right to return to the Crimea, from which they had been expelled to central Asia in 1944. The *Chronicle* now carried articles on their history and struggle, often referring readers to the Crimean Tatars' *Information Bulletin.* The activities of Ukrainian nationalists, Zionists, Lithuanian Catholics, and Uzbeks found their way into the *Chronicle* under sections with special headings like "The Jewish Emigration Movement" or "Persecution of Believers." Throughout its pages, the *Chronicle* maintained a judicious tone, even when it spoke of groups like the anti-Semitic and fascist Fetisov circle in Moscow, whose critique of the regime was abhorred by the *Chronicle*'s editors. When the leaders of the Fetisov group were sent to mental hospitals, the *Chronicle* commented that "to express satisfaction over the fact that the authorities have sent your intellectual opponents to a 'nut house' is immoral."

The *Chronicle* also managed to provide information from prisons and labor camps. After his conviction in 1967, Vladimir Bukovsky had not been forgotten. The fifth issue of the *Chronicle*, dated December 25, 1968, reported from his labor camp in central Russia:

In October Vladimir Bukovsky was concussed when a pile of timber collapsed on him. He was unable to work as a result, but was accused of malingering and put in a punishment cell. He started a hunger strike in protest. Against the usual rule he was put in a communal cell and his cellmates declared a ten-day hunger strike in support of him. Only after this was Bukovsky transferred to hospital for a while.

A year later, the *Chronicle* informed its readers that Anatoly Marchenko, the author of *My Testimony*, faced a further reprisal. His book appeared in the West while he was serving a one-year term in the camps. This infuriated the authorities, who immediately prepared a new case against him before the close of his term. The trial was held at his place of confinement. Although fellow prisoners who were called to testify could not recall hearing Marchenko utter anti-Soviet statements, prison guards testified, with a good deal of confusion, that he had declared that "there is no democracy in the U.S.S.R., freedom of expression, of the press, of creativity does not exist" and "the Soviet Union is violating the sovereignty of other countries, and Soviet troops were sent into Czechoslovakia to suppress freedom with tanks." For these statements his term at hard labor was extended an additional two years.

Marchenko was not expected to survive his term. Dutton, his American publisher, had little hope. On the back cover of a copy of *My Testimony* printed in 1971 we are told that "the author is reported to be still a prisoner, but it is thought unlikely that he will be heard from again." Marchenko, however, proved them wrong.

A short time before his release the authorities required Marchenko to choose where he would live for a year under administrative surveillance. Marchenko knew he would never be allowed to live in Moscow. He submitted the names of three cities, including Chuna, where Larisa Bogoraz had several months remaining of her own term of exile. Knowing she would stay with him if he joined her there, the KGB gave Marchenko permission to live in Chuna. He went there in August 1971. He and Larisa Bogoraz were married later that year.

As the *Chronicle* documented over the next four years, Marchenko tried to establish a normal life for himself and his family. In September 1972, he and Larisa moved to Tarusa, a city barely sixty miles from Moscow, where Marchenko rebuilt an old, dilapidated house they found there. That winter their son Pavel was born.

In Tarusa, Marchenko worked as a furnace stoker in a factory. The KGB, however, had not forgotten him. They often searched his house and harassed him at work, but Marchenko resumed his activity in spite of this pressure. He began to write fictional accounts of labor camp life and letters to world leaders such as Kurt Waldheim and Willy Brandt, alerting them to human rights violations. In response, on May 24, 1974, the KGB placed Marchenko under administrative supervision. He was required to be at home from eight in the evening to six in the morning. In addition, he was forbidden to go to restaurants or the cinema. If he wished to leave Tarusa, he first would need the permission of the police. And finally, he would have to report to the police every Monday at 6 P.M.

Marchenko barely tolerated such interference in his life, but he tried to fulfill the provisions set by the authorities out of concern for his family. At the same time, he continued his nonconformist activity. In July, Andrei Sakharov announced a hunger strike in support of Soviet political prisoners. Marchenko responded to this appeal by declaring a hunger strike of his own; he fasted for five days. Then, in August, the supervision became more severe. Several times Marchenko asked for permission to visit Moscow, once to bring his son to a doctor, another time to meet his mother at the train station. His requests were denied. A doctor examined Marchenko during this time, just before her own departure for the United States. She found him very weak; one ear was infected and filled with pus.

Nonetheless, as pressure from the KGB increased, Marchenko became more obstinate. On October 11, after being refused permission to bring his sick son back to Tarusa from Moscow, he declared himself free of the supervision. In November and again in December, he was fined by the courts for violating terms of the supervision. He knew the risks he faced. By law, "malicious violation" of administrative supervision constitutes a crime, punishable by up to two years in a labor camp. Still, he did not relent. On December 10, in a letter to Nikolai Podgorny, chairman of the Presidium of the Supreme Soviet of the U.S.S.R., Marchenko renounced his Soviet citizenship and declared his intention to go to the United States. At the end of December he was called to the visa office and encouraged to accept a visa for Israel. "If you insist on going to the U.S.," they warned him, "you'll end up being convicted for violation of supervision."

Marchenko refused to cooperate as a matter of principle. Again in February he was encouraged to submit documents for his emigration. And, once more in the visa office, he stood by his right to immigrate to the United States. The next day, February 26, his house in Tarusa was searched. The police seized rough drafts and other notes, together with manuscripts belonging to his wife. In violation of legal procedures, they refused to leave a protocol of the search. That night, Marchenko was arrested and taken to Kaluga Investigation Prison. At the time of his arrest, he declared an indefinite hunger strike and refused to cooperate with the investigation of his case.

Marchenko's behavior during this period — his appeals to the West, his refusals to accept a visa to Israel — reflect more than his obstinacy. Since the publication of *My Testimony*, he knew that his case was known in the West. His letters, also, addressed to Western statesmen or Soviet leaders, were often broadcast in Russian by the BBC or Radio Liberty. In his isolation, however, without genuine access to information, Marchenko, like many dissidents, could not properly judge how closely his activities were followed in the West. The radio transmits a good deal of information coming from the Soviet Union, making it seem as if the Western public actually knows and cares about internal repression. The Soviet government, in turn, reinforces this impression by making it difficult for dissenters to maintain contact with the West. Ironically, both the regime and its critics share an identical illusion, for the West, in general, is not thirsting for news from the Soviet Union. Marchenko made a tragic miscalculation. He believed that his appeals, his renunciation of Soviet citizenship, his insistence on immigrating to America, would compel the regime to relent. But he overestimated Western interest in internal Soviet developments.

Furthermore, Marchenko's character increased his willingness to challenge authority. After years of opposition and suffering he had come to believe firmly in the need to place himself in danger, as if only the reprisals he faced could confirm the legitimacy and justice of his behavior.

Marchenko's stubbornness, his allegiance to truth and opposition to injustice were not unique qualities. Other dissidents, too, oppose the regime, take risks, suffer arbitrary punishments. At the same time, most of them, notably those who are intellectuals, reserve a part of their energy and some of their time for personal or professional pursuits. They resist becoming full-time revolutionaries and hesitate to relinquish their creative ambitions and personal loyalties.

From the time of his arrival in Moscow in 1966, Marchenko transformed his life into a virtual crusade on behalf of Soviet political prisoners. As his involvement deepened, so, too, did his anger and intolerance. Friends who knew him in Moscow remember how his opinions hardened, how he came to view issues in starker, more simple terms. His life became synonymous with his cause. The restraints others experience, like the potential loss of employment, or the responsibility to one's family, did not move him. Even his love for his infant son did not deter him from refusing a visa to Israel. Principle alone dictated his behavior.

In part, Marchenko's attitude reflects his origins and the vicissitudes of his life. In contrast to virtually all of his fellow dissidents, he never completed his formal education. Since 1958, except for occasional periods, he has lived in labor camps, prison, or exile. Yet he also came to regard himself as a writer and a spokesman. Ironically, the authorities resented his social and intellectual pretensions. For the police, themselves members of the lower classes, Marchenko's familiarity with Jews and intellectuals was offensive; they knew how to remind him of his proper place. Marchenko, in turn, never learned to mitigate reprisals by the regime. His own defiance invited the harsh treatment that other dissidents learned to avoid.

Marchenko was prepared for prison. He kept mittens, warm socks, a toothbrush, and soap near the door. His wife had agreed to go to Moscow if he was arrested in order to be with family and friends. In jail he refused to answer questions, give fingerprints, sign documents. The guards beat him with keys, their boots, and their fists. The investigation itself was perfunctory; the officer in charge did not even know what material had been confiscated. Still, Marchenko waited five weeks for his trial to begin.

The whole time he continued his hunger strike. After eight days without food, he was dragged from his cell to be force-fed. He refused to walk by himself, to sit down, to open his mouth. His hands were manacled behind his back so tightly that his shoulders ached for weeks. When he resisted the spreader, they fed him through his nostrils. When the doctors came to inject glucose, he distorted his skin and muscles in order to impede the needle.

Marchenko describes his hunger strike and trial in his memoir, *From Tarusa to Siberia.* "My protest was a reaction to coercion, and the more brutal that coercion became, the more extreme became the form of my protest." His own conduct surprised, even repelled him. "Do I sit down on the stool voluntarily or allow strange hands to pin me down? . . . Each time the entire scene provoked in me an idiotic feeling. I could not define for myself at what point my refusal to submit voluntarily stopped being a protest and became simply asinine stubbornness." Once before he had attempted a hunger strike — in 1961, after his conviction for treason. He was force-fed and gave in the next day. Now he was more determined.

The trial took place in Kaluga on the thirty-third day of his hunger strike. The courtroom was open. Twenty of Marchenko's friends and relatives, including Andrei Sakharov, attended. Marchenko was led in by several guards. He looked bad. His wrists were handcuffed behind his back. At the defendant's bench he almost collapsed; the guards held him up. He told the court that his copy of the indictment had been taken away from him on the way to the courthouse, in violation of judicial procedure. In fact, he had not been informed that his trial was about to begin. The court disregarded this. Then Marchenko asked that his wife be allowed to defend him. The court denied his request, appointing a lawyer whom Marchenko had never seen. In response to these abuses, Marchenko refused to take part in the proceedings, reserving only his right to a final plea.

The trial then continued as predicted — Marchenko was charged with violating administrative supervision. Several policemen were called. No one cross-examined them. During a recess his wife and friends, claiming they could refute the accusations, asked the defense lawyer to call them as witnesses. At first he refused, but later he asked the court to allow them to testify. The judge denied his request, claiming they had been in the courtroom during the testimony of other witnesses.

Marchenko presented no defense; he spoke only to make his final plea.

... Neither the investigator nor the court has shown any interest in the fact that until October 11 I complied with the conditions of the supervision, and that I ceased to comply with them only when I was finally convinced of their humiliating character. After the summer, all my requests prompted by a concern for my family had been denied. I asked for permission to meet my mother — who is not only aged but illiterate — at the station in Moscow. I was refused. To visit my sick child in Moscow: refused. To see my aged mother off: refused. When my son got sick, and it was thought he might have scarlet fever, I asked permission to take him to Moscow, since at the time there was no pediatrician in Tarusa. For four days Volodin, the police chief, gave me the run-around: "Come back tomorrow; come back after lunch." Finally, on the fourth day, he told me bluntly that he had not received an answer. Who, I wonder, was supposed to answer that kind of request? After all, the law states that supervision is carried out by the regular police. I went

back once more. The deputy chief told me my request
had been denied. Then I told him I would refuse to
comply with the supervision, and took my wife and
sick child to Moscow. After that outrageous incident
I considered myself free from supervision. I issued a
statement saying that I had been outlawed in my own
country. I addressed that statement to the world public.
It is hard enough for one person to oppose a gang of
bandits, but it is even harder to defend oneself against
gangsters calling themselves the state. I do not repent
of what I did. I love freedom. But if I am living in a
state where concern for one's family and relatives, or
love for and devotion to one's child, are criminal, I
prefer a prison cell. Where else would I be tried for such
acts? I was put in a situation where I had to choose: to
renounce my family, or to become a criminal.

Marchenko was convicted. Surprisingly, the court sentenced him to four years of exile, a punishment more lenient
than the code allows. His wife and child could join him.
His fellow prisoners in Kaluga were amazed; hunger strikes
are not supposed to count. "You're going to be free," they
told him.

Another twelve days passed before he began his journey
to Chuna. The officers on the train did not know of his
hunger strike. He had to tell them himself, refusing his
rations. His dossier contained no word of it, although across
the front was printed in bold type: INCLINED TO SUICIDE.
He was not held separately, and no doctor accompanied
him — conditions required for hunger strikers. They refused
to recognize his protest, so he was not force-fed. In crowded
trains, at switching points, in halls full of convicts, Marchenko was treated like the other prisoners: forced to drag
his mattress, to stand long hours. He was in the eighth week
of his hunger strike, and his last reserves of strength abated.
After eight days in transit, he could no longer move. In the

corridor, a guard argued with his boss, refusing to answer for a prisoner's impending death. Marchenko realized it was time to relent. He broke his strike the next morning, chewing slowly on a spoonful of gruel.

His deportation lasted another month. Arriving in Chuna, Marchenko issued a statement through his friends in Moscow. He thanked all those who spoke out in his defense.

Although the *Chronicle* has focused its attention on individual dissidents, other matters relating directly to Stalin's legacy also are mentioned. Occasionally, notes appear on the purge trials of the 1920s and 1930s. The struggle of the Crimean Tatars and other national minorities, the ideological constraints on science, the backward state of Soviet agriculture, all reflect the inability of the present regime to come to terms with its own past. While these and other problems permeate Soviet society, they gain no attention in the official press.

The principal goal of the *Chronicle of Current Events* has been to challenge the regime's control of information. It therefore has been eager to report on a wide range of nonconformist activities, involving everyone from anti-Stalinist Marxists to liberal reformers and evangelical Christians. But the *Chronicle* avoids commenting on its own reports, wishing to stand apart from the ideological tensions that arise among the dissidents themselves. Consequently, it is not a useful source of information for the debates — on détente, emigration, or the future of Russia — that have shaken the dissident community.

In 1974, for example, in the midst of increased repression, three leading figures — Alexander Solzhenitsyn, Roy Medvedev, and Andrei Sakharov — engaged in a polemical debate over détente. Its contours reflected long-standing attitudes toward Russian history, the country's relation to the West, and the future Russia should seek. Sakharov and Solzhenitsyn especially represented the views of a substantial group of dissidents. Many people responded on their own, attacking, supporting, circulating a flurry of essays in *samizdat*. While the *Chronicle* occasionally mentioned their appearance and described their contents, it paid little attention to the whole debate. At the same time, by not commenting on these and other issues, the *Chronicle* gained the confidence of diverse groups. For in a society where genuine information is precious and tolerance is rare, the *Chronicle* has tried hard to avoid compromising the integrity of its reports with editorial comment.

The *Chronicle*'s focus remained on events within the activist community. These reports exposed an ever-increasing pattern of reprisal against people who signed appeals or who circulated literature not approved by the authorities. The mathematician Ilya Burmistrovich received three years in a labor camp for circulating works by Yuli Daniel and Andrei Sinyavsky. The *Chronicle* described his trial for its readers. A group of foreigners was convicted for passing out leaflets to Soviet citizens. According to the *Chronicle*, one witness told the court, "I saw the word freedom — and I knew it meant some kind of provocation." The *Chronicle* learned of arrests and trials throughout the country and provided its readers with useful details of the regime's repressive controls.

One episode in particular, the arrest and hospitalization of General Pyotr Grigorenko, altered the direction of the human rights movement.

Until his arrest in Tashkent on May 7, 1969, General Grigorenko was one of the dominant figures among the Moscow activists. Born in the southern Ukraine in 1907, Grigorenko was the first in his village to join the Komsomol. During World War II Grigorenko became a distinguished soldier. Twice wounded, he received the Order of Lenin, two Orders of the Red Flag, and numerous medals. After the war he began a career as a military strategist, working for seventeen years in Moscow's Frunze Military Academy, first as chairman of the research department and then as head of the cybernetics department. He was promoted to major general in 1959.

For more than thirty years Grigorenko served the Communist party as a devoted follower of Stalin. Not until Khrushchev's speech in 1956 did his views begin to change, but even then he resolved to reform the Party within the framework he believed Khrushchev himself established. By 1961, however, Grigorenko saw indications of a new, personal dictatorship and decided to warn his colleagues. At a Party conference in Moscow he criticized the proposed Party program because it did not contain guarantees against the rise of a new "cult of personality." The chairman of the meeting interrupted and asked that Grigorenko be deprived of the floor, but the audience of about two thousand Party members voted to allow him to continue. The speech was neither seditious nor anti-Soviet. Grigorenko called for the restoration of "Leninist principles," free elections, and guarantees against a new one-man dictatorship.

For this lack of discipline, he was given a Party reprimand, suspended from his job, and six months later demoted and assigned to Ussuriisk, a small town near Vladivostok. In addition, he was not permitted to defend his doctoral dissertation.

Grigorenko's transfer to the Far East did not persuade him to recant, as the authorities hoped it would. Still determined to return the Party to what he considered its original principles, he formed an underground organization called the Union of Struggle for Revival of Leninism. At the time there were many similar neo-Marxist or neo-Leninist groups discussing how the Party went wrong under Stalin or attempting to reach the population through leaflets. Almost invariably they were exposed, their members arrested and sent to the camps. Grigorenko's efforts ended no differently. His pamphlets, on the shooting of workers in Novocherkassk or the shortage of bread in large parts of the country, were distributed in Moscow. Ironically, a year and a half later, after Khrushchev's removal, Brezhnev gave an explanation similar to Grigorenko's for the bread shortage. But in 1964 Grigorenko was arrested for his premature remarks, accused of "anti-Soviet propaganda," and sent to a mental hospital in Leningrad.

The investigators had asked him what he hoped to accomplish alone, for no one else in the country shared his views. In the hospital, however, he stayed in a ward with other political prisoners, each of whom had been given the same admonition. Among the prisoners Grigorenko met was Vladimir Bukovsky.

Grigorenko spent a year in the hospital, gaining his release after Khrushchev's fall from power. The doctors were afraid he was connected to the Party leaders who had overthrown Khrushchev. A week after Grigorenko's release in late April 1965, one psychiatrist even sent a telegram congratulating him as a great Bolshevik. Four years later, in 1969, with the authorities about to declare him insane again, his wife reminded the same doctor of his telegram. The doctor insisted, in vain, that it be destroyed.

Grigorenko took an active part in the initial events of the human rights movement during his four years at large. He was a familiar figure at courthouse vigils. His eloquent appeals on behalf of imprisoned friends circulated widely in *samizdat*. His speeches, especially on behalf of the Crimean Tatars, were notably frank and defiant.

Grigorenko became acquainted with the Crimean Tatars through his friend Alexei Kosterin. Like Grigorenko, Kosterin had been a loyal Communist. (He had joined the Party in 1916; he also served three years in jail and in exile for revolutionary activity under the czar.) Under Stalin, though,

Kosterin experienced the new regime's arbitrary nature. Arrested in 1937 at the height of Stalin's purge of the Communist party, Kosterin spent seventeen years in prison and exile, accused of being an "enemy of the people." During his years in exile, Kosterin came in contact with ethnic minorities who had been deported from their homelands. After he returned to Moscow in 1955, Kosterin did not forget them. He knew their representatives in Moscow and often visited their communities in exile.

Grigorenko met Kosterin in 1965; their disgust for the regime and their shared belief in Communist ideals secured an immediate friendship. Soon after, Grigorenko took up the cause of the Crimean Tatars. The younger Tatar activists would visit him, seeking his advice about demonstrations, strikes, and means to reach international agencies. At a dinner in honor of Kosterin's seventy-second birthday in 1968, Grigorenko addressed the Tatar guests, urging them to demand their rights and adopt aggressive methods of protest.

Alexei Kosterin died a few months after the invasion of Czechoslovakia. Just before his death he had resigned from the Party; without his knowledge, he had also been expelled from the Writers' Union. At the funeral Grigorenko again refused to restrain himself. In the presence of hundreds of Crimean Tatars, Chechens, and Volga Germans—some of whom had traveled thousands of miles to attend—Grigorenko expressed his debt to Kosterin for turning "a rebel into a fighter." The Tatars were no less devoted to Grigorenko. The following year two thousand Crimean Tatars signed an appeal to Grigorenko, asking him to represent their cause at a trial of Tatar leaders in Tashkent.

The regime found numerous means to retaliate. During his hospitalization in 1964, Grigorenko was reduced in rank and expelled from the Party, although a "sick man" should not be considered legally responsible for his actions. His right to a military pension was also rescinded. After his release, Party members came to his aid, believing his earlier criticism of Khrushchev would hold him in good stead with the new leadership. For a time he worked as a foreman and lecturer at a Party school. When necessary, though, the regime found it convenient to recall his ill health. At the trial of Galanskov and Ginzburg in January 1968, the judge would not allow him to appear as a defense witness, declaring him unfit due to mental unbalance.

Grigorenko was especially angered by this treatment. In a letter to Andropov, the head of the KGB, he insisted "on one thing only, that they treat me either as a mentally competent person or as a mentally incompetent one, in order not to make of me a 'psychiatric hermaphrodite' — for certain ends insane, for others — completely normal."

Before his arrest the regime tried to compromise his influence and his reputation. Rumors were circulated at Party meetings that he was really a Jew. A letter, allegedly signed by Crimean Tatars, warned their compatriots that Grigorenko was an insane "anti-Sovietist."

The authorities decided to lure Grigorenko away from Moscow in order to arrest him. On May 2, 1969, he received a call that the trial in Tashkent of the Tatar leaders was about to begin. Grigorenko at once flew to central Asia. But the trial had not been scheduled. Grigorenko stayed in Tashkent, where he was arrested on May 7. On the same day searches were conducted at seven apartments in Moscow. In addition to *samizdat*, all typewriters, notebooks, personal correspondence, and photographs were confiscated. The investigators wanted to know if Grigorenko had passed on documents containing "deliberate fabrications" and if anyone had noted signs of his mental derangement.

In Tashkent and in Moscow, Grigorenko's supporters came to his defense. Crimean Tatars set up pickets in front of the prison, demanding his release. In June a group of

Tatars staged a demonstration in Moscow's Mayakovsky Square. Among their demands was the release of Grigorenko. They were detained, then released that afternoon. The World Communist Conference was meeting in Moscow at the time; it seemed an inconvenient occasion for the arrest of peaceful demonstrators.

Two weeks after Grigorenko's arrest, the Action Group for the Defense of Civil Rights was formed. For several years Moscow activists frequently had discussed whether to establish such an organization. Each time the idea had been rejected. It was considered too dangerous, liable to provoke immediate reprisals and therefore useless. After the arrest of Ivan Yakhimovich in March 1969, Grigorenko suggested to his colleagues that a committee be formed to defend Yakhimovich and to explain the movement's goals in general. Again, the idea was dropped, this time after intense debate.

Grigorenko's own arrest, however, changed people's minds. It is not clear why. The shock of his arrest and the threat of his incarceration in a mental hospital may have convinced his colleagues that discrete protests would not be a sufficient response.

At the time of his arrest, seven issues of the *Chronicle of Current Events* had appeared in Moscow. They reflected sustained and coordinated activity by many people, in different parts of the country and among various sectors of the population. The *Chronicle* embodied one aspect of the movement's maturity — its ability to collect and circulate information — but it was not signed and referred in vague terms to "a movement for civil rights in the U.S.S.R." Many activists realized that, at some point, they would have to present a more formal, programmatic outline of their goals and lend a structure to their cause.

The Action Group was a defiant but incomplete attempt to do this. In contrast to earlier appeals, which had been sent to Soviet officials, western Communist parties, or to "world public opinion," the Action Group's first announcement was addressed to the United Nations Commission on Human Rights. The petition outlined a broad range of abuses and requested the world body to intervene, "believing that the defense of human rights is the sacred duty of this organization." The petition referred to numerous political trials, including those of Sinyavsky and Daniel, Bukovsky, Galanskov and Ginzburg. It brought up the Crimean Tatars, whose cause remains little known in the West. It mentioned the trials of Soviet Jews who desired to immigrate to Israel — an issue that had yet to assume wide-scale dimensions. It called attention to "an especially inhuman form of persecution: the confinement of normal persons in psychiatric hospitals because of their political convictions." Both Ivan Yakhimovich and Pyotr Grigorenko, whose recent arrests were also mentioned, would be subjected to this form of reprisal.

Fifteen people signed the petition as members of the Action Group. Among them were Natalya Gorbanevskaya, Pyotr Yakir, and Anatoly Yakobson, leading figures among Moscow activists. Other members included Vladimir Borisov, a worker from Leningrad, Mustafa Dzhemiliev, a Crimean Tatar worker from Tashkent, Leonid Plyushch, a mathematician from Kiev, and Genrikh Altunyan, an engineer from Kharkov. In addition, thirty-nine people supporting the Action Group's initiative signed the petition. They, too, included widely known figures, like Alexander Esenin-Volpin as well as activists from cities other than Moscow.

Those who signed the petition did not know they would be identified as members of an organization. Without consulting their colleagues, Pyotr Yakir and Victor Krasin had added the name of the group above the list of signatures. The letter had been a joint effort, but it was not intended to be the first declaration of an organized committee. Many dissidents were angered by the unilateral action of Yakir and Krasin, but the letter itself seemed so effective that no one wanted to undermine it by disavowing his or her signature. In addition, within a short time the signatories overcame their anger and issued new appeals as the Action Group.

The Action Group did not remain in existence for long. Within a half year of its first appeal, many members were harassed and arrested. Victor Krasin was sent into exile, charged with "parasitism." Natalya Gorbanevskaya was confined to a mental hospital, accused of circulating the *Chronicle*. Genrikh Altunyan was arrested in Kharkov, charged with "anti-Soviet slander," and given three years in the labor camps. Other members were subjected to interrogations, searches, and threatening letters.

Although the Action Group helped to publicize Soviet abuse of human rights and gave the impression that the human rights movement itself was becoming an organized political opposition, in actuality the group hardly existed as a formal committee. True, its members were among those most responsible for collecting information and circulating appeals. They were at the center of the network that linked nonconformist intellectuals in different cities. Western journalists knew many of them as reliable sources of news otherwise impossible to obtain. Yet the Action Group was little more than the list of those who signed their names together. As the regime picked up one member after another, the list of signatures on the group's appeals grew smaller, until the appeals no longer were issued at all.

Regrettably, the formation of the Action Group may have invited the authorities to arrest its supporters sooner than some of them, at least, would have been detained. At the same time, the members were not able to mount a challenge to the regime that would have justified the obvious risk they took by identifying themselves as an organized group. In subsequent years, other dissidents would remember the example of the Action Group and prepare their organizational activity with greater care.

The human rights movement involved people of diverse backgrounds and temperaments. Not every dissident participated in demonstrations, signed petitions, or contributed to the *Chronicle*. The response of the regime also affected their choices. Demonstrations, especially with signs or banners, often led to imprisonment. Petitions more and more frequently led to reprisals against those who signed or circulated them. (By early 1968, nearly two thousand people had signed various appeals. By late spring, however, as the regime took administrative measures against many of them, fewer people affixed their names to protests.) The government deliberately acted without consistency or logic, keeping its critics off balance. One dissident might be imprisoned while another would be ignored entirely for participating in similar activity. At times the regime's behavior provoked unpleasant suspicion. In addition, while the attention of the West most often focused on group petitions or the occasional demonstration, the emerging movement permitted many individuals to fashion roles for themselves that were not easily understood in the context of Soviet society.

In the late 1960s, Andrei Amalrik became a widely known dissident writer. Like Ginzburg, Amalrik also befriended unofficial artists. In 1965, a collection of his plays displeased the authorities, and he was exiled from Moscow as a parasite. (His first book, *Involuntary Journey to Siberia*, described his life among the impoverished peasants of a collective farm.) He returned to Moscow in 1966, and while shying away from organized protest — he neither attended demonstrations nor signed group petitions — he was a familiar figure among Moscow activists. During the trial of Galanskov and Ginzburg, he provided moral and practical support to their families, trying (unsuccessfully) to arrange meetings with foreign correspondents. In July 1968 he and his wife demonstrated with posters outside the British embassy, protesting Britain's and the U.S.S.R.'s military aid to the Nigerian government for use against the Biafran rebels. A year later Amalrik finished his essay, "Will the Soviet Union Survive until 1984?" By exploring the challenge posed by the human rights movement and other disaffected groups, as well as the emerging threat from China and the regime's inability to nurture economic growth, Amalrik fashioned a startling essay on the country's future.

Its appearance generated widespread speculation. Just as the work of "Abram Tertz" a decade earlier seemed too contemporary for a Moscow writer to have produced, so Amalrik's essay, which was unlike the work either of established Soviet writers or of other *samizdat* critics, raised questions about his trustworthiness. Furthermore, after his essay reached the West under his own name he remained at large, seemingly immune from the regime's anger.

Rumors soon circulated that Amalrik had been compromised by the KGB. An American reporter, Henry Bradsher of the Washington *Evening Star*, questioned Amalrik's integrity, compelling the young writer to respond with an open letter, "I Want To Be Understood Correctly." As always, Amalrik bluntly defined the problem: "Several decades of terror gave rise in my country not only to an atmosphere of fear but an attendant atmosphere of universal distrust and suspiciousness. Consequently when people appeared who dared to do what no one had dared to do earlier . . . there were rumors about nearly all of them that if they were acting so boldly it must be by permission or on the instructions of the secret police." Amalrik understood that Soviet life nurtured questionable instincts and that people are likely to say upon seeing an honest man, "He has not yet been arrested — that is very suspicious" rather than "Thank God he has not yet been arrested, that means there is one more free man on earth." Amalrik, unfortunately, did not remain a free man for long. Arrested in 1970, he was convicted of "anti-Soviet fabrications" and sentenced to three years in the labor camps.

Other dissidents in Moscow developed expertise in Soviet legal procedure. Men like Boris Tsukerman, Leonid Rigerman, and Valery Chalidze responded to numerous violations of Soviet law *by the regime.* Tsukerman became famous for his correspondence with Soviet postal authorities and with other government institutions. The dissidents referred to his collections of letters as "juridical symphonies." When Tsukerman noted a violation of law, he would write a complaint to a governmental body, which would either not reply or send one that demonstrated ignorance of the law. Tsukerman would not allow the matter to rest. He would write to the next-higher agency, pointing out the subordinate body's indifference to legality. Several times he proceeded in this way until he reached the office of the procurator general.

Chalidze also assumed a prominent role among the "legalists" in Moscow. Trained as a physicist, Chalidze learned of the initial demonstrations and protests through his friend Alexander Esenin-Volpin, whom he had met in 1955 when they both attended a seminar on mathematical logic at Moscow University. Although Chalidze had studied legal philosophy and comparative legal systems, Soviet law did not interest him for a number of years. With the advent of open, legal protest, though, he realized that Soviet law could be approached seriously. Still, he did not openly join the dissident struggle until 1968, when Volpin was arrested and sent to a mental hospital. Chalidze wrote to Premier Alexei Kosygin, urging his friend's release. When Volpin returned home, Chalidze decided to take an active part in the movement.

At that time, the spring of 1968, many people faced harassment and persecution for signing appeals to government officials. Chalidze recognized that the act of petitioning one's own government, quietly and respectfully, is an act of loyalty, but the regime chose to react illegally. So, with Volpin, Chalidze wrote a short "Memorandum on Loyalty," placing their views within a strict legal framework. Although the memorandum did not circulate widely enough in *samizdat* to have been preserved, it served a useful purpose for Chalidze. As he collected signatures he was able to see who would be open in the future to his way of thinking and who could not support his manner of approaching the authorities. There were dissidents, after all, who believed it was foolish to speak of laws to "bandits." Chalidze understood their criticism, but by temperament and intellectual disposition he was committed to a legalist approach.

Chalidze decided to devote three years to work as a legal expert. In the first year, he intended to study Soviet law; in the second, he hoped to start a journal where legal issues could be discussed; and in the third, he planned to organize a small investigative association that could assume responsibility for the journal, allowing him to return to his work in physics. Chalidze fulfilled all his plans except the last, for he was not able to relinquish his legal work as easily as he originally had hoped.

Chalidze worked quietly at home and in the library for a year. He wrote several articles, including one on restrictions in Soviet law according to class affiliation and another that analyzed United Nations documents on civil rights and explored the Soviet constitution and its application in practice. Chalidze felt it important to demonstrate that "laws can be understood as they are written and not necessarily as they are interpreted by the authorities." He also encouraged his colleagues to place Soviet law in an international context, pointing out that the Soviet government has signed numerous conventions and covenants. In subsequent years, especially after accords were signed by thirty-five nations at the Conference on Security and Cooperation in Europe in Helsinki, other dissidents would exploit the regime's hypocrisy, which Chalidze elegantly described: "On the one hand a state makes commitments to guarantee human rights on its own territory, while on the other hand it tells those to whom the commitment was made that securing human rights is exclusively its internal affair."

Chalidze took up the next part of his plan in August 1969 by circulating the first issue of his journal, *Social Problems*. Most of its articles approached legal issues theoretically. Gradually, though, as Chalidze became more involved in specific cases, his journal published discussions and petitions relating to the defense of particular rights. Unlike the *Chronicle of Current Events*, which did not give the names of its editors or contributors, Chalidze would not include anonymous or pseudonymous articles in *Social Problems;* in addition, his own name, address, and telephone number appeared on the title page of each issue.

While Chalidze pursued his theoretical studies, he also tried to influence the behavior of his fellow dissenters. "In practical terms," he wrote in his book *To Defend These Rights,*

> this means keeping people out of jail. . . . Thus it was important to study court practices and to let people know what acts, even though lawful, might cause their arrest. It was also useful to work out methods of acting that minimize the risk of unlawful repression and to recommend these as substitutes for methods that almost always provoke such repression. . . . Not

that I was exceedingly insistent, since I recognize an individual's right to any action consistent with law as well as the right to self-sacrifice for its own sake, or sacrifice for the great cause of liberty. I recognized an individual's right to sacrifice only himself, and this stand did not satisfy many who were convinced that great causes demand sacrifices. I was often lectured on the grandeur of sacrifice, on the inevitability of many sacrifices for freedom's sake, on sacrifice as an essential quality of the Russian soul. Alas, I could neither accept nor understand these values. I held to my own principle, and I believe I was successful in preventing several demonstrations, the organization of tens of committees, the publication of quite a few sharp protests, and even one self-immolation.

Following the invasion of Czechoslovakia, Chalidze stayed up all night trying to convince a group of dissidents not to demonstrate in Red Square. Only Larisa Bogoraz stubbornly resisted his arguments. And in 1970, Chalidze learned of a Jewish man who intended to kill himself and his pregnant wife to protest the regime's refusal to grant them exit visas. Chalidze reminded the fellow of similar attempts at self-immolation, when the victims survived only to face confinement in psychiatric hospitals. This example persuaded the man not to make the attempt.

Chalidze did not participate in the dissident community as others did. He avoided the long and raucous meetings. He discouraged casual visiting and preferred that people make appointments. To many dissidents he seemed like a bureaucrat, and they disliked him for his manner of working. Chalidze felt the need to guard his time carefully, though, for in addition to his new career as a legal expert he was still working as a physicist.

Chalidze began the third part of his plan in the fall of 1970. He, his close friend Andrei Tverdokhlebov, and the physicist Andrei Sakharov announced the formation of the Moscow Committee for Human Rights. Chalidze had met Sakharov the previous year. Together they had issued appeals on behalf of General Grigorenko and Zhores Medvedev, the distinguished biologist who was confined to a mental hospital for several weeks in June 1970.

Chalidze and his colleagues carefully outlined the committee's principles. For years, the regime had been convicting people for forming organizations, even when none existed. Chalidze himself had dissuaded activists from forming committees. The example of the Action Group for the Defense of Civil Rights also reinforced their caution. Although it did not really exist as an organization, its members faced immediate reprisals, for the government felt provoked by the very title over the list of signatures.

Chalidze, Sakharov, and Tverdokhlebov presented the regime with a troublesome predicament. From the outset the Committee for Human Rights defined itself as "a creative association acting in accordance with the laws of the land." It offered "consultative assistance" to the government on human rights problems and "creative assistance to persons engaged in constructive research into the theoretical aspects of the human rights question and in the study of the specific nature of this question in a socialist society." It also declared itself ready for contact with other public and international nongovernmental organizations "as long as their activities are based on the principles of the United Nations and are not aimed at harming the Soviet Union."

Chalidze's experiment did not please the regime. On February 15, 1971, Chalidze and Tverdokhlebov were invited separately for talks with the head of the Department of General Surveillance of the Moscow procuracy. As might be expected, they were warned of the committee's illegal nature. Chalidze replied a few days later, describing in meticulous logic the inapplicability of the statutes that the authorities claimed made the committee illegal. Chalidze even challenged the authorities to institute legal action, "as this would make it possible to examine, in open judicial debate, the state of the law and of current practice regarding the right of association."

Some dissidents also disapproved of the committee's initial statement. It seemed too theoretical, too formal. The suggestion that the committee would be willing to engage in "consultative assistance to the organs of government" seemed ludicrous. Most dissidents understood and accepted the need to use the law as a means to embarrass the government. It seemed like a charade, though, to oppose specific violations of law but not to oppose the general absence of rights in a police state, where the law could be ignored with impunity by government officials. Those who criticized Chalidze could not pretend to live in a normal society. If the regime was based on force (and not on law), they could not point to laws and hope to persuade the regime to observe them.

The opinion of these activists notwithstanding, the Committee for Human Rights advanced the movement a great deal. It was the first association among the dissidents to assert and maintain its existence in a productive manner. It also came to the attention of numerous ordinary citizens, who approached the committee for help, believing it to be a type of legal aid society. This was the most tiresome part of its work. People visited members' apartments at all hours of the day and night, even from cities thousands of miles from Moscow. Only a very small percentage — perhaps one in twenty-five visitors — brought a case that was worthwhile pursuing. Most of the claimants asked for assistance in matters well outside the committee's competence. In one typical example, a man wanted help finding an apartment in Kazakhstan and insisted on at least receiving a supporting letter from Chalidze. Many people left disappointed.

The committee itself took up only general questions, among them compulsory confinement in psychiatric hospitals, the right to a defense attorney, and the right of the Tatars to return to their native Crimea. In the fall of 1971, the committee submitted an appeal to the Fifth World Congress of Psychiatrists meeting in Mexico City, calling upon the doctors to promote international legal guarantees for the mentally ill.

Individual members of the committee pursued cases on their own initiative. Chalidze and Sakharov issued statements on numerous trials. Boris Tsukerman, who was affiliated with the committee, helped a large group of believers in Narofominsk who had been denied the right to open a church. After Tsukerman immigrated to Israel in January 1971, an article in a local newspaper defamed several women who headed the religious group. They wanted to file suit for libel but they could not find a lawyer with the courage to help them; one lawyer had already been intimidated by the authorities. Chalidze accepted the case, filing a petition in court and then following up with an appeal. (Because it was a civil matter, Chalidze had the right to file petitions and to act as the lawyer for the believers.) No court would allow a hearing on the question of libel. Still, the work of Tsukerman and Chalidze exposed a total lack of regard for legality at various levels of government.

In spite of his original plan, Chalidze was not able to relinquish the legal work he had begun. The regime had already made it impossible for him to continue his research in physics; in the fall of 1971 he resigned from his institute. Gradually, though, the endless stream of visitors and the constant pressure to issue appeals overwhelmed him. The regime, too, increased its harassment of him as part of a general campaign against the dissidents that reached its height in 1972 and 1973. Exhausted and under tremendous pressure from the authorities, Chalidze resigned in September 1972 from the Committee for Human Rights.

By 1972, many dissidents, and not only activists in the Jewish emigration movement, were leaving the Soviet Union. Some emigrated out of a heartfelt desire to live elsewhere; others were given the cruel choice of emigration or imprisonment. Chalidze did not consider leaving the country. He did know, however, that New York University had invited him to present a lecture, though he never received their letter. Near the end of the summer of 1972, attorney Sam Dash (who would later be a counsel during the Senate Watergate hearings) visited Moscow and invited Chalidze to Georgetown University in Washington, D. C. Chalidze submitted the invitation to OVIR (the agency that handles tourist and emigration visas), expecting to receive a refusal.

It soon became apparent that he might be allowed to go. In November, he became the first dissident to receive a travel visa and to leave the country on a Soviet passport. (Emigrants relinquish their Soviet citizenship and leave with exit visas.) After two weeks in America, Chalidze grew worried about being allowed to return, in which case, in order to achieve an important precedent — the right to return to one's country — he would have gone back. But he was still tired and not eager to return to the fracas. The regime soon resolved his dilemma. On December 13 he was informed that the Supreme Soviet had deprived him of Soviet citizenship, forcing him to remain in exile.

The human rights movement began as an attempt by the friends of Andrei Sinyavsky and Yuli Daniel to help them gain a fair trial. As more people joined the struggle, the movement gradually expanded its concerns to a broad range of issues, but the defense of friends and colleagues has remained at the center of the movement's work. As projects like the *Chronicle of Current Events* succeeded, the regime felt increasingly hard pressed to retaliate. Among its most cynical reprisals was the imprisonment of dissidents in psychiatric hospitals.*

Many well-known dissidents faced confinement in psychiatric hospitals before the human rights movement was able to systematically expose the practice. General Grigorenko met Vladimir Bukovsky in a Leningrad hospital in 1964. Natalya Gorbanevskaya was transferred against her will from a maternity clinic to a mental hospital in 1968. Over a nineteen-year period beginning in 1949, Alexander Esenin-Volpin was interned five times in psychiatric hospitals. His last confinement occurred in February 1968, after he protested the trial of Yuri Galanskov and Alexander Ginzburg. That winter, Volpin also had applied for a visa in order to attend a scientific conference in the United States. His detention provoked a large-scale reaction. Ninety-nine Soviet mathematicians and scientists protested to the Ministry of Health, the procurator general, and the chief psychiatrist of Moscow, claiming that Volpin's forced confinement was a "flagrant violation of medical and legal norms." Their petition was the first to object to psychiatric internment of a specific dissident. Though a number of the signatories were demoted or dismissed from their positions and nearly all were denied the right to attend conferences abroad, the petition helped to limit Volpin's detention to three months.

The *Chronicle of Current Events* also exposed the abuse of psychiatry. In its first eleven issues, from April 1968 to December 1969, the *Chronicle* reported the cases of twenty-seven dissidents interned in special psychiatric hos-

---

*For a detailed and comprehensive report on the abuse of psychiatry in the Soviet Union, see *Psychiatric Terror* by Sidney Bloch and Peter Reddaway (Basic Books, New York, 1977).

pitals. The regime had reasons for adopting this form of punishment. The trials of dissidents had been designed not only to punish individuals but also to intimidate and discredit the movement as a whole. To its chagrin, the government achieved the opposite results. Each trial became the occasion for renewed protest. Transcripts would surface in Moscow and in the West. A campaign of resistance continued to grow in the labor camps also. The regime seemed helpless; it could not arrest more culprits without initiating shameful publicity about itself.

The authorities hoped to resolve their dilemma by declaring dissenters insane. A defendant could be judged "unfit to plead," then tried in absentia behind closed doors; it would be much harder for the movement to campaign for his or her release. There would always be a lingering doubt that someone was insane, and the authorities could deny responsibility, referring all questions to its cadre of eminent doctors.

Also, the fear of hospitalization with the genuinely insane — and the threat of treatment with neuroleptic drugs — was more acute than the fear of imprisonment or exile. Prison terms come to an end, but termination of psychiatric treatment depends on the "health" of the patient. As the *Chronicle* made clear, the doctors treated dissidents with cynical contempt. General Grigorenko was asked, "Why did you protest?" His response, "I couldn't breathe," was taken as evidence of psychopathology.

Another victim was biologist Zhores Medvedev. On May 29, 1970, Medvedev was forcibly removed from his home in Obninsk by two psychiatrists and three policemen. He was held for nineteen days, questioned, diagnosed, and threatened. The doctors asked mostly about his writings. His two books, *The Rise and Fall of T. D. Lysenko* and *The Medvedev Papers*, exposed the political manipulation and control of the country's scientific life. The doctors, however, took these writings as a sign of "sluggish schizophrenia" accompanied by "paranoid delusions of reforming society." By "combining scientific work in his field with publicist activities" Medvedev was diagnosed as a split personality. His work in gerontology had gained him an international reputation, but involvement in two seemingly unrelated activities was taken as evidence of mental illness. The diagnosis was so ludicrous that it gave rise to the ironic term "the da Vinci syndrome."

The KGB could not have foreseen the storm that accompanied Medvedev's confinement. From the outset of his arrest, his twin brother Roy pressed the authorities to justify Zhores's detention. Scientists in Moscow as well as many in the West bombarded Soviet officials with protests. Andrei Sakharov visited the Institute of Genetics, where an international conference was taking place, to request the delegates' intervention. Alexander Solzhenitsyn also condemned Medvedev's detention. His appeal, "This Is How We Live," gained widespread attention. In characteristic fury, Solzhenitsyn wrote:

It is time to think clearly: the incarceration of freethinking healthy people in madhouses is SPIRITUAL MURDER, it is a variation on the GAS CHAMBER, but is even more cruel: the torture of the people being killed is more malicious and more prolonged. Like the gas chambers these crimes will NEVER be forgotten, and all those involved in them will be condemned for all time, during their life and after their death.

The authorities backed down. Zhores Medvedev was released on June 17, nineteen days after being detained. The doctors recommended outpatient supervision and employment for their patient. Medvedev, though, had great difficulty finding a job. Later, he was prevented from attending scientific conferences in Kiev and Moscow; in Kiev, the KGB took him to a train station and ordered him to leave the city. In January 1973, Medvedev accepted an invitation from a distinguished laboratory in England, an action approved by the director of his own institute in the Soviet Union. Eight months after his arrival in London, Medvedev, like Chalidze before him, was stripped of his Soviet citizenship for spreading "slanderous materials discrediting the Soviet state and social system."

Although the cases of Grigorenko and Medvedev and the appeals by Sakharov and Solzhenitsyn provided ample evidence of psychiatric abuse, many Western doctors seemed less convinced; amid the numerous protests, none had been from individual psychiatrists or from official psychiatric associations. Only in January 1971 did the Canadian Psychiatric Association become the first official body to condemn the confinement of healthy people for their nonconformist political views. Still, many psychiatrists wanted first-hand evidence. They would not have long to wait.

In January 1970, Vladimir Bukovsky returned to Moscow after serving a three-year term in a labor camp. He was then twenty-eight years old. Except for brief periods at liberty, he had passed the previous seven years in jails, psychiatric hospitals, and labor camps. He was tired and resolved not to go back to prison. For a time he restrained himself, determined to live his "fill of life after the gray monotony of the camp." Bukovsky, though, could not stay out of the fray for long.

During his latest term, conditions in Moscow had changed considerably. The *Chronicle of Current Events* had begun. National movements among the Ukrainians, Crimean Tatars, the Lithuanians, the Volga Germans, and the Jews had sprung up. Each had different aims. All were in touch with Bukovsky's friends in Moscow. "There were more people, there was more publicity, and the people came from higher

up in the social scale: professors, academicians, writers —
not to be compared with us striplings of the early 1960s,"
Bukovsky recalls in his memoir.

All they had achieved, though, was threatened by the regime's confinement of dissenters in mental hospitals. Bukovsky himself had experienced this treatment. Now his friends
were in special psychiatric hospitals, while others were
frightened by a similar threat. The Medvedev case also
confirmed Bukovsky's fear. The dissidents knew of hundreds
of such cases — the worker Borisov, the bricklayer Gershuni —
but who would come to their defense? After Medvedev's
detention, the Soviet academic world was up in arms because
the repression had reached their doorstep. Although
Medvedev was soon released, how would the others gain
their freedom?

Bukovsky made his first step in May 1970. He gave a
television interview to Bill Cole, the CBS correspondent in
Moscow. It was not easy to arrange. With about twenty of
his friends, including wives and children, he and Cole went
for a picnic in the woods in order to distract the KGB.
Agents hovered nearby, unaware of Bukovsky's intentions;
they did not want to miss his departure. In the interview,
Bukovsky summarized his career as a dissident, then recounted in stark detail the psychiatric confinement of
healthy people.

Still, Bukovsky was determined to do more. As a primary
source of information for Western reporters, he was careful
to maintain his credibility. Once he told Anthony Astrachan
of the Washington *Post* about a severe food shortage in
Ivanovo, an industrial city of half a million inhabitants not
far from Moscow. Bukovsky knew that Premier Kosygin had
to go there in order to forestall strikes among the workers,
but he asked Astrachan not to use the information until he
could document it.

Bukovsky approached the abuse of psychiatry with the

same care. He understood that the regime insisted that non-specialists could not dispute the conclusions of trained forensic psychiatrists, so he decided to assemble documentation, including the testimony of witnesses and the diagnoses of Soviet doctors. Then he would find honest specialists who could evaluate the material.

It was an audacious project. For months, Bukovsky tracked down information. He was able to obtain reports of the official psychiatric commissions that examined several dissidents. Bukovsky also knew sympathetic psychiatrists in Leningrad and at the Serbsky Institute in Moscow, where most of the dissidents were judged insane; they, too, gave him useful material.

Along with this documentary evidence, Bukovsky arranged interviews with former psychiatric prisoners and their families. He found evidence of new, special hospitals and photographs of the doctors. He planned to reconstruct the history of psychiatric abuse, under Stalin and then under Khrushchev and Brezhnev.

The expert findings were the most shameful evidence he uncovered. A panel of doctors in Tashkent found Grigorenko fully healthy and recommended against further examinations. He had to be transferred to the Serbsky in Moscow, where his paranoia, "accompanied by reformist ideas," could be detected.

In the case of Ivan Yakhimovich, the conclusion contradicted the description of the patient. As chairman of a collective farm, Yakhimovich had been a dedicated Communist. The report lauded his stubborn belief in Communist ideals. Then the Riga doctors abruptly concluded that he needed compulsory treatment in a hospital. The court also had to send Yakhimovich to the Serbsky, where a second opinion quickly resolved any ambiguity.

Bukovsky needed honest specialists to evaluate the material. Many prominent psychiatrists shared his concern but refused to relate their own findings publicly. Although young psychiatrists offered to help, Bukovsky feared it would be too easy to dismiss their opinions. They could not interview the patients themselves and would have to rely on documents and hearsay. One psychiatrist in Kiev, Semyon Gluzman, got word to Bukovsky that he was willing to help. Bukovsky sent him the material on Grigorenko through Leonid Plyushch, who often served as a courier of *samizdat* between Kiev and the capital. Gluzman distributed his critique of the Grigorenko case and was soon arrested.

Bukovsky's final hope was an appeal to Western psychiatrists. On January 21, 1971, he sent the material abroad, asking Western doctors to determine whether the findings described mental illness in any of his friends. Bukovsky also wanted the issue placed on the agenda of the forthcoming World Congress of Psychiatrists scheduled for Mexico City. Regrettably, the congress was unwilling to respond to Bukovsky's appeal, and it was not until August 1977, in Honolulu, that the World Psychiatric Association finally voted to condemn Soviet abuse of psychiatry. By that time, Bukovsky was no longer in the U.S.S.R. Arrested in March 1971, he was convicted of "anti-Soviet agitation and propaganda." Sentenced to seven years of imprisonment and five years of exile, Bukovsky would serve barely half his term. In December 1976, the Soviet government exchanged him for the Chilean Communist leader Luis Corvalan.

Bukovsky's trial, in January 1972, came at a time when the regime was determined to crush the human rights movement altogether, beginning with the *Chronicle of Current Events*. With its growth (by the early 1970s, the *Chronicle* included reports from all parts of the country and had increased in size from about fifteen pages to more than fifty pages), the *Chronicle* became a primary target of the KGB. People found with copies in their homes faced serious reprisals. The dissidents made special arrangements in producing it. Under the direction of literary critic Anatoly Yakobson, material was compiled every two months in a different apartment. For three, sometimes four days, the editors stayed inside, rewriting material, organizing it, and typing it. Once, some activists secured the use of a mimeograph machine, but only one issue was reproduced on it. It was too dangerous and, given the circumstances under which they worked, too complicated to use again.

In 1972, the KGB was ready to launch a major crackdown on the *Chronicle*. The dissidents believe the regime decided at a special high-level meeting, on December 30, 1971, to eliminate the *Chronicle* and two other *samizdat* journals, the *Ukrainian Herald* and the right-wing, nationalist *Veche*. Between January and May, hundreds of searches were carried out in Moscow, Leningrad, Vilnius, and Novosibirsk. Many activists were arrested in an attempt to break up the network of contacts; more than a hundred people were arrested in the Ukraine alone. For the first time, an issue of the *Chronicle*, number 27, dated October 15, 1972, appeared more than two months after the previous one, which had come out in July.

The most tragic aspect of the crackdown, however, emerged with the arrests of Pyotr Yakir and the economist Victor Krasin. Both men had survived Stalin's labor camps when they were younger. Now, isolated and threatened with execution as traitors, they began to give evidence against their colleagues. On November 4, 1972, Yakir's daughter was allowed to visit him. The *Chronicle* later reported:

> According to P. Yakir, he has changed his attitude toward the democratic movement and his own activity. His active cooperation with the investigators has become clear. According to what Yakir said, the material presented to him by the investigators has convinced him of

the tendentious character and objectively harmful position of the *Chronicle of Current Events* and of the presence therein of factual inaccuracies and even direct distortions. He also declared that each future issue of the *Chronicle* would make his and Krasin's eventual prison terms longer, and that as each *Chronicle* appeared new arrests would result. The investigators confirmed the latter statement, pointing out that those arrested would not necessarily be those directly participating in the publication of the new issue.

Pyotr Yakir and Victor Krasin related everything they knew about the workings of the *Chronicle* and *samizdat*, and what they did not know themselves they made up and told the KGB anyway. They made the movement appear more formally organized, more structured than it actually was.

Yakir, for example, claimed that Lyuda Alexeeva, who had helped the *Chronicle*'s editors since its inception, had been present at a meeting in 1968 when it was decided to start the journal. He added that Lyuda then took charge of the *Chronicle*'s "Ukrainian department." Actually, the testimony reflected Yakir's own desire to satisfy the KGB, which was always looking for conspiracies. There had never been a special meeting to discuss the *Chronicle*, although numerous discussions took place before Natalya Gorbanevskaya actually began it. When the KGB interrogated her, Lyuda Alexeeva told them to check their own tapes and files to learn if she was there that day, rather than trust the testimony of Yakir and Krasin; the KGB never asked her about the meeting again. As for a "Ukrainian department," Lyuda had passed on much material about events in the Ukraine as well as about other occurrences, but the *Chronicle*'s work was never so formally structured; a Ukrainian department simply never existed.

Krasin's behavior was even more upsetting to his former colleagues. For several years, many felt that Krasin had tried to politicize the movement. He often caused profound disagreements with other people. Krasin saw himself as a leader of the movement, while the others understood that the movement had no particular "center" or leadership, but relied on the moral consciousness of each person. No one asked others to do things; instead, people did what they felt obliged to do. In his understanding of the movement and in his testimony to the KGB, Krasin betrayed these principles. At one point, it is believed, he asked his interrogators to write *democratic movement* with capital letters, as if, like the KGB, it was an established organization and he was entitled to negotiate on its behalf.

For a time the human rights movement appeared to be broken. Over two hundred people were interrogated and urged to cooperate. Many activists had personal confrontations with Yakir or Krasin under the eyes of KGB interrogators. Yakir sent a letter to Andrei Sakharov, warning him not to allow his name to be used "for purposes of propaganda against our homeland." Krasin addressed a letter to his "friends who are free." In the letter Krasin stated that the "Democratic Movement" had taken a direction dangerous to state authority, and the state was entitled to defend itself. The *Chronicle* summarized his message:

The defeat of the "Democratic Movement" should be acknowledged. The cessation of all opposition activity is not sufficient to save people from repressions. The authorities require guarantees, and these guarantees can be assured only by all-round cooperation with the investigation. Krasin calls upon people to overcome the psychological barrier and testify freely, not only about their own activities but also about those of others.

A handful of dissidents gave in. Faced with damaging testimony by Yakir and Krasin and threatened with prison terms, they began to cooperate with the investigation. Krasin's wife, Nadezhda Emelkina, revealed information about the *Chronicle*. Irina Belogorodskaya was arrested in connection with issue 27 of the *Chronicle*, although she had not taken part in producing it. Soon thereafter she, too, divulged information about her friends.

In Moscow, many who knew the activists from a distance reacted cynically. For years they had refused to participate in the movement for fear of endangering themselves or losing privileges the regime dispensed in order to nurture their dependence. Now the dissidents did not seem so courageous or so different from themselves.

The regime tried to capitalize on this dispirited and confused atmosphere. It hoped to compromise other prominent dissidents and further discredit the movement. Vladimir Bukovsky was brought to Moscow from prison. Ostensibly, the KGB wanted to question him about Case 24, the *Chronicle* investigation. In reality they wanted Bukovsky to recant. He refused. They tried to fashion a compromise, offering to send him abroad if he would promise not to "make noise" in the West. Bukovsky accepted their offer with one condition: the KGB would have to acknowledge that they had imprisoned healthy people in psychiatric hospitals, release them all, and stop the practice altogether. The KGB returned Bukovsky to Vladimir prison.

Victor Krasin also betrayed a colleague with information that the KGB was not even looking for. By 1972, the British scholar Peter Reddaway had prepared a one-volume compilation in English of the first eleven issues of the *Chronicle*.* Krasin had a set of galley proofs concealed near his apartment. (The galleys had been sent to Moscow for proofreading

*See *Uncensored Russia* (American Heritage, New York, 1972).

by the dissidents themselves.) It had been Krasin's responsibility to arrange for their return to England, with the corrections included. But Krasin neglected to do it before his arrest in September 1972. He revealed the hiding place to the KGB, which, in turn, accused Gabriel Superfin of writing the corrections. Superfin was a young historian of literature who had helped Anastas Mikoyan, a veteran Bolshevik and government official, prepare his memoirs. The KGB assumed Superfin harbored an archive for the *Chronicle* in his apartment, but none was ever found. At his trial, the court found the galley-proof corrections to be in his handwriting and sentenced him, for this and other activity, to five years of imprisonment and two years of exile.

The dissidents were not sure how to respond to Case 24, in particular to the threat of arrests for each new issue of the *Chronicle*. Some were willing to publish the *Chronicle* and face the consequences for themselves. Others argued that publication would have to be interrupted, for no one had the right to endanger other people. It was feared that Anatoly Yakobson, who was no longer editing the *Chronicle*, would be arrested and held responsible for the next issue. In other words, to increase the moral pressure the authorities seemed willing to arrest someone who was not directly involved. Faced with this threat, the dissidents backed down. The *Chronicle* did not appear again until May 1974.

Many in the West wondered if the editors were among those arrested. At the beginning of 1973, at the initiative of Khronika Press in New York, a counterpart to the *Chronicle*, entitled *A Chronicle of Human Rights in the U.S.S.R.*, was begun. In the spring of 1974, the editors, who now included Valery Chalidze, received a written message from Moscow. In it, the *Chronicle of Current Events* announced a correction to an article published three years earlier. A prisoner named Baranov had been shot and reportedly killed when he threw himself against a prison camp's barbed wire.

In reality, "he received three firearm wounds: one in the chest and two more, probably in the legs. The wounds were not fatal — Baranov survived."

The editors apologized for this "unintentional error which resulted from the extraordinarily complicated conditions of receiving information from penal camps." They urged that the correction be published, for the earlier report of Baranov's death was now regarded by the KGB as "deliberately false and slanderous" and a basic charge against the *Chronicle*.

On August 27, 1973, Yakir and Krasin went on trial for "anti-Soviet agitation and propaganda." They admitted their guilt and repented their involvement in anti-Soviet activity. One witness, psychiatrist Andrei Snezhnevsky, informed the court of his embarrassment, during international conferences, over reports in the *Chronicle* that healthy people were kept in Soviet mental hospitals because of their political ideas. Snezhnevsky assured the court that no such practices occurred. A week after their trial, the defendants appeared at a news conference with foreign journalists and repeated their belief that information in the *Chronicle* was "libelous." Part of the conference was broadcast over Soviet television, and one of the viewers was General Pyotr Grigorenko, watching from the mental hospital in Chernyakhovsk.

In the period before and after the Yakir-Krasin trial, the dissidents also had to endure the deaths of two of their colleagues. Yuri Galanskov, who had been sentenced in 1968 to seven years in a labor camp, died in November 1972 at the camp complex in Mordovia. Even before his arrest, Galanskov was troubled by a serious case of ulcers; his condition grew worse in the camp. He hardly received medical care, and requests for a special diet were ignored. In the fall of 1972 he developed peritonitis after an operation in a camp hospital. Physicians were called but it was too late. The *Chronicle of Current Events* was not able to publish its report as well as an obituary from his fellow inmates until May 1974, when it resumed publication.

The death of Ilya Gabai was even more unexpected. Since the late 1960s he had been a well-respected figure in Moscow, known for his poetry and his devotion as a teacher. The *Chronicle* called him "an exceptionally compassionate man with an unrelenting sense of personal responsibility — the embodiment of a moral presence." Through General Grigorenko, Ilya Gabai (who was a Jew) became involved in the defense of the Crimean Tatars, for which he served three years in the camps. Released in May 1972, he was subjected to frequent interrogations but refused to cooperate. Gabai had been close to Pyotr Yakir and Yakir's betrayal dumbfounded him. After his trial Yakir was exiled to Ryazan. Gabai wanted to visit him, to talk with him, but he never made it to Ryazan. The effects of prison, interrogations, searches, and the lack of regular work may have unhinged him. On October 20, 1973, he committed suicide by jumping from the balcony of his apartment.

Half a year later, in April 1974, his wife Galya Gabai left the Soviet Union. Many dissidents were also leaving that spring. The movement seemed defeated. On the afternoon before her departure, a young man visited her apartment. He had heard of her, probably from Western radio broadcasts. He and his friends wanted to organize a group to struggle for rights, and they wanted her to lead them. Galya could not accept, she told him, because she was leaving the next day for Vienna. He did not expect that reply. She imagined his fate — prison, exile, or death — and advised him to read Pushkin, that it would be more useful. He looked at her as if she were crazy, and she understood that all she could tell him would be useless.

For the regime and for its opponents the drama was about to resume. Not everyone had been arrested, but the authorities tried to compromise those who were still at large. In January 1974, three Moscow dissidents — Tatyana Velikanova, Sergei Kovalyov, and Tatyana Khodorovich — issued a public statement describing the regime's attempt to buy their cooperation. In return for their silence, an imprisoned friend would have things easier, or even be released. But both the prisoner and his warrantor must remain silent. The three dissidents rejected the offer and vowed not to cooperate with this "hostage system."

The three took an even bolder step in May. At a press conference held in Andrei Sakharov's apartment, Velikanova, Kovalyov, and Khodorovich handed issues 28, 29, and 30 of the *Chronicle* to Western correspondents. At the same time, they made the following statement:

> As we do not consider, despite the repeated assertions of the KGB and U.S.S.R. court instances, that the *Chronicle of Current Events* is an illegal or libelous publication, we regard it as our duty to facilitate as wide a circulation for it as possible.
>
> We believe it is essential that truthful information about violations of basic human rights in the Soviet Union should be available to all who are interested in it.

Ten days later, number 31 appeared. Issued on the thirtieth anniversary of the expulsion of the Crimean Tatars from their homeland, it consisted entirely of material on their persecution and their struggle to return. From the material in these four issues, it was obvious that while the *Chronicle* had not appeared for nearly two years, information was being routinely collected and edited.

The authorities could not ignore the revival of the *Chronicle*. At the end of December 1974, Sergei Kovalyov was arrested. A distinguished biologist, whose work on the electrophysiology of muscles and the control of the heartbeat had earned him an international reputation, Kovalyov had been an active figure among the dissidents. The regime blamed him for the revival of the *Chronicle* and accused him of contributing material to the *Chronicle of the Lithuanian Catholic Church*, a *samizdat* journal modeled directly on the *Chronicle of Current Events.*

Kovalyov's trial, held in Vilnius, Lithuania, began on December 9, 1975, the day before Andrei Sakharov was awarded the Nobel Prize for peace in Oslo. Sakharov, however, was outside the Vilnius courthouse, trying in vain to enter. From others who managed to attend, we know that for the first time the prosecution made an attempt — however falsely and under procedures that were obviously rigged — to show the libelous character of the *Chronicle of Current Events.* Doctors were even brought from prison hospitals to contradict allegations in the *Chronicle.* Kovalyov, however, was not permitted to cross-examine them fully, and the court would not allow him to call witnesses, such as the wife of Leonid Plyushch, who could corroborate disputed information in the *Chronicle.* (Plyushch had been placed in a psychiatric hospital in Dnepropetrovsk.) Kovalyov was convicted of anti-Soviet agitation and sentenced to seven years in a labor camp to be followed by three years of internal exile.

Since the revival of the *Chronicle* in 1974, it has become increasingly unlikely that the regime will take measures to suppress it completely. As each new issue demonstrates, the *Chronicle*'s sources of information extend to the most remote areas of the provinces, as well as to institutes of higher learning and upper echelons of the Party and government. (Recent issues have been close to two hundred pages long.) Many people who have never signed appeals now supply information on a regular basis to the *Chronicle.* The regime and perhaps even the *Chronicle*'s editors do not know their identities.

Furthermore, its network of readers would be too difficult to unravel. For a time, especially in the beginning, the *Chronicle* relied on contacts made in the labor camps in order to know who in other cities would be interested in such information. Without these contacts, dissidents in one city or within one circle of acquaintances would be hard pressed to meet other people with similar ideas. Now that isolation has been overcome. And the regime will not easily find another Yakir or Krasin, who knows so much and could be broken into betraying his friends.

Finally, the *Chronicle* is no longer the primary target of the KGB. In recent years, the Helsinki Watch Groups in Moscow, Kiev, Vilnius, Tbilisi, and Yerevan have drawn the most attention. Their reports on violations of the Helsinki Accords (much of the information is also summarized in the *Chronicle*) seemed too threatening for the authorities to ignore. Members of the groups publicly announced their participation and signed the reports. Many have either been arrested or permitted to emigrate. In the camps, too, the regime faces a continuing campaign among its political prisoners. As the *Chronicle* has reported, inmates in labor camps and prisons are demanding that their status be distinguished from that of common criminals, that forced labor be eliminated, and that contacts with their relatives not be disrupted at the whim of the jailers. Highlighted by hunger strikes and petitions that reach Moscow, news of these protests, too, makes its way to the West.

Despite this intense level of nonconformist activity — which is punctuated every year with the appearance in the West of novels and books from authors who write and live in the U.S.S.R. — Western observers periodically report on the collapse of the Soviet human rights movement. For some, its seeming lack of contact with workers spells its doom. For others, the arrest or expulsion of prominent dissenters means the movement will be left helpless, without leaders to guide it.

The history of the *Chronicle of Current Events* belies such conclusions. After decades of official hypocrisy, mass repression, and isolation, it is not surprising that, once the terror itself abated, a movement dedicated to simple justice and truth should arise. The *Chronicle* has been the voice of that movement. When it emerged in the late 1960s, other, more compelling events were occurring — in France, in Czechoslovakia, and in the United States. Only the *Chronicle*, however, has managed to survive and mature with its original values intact. As it continued to appear, its style grew more confident and expansive; in recent issues it has even attained a unique eloquence, in spite of its objective manner and complete lack of rhetorical excess. Other journals, like Herzen's *Bell* and Lenin's *Spark,* played major roles in the seismic shifts of Russian history. Both were produced in western Europe, then smuggled into the country. Both reflected the circumstances of czarist rule, the importance of an émigré community enamored of Russia, and the debate over her future. While today's human rights movement has similar preoccupations, the violence of Soviet history has led the dissidents to reject the politics of conspiracy and extremism that marked dissent under the czar. Instead, the movement has transformed the climate of Soviet intellectual life and the manner in which Russia is perceived abroad in a way no better exemplified than in the growth and achievement of the *Chronicle of Current Events.*

5

ZIONISTS AND DEMOCRATS

MORE THAN 200,000 Jews have left the Soviet Union since the early 1970s, making the emigration movement the most successful campaign of dissent in Soviet history. While the Jews have pursued one particular goal — the right to leave — they have received inspiration and support from the human rights movement, whose activists regard emigration as a fundamental human right. Nonetheless, the relationship between the two movements has fluctuated between periods of cooperation and isolation because the Zionist activists, particularly at the outset of their struggle, were sure that common action with dissidents would inhibit their chances of leaving. They believed that emigration did not relate directly to matters of internal reform and that support for the broader aims of the human rights movement would weaken their own cause.

The relationship has been further complicated by the presence of numerous Jews among the democratic activists. Well-known figures such as Pavel Litvinov, Larisa Bogoraz, Victor Krasin, Pyotr Yakir, Boris Tsukerman, Anatoly Yakobson, and Ilya Gabai are Jews. Intermarriage is common among Moscow intellectuals; many of the activists, like

Natalya Gorbanevskaya, were born to Jewish fathers or, like Alexander Esenin-Volpin, to Jewish mothers. Few regarded themselves as Jews in any active sense. Growing up in Moscow, they knew little if any Yiddish. They had never entered a synagogue or acknowledged a personal connection to Jewish history. Instead, they cultivated a profound devotion to the Russian language and made Russian literature the source of their cultural and moral education. In her essay "Do I Belong to the Jewish People?" Larisa Bogoraz expresses a common condition:

> Who am I now? Who do I feel myself to be? Unfortunately, I do not feel like a Jew. I understand that I have an unquestionable genetic tie with Jewry. I also assume that this is reflected in my mentality, in my mode of thinking, and in my behavior. But this common quality is as little help to me in feeling my Jewish identity as similarity of external features — evidently, a more profound, or more general, common bond is lacking, such as community of language, culture, history, tradition; perhaps, even, of impressions, unconsciously absorbed by the senses: what the eye sees, the ear hears, the skin feels. By all these characteristics, I am Russian.
>
> I am accustomed to the color, smell, rustle of the Russian landscape, as I am to the Russian language, the rhythm of Russian poetry. I react to everything else as alien.

She and her colleagues were not indifferent to anti-Semitism, though. Among Russian intellectuals, anti-Semitism has always been a personal touchstone, setting off liberal thinkers from reactionaries, but for most of the Jewish democratic activists, the "Jewish problem" was not even near the center of their consciousness.

They had friends, however, who thought differently. In the camps at Kolyma, Victor Krasin had met Zionists, among them a student named Vitaly Svechinsky. After World War II, when Soviet anti-Semitism increased and the state of Israel was founded, many young Jews wanted to help Israel in its war of independence. Svechinsky and a group of friends planned to cross the southern border into Turkey, but an informer exposed them. Svechinsky and two schoolmates were arrested, charged with treason, and sentenced to ten years in the camps.

Two years after Stalin's death, in 1955, Svechinsky and his friends were brought back to Moscow for a new trial. Convicted again, their sentences were reduced to five years — the time they already had served — and they were released. Svechinsky then studied architecture in Moscow until 1959, when, with his degree completed, he returned to Kolyma. The camps had been closed and a small city established near Magadan. Svechinsky felt more comfortable there, living among his friends from the camp. He would visit Moscow once or twice a year. As the 1960s progressed, he could see that something was beginning. People spoke more openly about the life around them. There were protests. One could sign an appeal and remain at liberty.

On one visit to Moscow, Svechinsky met Pavel Litvinov and Natalya Gorbanevskaya through their mutual friend, Victor Krasin. They spent New Year's Eve, 1968, together, talking all night about prison life. In the morning they remembered a Russian superstition: if you speak of camp on the New Year, then camp awaits you. (Litvinov would be arrested in August, Gorbanevskaya and Krasin in 1969.)

Svechinsky joined the democratic activists for a brief time. Through his friendship with Litvinov, he signed an appeal for Yuri Galanskov and Alexander Ginzburg and then collected more signatures on his own. As the petition grew, he saw that a great majority of the signers were Jews. This bothered Svechinsky. It reminded him of the period before the Revolution when, as even Soviet historians acknowledge, Jews comprised a quarter to a third of the organizers of all the revolutionary groups. The Zionists were a minority faction, while most politically active Jews argued that a revolution would obviate the need for a Jewish homeland in Palestine. Svechinsky saw history repeating itself. Although he admired his Moscow friends, he could not help but feel that the human rights movement could not resolve the Jewish condition in Russia. So he decided to stop participating in the movement and to look for means to reach and to rally his fellow Jews.

From his contacts in the labor camps, Svechinsky knew Jews throughout the country who shared his Zionist dream. As far back as 1948, the arrival in Moscow of the first Israeli legation, headed by Golda Meir, provoked a tumultuous welcome. When Mrs. Meir attended Rosh Hashana services on October 16, 1948, tens of thousands of worshipers greeted her. Shouts of *"am yisrael hai"* ("the Jewish people lives") echoed through the streets. In the Georgian Republic a large community of Jews continued to follow traditional customs. Life in Georgia is generally far more tolerant, and the Jews have been able to maintain synagogues and kosher slaughtering houses. In the capitals of the Baltic republics, where the Red Army took control in 1940, many Jews still spoke Yiddish and Hebrew. Compared to Jews in Leningrad or Moscow, the Jews of Riga and Vilnius were much less assimilated. By the 1950s there were underground Zionist seminars in both cities, whose members circulated information about Israel and Jewish history. Within a few years Zionist activists were translating books into Russian and creating a wide network of *samizdat* readers.

One of the most popular books was *Exodus* by Leon Uris. Translations were made independently by groups in different cities; the novel also surfaced in a Mordovian labor camp in 1963, where prisoners, Jewish and non-Jewish, translated it together.

While the most explicitly Jewish activity flourished in Georgia and the Baltic republics, in Moscow, too, young Jews looked for opportunities to express their defiance. Beginning in 1958, thousands of them gathered at the synagogue each year on the eve of Simchas Torah, a Jewish holiday marked by singing and dancing. They circulated Jewish *samizdat* and maintained informal contact with officials at the Israeli embassy. Contact with Israelis was especially coveted. In 1957, Moscow Jews searched out Israeli delegates to the International Youth Festival. In 1966, thousands cheered Israeli singer Geula Gil. (In Riga her concert provoked a riot. The audience of three thousand people refused to leave the hall, insisting on their desire to sing Israeli songs. The police threatened mass arrests. A teenage girl was detained. Young Jews rushed the police car; with the crowd out of control, the police backed down. The girl was not released, the crowd was eventually dispersed, but the police did not make mass arrests.)

There had always been individual Jews, mostly elderly, who wanted to join relatives or who retained strong religious motives for living in Israel. But the idea of mass emigration seemed out of place. Activists like Vitaly Svechinsky did not foresee the possibility of widespread applications for visas to Israel. For Svechinsky the dream of leaving would deflect Jews from confronting their place in Soviet society. He wanted to encourage Jews to be Jews and to insist on their rights as a recognized Soviet nationality. In a sense he wanted an internal Jewish revolution. With this in mind he helped to organize a Hebrew *ulpan* in Moscow. (*Ulpan* is a Hebrew word for an intensive language school.)

By the late 1960s, however, several events transformed the emerging national activity into a broadly based movement to emigrate. The Six Day War in June 1967 aroused intense feelings of pride and solidarity. Among religious Jews in Georgia and the Baltic republics the desire to live in Israel became overwhelming. The Soviet government reinforced this desire to leave by sponsoring an anti-Zionist campaign whose demented propaganda in the official press included caricatures similar to those that appeared in Julius Streicher's Nazi paper, *Der Stürmer*. The regime also intensified its discrimination against Jews, limiting their admission to universities and curtailing their opportunities for professional advancement. For Jews with secure positions, the restrictions compelled them to assess their children's future and to decide, often with great reluctance, to emigrate.

Events in Eastern Europe transformed emigration into a necessary and achievable goal. In Poland, the faltering regime of Wladyslaw Gomulka forced several thousand Jews to leave the country, making them a scapegoat for the government's problems. This "Polish variant" set a new precedent in Eastern Europe and gave Soviet Jews hope that their government, too, would permit emigration.

The invasion of Czechoslovakia was also an important and often overlooked factor. Many Jews, especially in Moscow, followed events in Czechoslovakia with profound interest. Excited by the upsurge in dissent in their own capital and by reports of liberalization in Prague, the invasion destroyed their hopes for a reasonable future in the Soviet Union and made the idea of emigration a necessity.

Furthermore, the regime made it seem as if Jews had penetrated the Czech government. Soviet newspapers stressed the Jewish origin of some Czech leaders, like Otto Shick, whose proposed economic reforms worried the Kremlin, and Ernst Goldshtuker, the head of the Czech Writers' Union. This propaganda also reinforced the desire to leave.

The emigration movement coalesced as Zionists in the Baltic republics found allies among Jewish activists in

Moscow. The Zionists in Riga and Vilnius had carried on underground activity for over a decade. Already alienated from the surrounding population, they took pride in their struggle for self-determination and were, in general, especially anxious to avoid common action with the human rights movement.

Many of their colleagues in Moscow, however, were friendly with dissidents and had been involved to varying degrees in the movement's initial protests. Vitaly Svechinsky, Roman Rutman, and Mikhail Zand — early figures in the emigration struggle — had close ties to dissidents. Vitaly Rubin, a scholar in ancient Chinese philosophy, would become a well-known spokesman for the emigration movement. In the late 1960s, though, he signed a protest against the trial of Galanskov and Ginzburg. Meetings with dissidents took place in his apartment. His sister Maria Rubina helped Natalya Gorbanevskaya type the original manuscript of *Red Square at Noon,* her account of the demonstration against the invasion of Czechoslovakia.

Through personal contacts, the dissidents in Moscow gradually learned the extent of Jewish disaffection in the country. Pyotr Yakir became the main channel of information on Zionist activity. Beginning with its sixth issue, dated February 28, 1969, the *Chronicle of Current Events* described a new phenomenon for its readers: the surge of Jewish national expression in cities across Russia.

Under the heading, "The Case of Boris Kochubievsky," the *Chronicle* reported the persecution of a Jew who had requested a visa to Israel. Born in Kiev, Kochubievsky became a radio engineer. Although he was an assimilated Jew, he knew that his family had suffered from succeeding episodes of anti-Semitism and repression. One relative had been shot by the Bolsheviks during the civil war. Another perished during Stalin's purge of the military. His grandparents were killed by Ukrainian nationalists after the German invasion, while his father, a Red Army major, was murdered at Babi Yar.

After the Six Day War, Kochubievsky could not restrain his pride in the Israeli victory. At factory meetings and during a ceremony at Babi Yar, he expressed support for Israel, defying official attempts to silence him. He married a Russian woman in June 1968, and they both soon applied for visas to Israel. The visas were granted in November, after they had initially been refused. But on the day they went to the OVIR office to pick up their documents, their apartment was searched. A week later, Boris Kochubievsky was arrested, charged with "anti-Soviet slander."

His trial was held on May 13, 1969, in the same court where Mendel Beilis, in a notorious example of czarist persecution, was acquitted in 1913 of the ritual murder of a Christian child. Leonid Plyushch, a dissident activist in Kiev, brought news of Kochubievsky's trial to the *Chronicle* in Moscow. For several issues the *Chronicle* provided details of the case, including this remarkable exchange between the prosecutor and the defendant regarding World War II:

PROSECUTOR: You know what we were fighting against?
KOCHUBIEVSKY: Fascism.
P: And what were we fighting for? Was it freedom?
K: Yes.
P: Did we win?
K: Yes.
P: Well, there you are, then, we have freedom.

By exposing the character of the proceedings, the human rights activists offered the Jews a means of protesting their condition. In every issue of the *Chronicle* since February 1969, a section concerning the Jewish emigration movement has included reports of petitions and letters, of hunger strikes, searches, and trials, attesting not only to the courage of the Zionists but to the solidarity of the democrats with a group of people who, after all, had despaired of a change in Soviet policies and now wished only to leave.

Acting on the assumption that the Soviet government was sensitive to public opinion, the Zionists accepted the strategy of their friends in the human rights movement. Between 1968 and 1970, almost two hundred petitions, some signed by as many as ninety people, were sent to government officials and international agencies.

Several of the most notable letters were not written by Jews themselves. In the fall of 1969, a non-Jew named Victor Fedoseyev became active in the Zionist struggle. Fedoseyev's wife, Rakhel Koliaditskaya, was Jewish; her parents had fled Russia after the Revolution and settled in China. After World War II, her father left for Palestine while her mother, Dora Koliaditskaya, returned to Russia, taking Rakhel with her. By the late 1960s, Dora Koliaditskaya was trying to remedy her mistake. She applied for an exit visa, wishing to reunite with her husband in Israel after a separation of twenty years. Her daughter and son-in-law joined her in Moscow in 1968; they, too, wanted to leave.

Like his wife, Victor Fedoseyev had grown up in China. His father had been sent there to help build railroads, and with the outbreak of war with Japan the family had been forced to remain in Shanghai. His parents returned to Russia in 1945; Victor, who was then sixteen, decided to become a merchant seaman. He traveled extensively, including several trips to the United States, before returning to live in the Soviet Union. Victor's personal contact with the West and his linguistic skill — he knew Russian, Chinese, English, and French — were valuable assets to the Zionist movement. By 1969, when open letters and petitions began to circulate widely, the movement called upon his talents.

Not all the Zionist activists, however, approved of his participation in their movement because he was not Jewish.

When Fedoseyev's letter to U Thant — referred to as the "Letter of the 25" — was completed, David Drabkin, one of the most active Moscow Zionists, refused to sign it. Drabkin, an industrial engineer by profession, opposed any contact with the human rights movement. He himself had written angry letters to Soviet officials, including a renunciation of Soviet citizenship. He would also begin a Hebrew *ulpan*, announcing his classes with posters in subway stations and other public places. After a good deal of pressure, Drabkin signed the letter to U Thant — his name appeared first on the list, where, according to custom, the author usually signs — but Victor Fedoseyev did not sign the letter, not wanting to reveal that a non-Jew had composed a letter for the Jewish movement.

Fedoseyev's involvement grew more intense in 1970. Inspired by the example of the *Chronicle of Current Events*, the emigration movement decided to publish its own journal. Again, Fedoseyev's energy and talents were utilized. With the help of Vitaly Svechinsky and other activists, Fedoseyev prepared four issues of *Iskhod* (Exodus). Modeled directly on the *Chronicle, Iskhod* contained collective appeals and petitions, records of house searches, and reports of the December 1970 hijacking trial in Leningrad. The cover page, too, reflected the influence of the human rights movement. Below the title, the editors included article 13 of the Universal Declaration of Human Rights ("Everyone has the right to leave any country, including his own") and a verse from Psalm 137 ("If I forget thee, O Jerusalem, Let my right hand forget her cunning"), which Jews have recited for thousands of years.

In an interview with Leonard Schroeter for his book *The Last Exodus,* Fedoseyev showed an intimate understanding of the Jewish problem in the Soviet Union:

> It was important to publish *Iskhod* because the main achievement of the Soviet regime upon Jews was that

they were deprived of the *word*. You can't buy a Bible which speaks of the history, morals, and religion of the Jewish people nor can you read and learn about Jewish culture and life. A people deprived of the *word* face assimilation; to stop assimilation, to recreate a nation, a people must know and read the *word*. In the Bible, the exodus of Jews from Egypt is reported as a migration. What if it had never been reported? What if the Jews had been denied knowledge of their heritage? Jewry is great and strong because it recorded everything that happened. We needed to record every word — the *word*. That was the most important task for us; we had to report the events of Soviet Jewry for those who wished to avoid assimilation; for those who wanted to know their rights and to know how to struggle; and for those who would support and encourage the Jewish repatriation movement. This is the second exodus of the Jews. This was the reason for the journal and the reason for its name.

Fedoseyev was not the only non-Jew to play a significant role in the emigration movement. Valery Chalidze was often approached for help and advice, and he responded sympathetically from the outset of the movement. As he remarks in his book *To Defend These Rights*, "Any mass restrictions of rights affecting Jews attracts the attention of 'world public opinion,' since historically any form of restriction on the rights of Jews is a critical question for our civilization." As a matter of principle, Chalidze looked into numerous cases involving Jews. He accepted power of attorney for Jonah Kolchinsky, a nineteen-year-old Kharkov Jew who was inducted into the army after renouncing Soviet citizenship and declaring his desire to live in Israel. Chalidze asked the minister of defense to have Kolchinsky demobilized. That same year, in 1971, Chalidze appealed on behalf of Joseph Mendelevich, one of the convicted conspirators in the hijacking case. Mendelevich was an observant Jew.

Prison officials harassed him, preventing him from wearing a skullcap according to religious tradition. This time, Chalidze wrote to the minister of internal affairs, asking him to explain to the camp officials that according to the Soviet constitution citizens are guaranteed freedom of worship. In another case involving the prisoner Yuri Vudka, camp officials terminated a visit from his wife because they were conversing in Yiddish, the recognized language of the country's Jewish minority. Again Chalidze sent a complaint to the authorities and helped to publicize the abuse.

One case that absorbed much of Chalidze's time involved Dora Koliaditskaya, the mother-in-law of Victor Fedoseyev. She took on Chalidze as her legal adviser when her application for a visa was refused. Chalidze filed petitions in various courts, citing her rights under international law to be reunited with her husband. Although the case did not succeed in the courts, she was permitted to leave with Fedoseyev and her daughter in February 1971.

As more Jews applied for visas, the regime tried in vain to discourage applications. More and more articles appeared in the press, condemning life in Israel and praising the Soviet Union as a haven for its Jewish minority. Zionism was already a principal target of Soviet propaganda, an enemy ideology whose followers were traitors to the Soviet motherland. In part, the propaganda campaign was designed to reassure the regime's Arab clients; it was also a thinly disguised warning to its Jewish citizens. The authorities, however, were reluctant publicly to acknowledge that a Jewish national movement was growing.

But on March 4, 1970, the regime reversed its façade of indifference. Leonid Zamyatin, head of the Press Department of the Foreign Ministry, introduced forty Soviet Jews at a press conference attended by both foreign journalists and the Soviet press. The Soviet media treated the conference as a major event. It was broadcast on radio and television, then, within a week, repeated three times on television.

The participants included the country's highest ranking Jewish official, Vice-Premier Venyamin Dymshits. Several military officers and academicians also took part. Alexander Chakovsky, the editor of *Literaturnaya Gazeta,* the journal of the Writers' Union, appeared, as did the ballerina Maya Plisetskaya, the violinist Leonid Kogan, and the comedian Arkady Raikin. Aside from these familiar figures, the regime produced doctors, scientists, and workers. In its opening statements and in response to questions, the group repeated well-worn claims: that Israel had begun a subversive campaign against socialist countries, that Soviet Jews enjoyed economic and educational advances, that anti-Semitism did not exist in Soviet society, and that Jews, as well as the whole of mankind, should be grateful to the Soviet Union for saving the world from Fascist slavery in World War II. Any suggestion that Jews wished to leave the Soviet Union was propaganda.

A group of Moscow Jews reacted immediately. Their response, known as the "Letter of the 39," was one of the movement's most publicized and effective petitions. Dated March 8, 1970, the letter was addressed to Leonid Zamyatin, who directed the press conference. In an opening statement, the activist Jews contrasted their beliefs with the smug complacency of the regime's adherents:

> We are those Jews who insist on their desire to leave for Israel and who are being constantly refused by the Soviet authorities.
>
> We are those Jews who have more than once addressed open statements to the Soviet press, but whose letters were never published.
>
> We are those Jews who had not been invited to the press conference on March 4 of this year and who had not been asked to express their views.

In the attached declaration, the activists responded in detail to the major themes of the press conference.

... No references to completely equal and joyful labor with Russians and no examples of a brilliant military or social career can divert our attention from the problem, for in this, Russians remain Russians, and Jews cease to be Jews. Forcible assimilation in this case does not mean, for example, that reading Jewish books is prohibited. It means that young Jews do not know how to read Jewish books because there are no schools in the Soviet Union where a Jewish language is taught. . . .

One of the basic issues of the question in the U.S.S.R. is a guarantee of the right of repatriation. The Soviet Union does not recognize that right, and many thousands of Soviet Jews who want to leave for Israel are being refused.

We shall insist on our right to decide our own destiny, including the choice of citizenship and country of residence. We ourselves are capable of assessing all the possible difficulties awaiting us concerning military events, change of climate or of social order.

The present state of our citizenship includes the right of the state to demand from us no more than obeying the laws, and our claims to freedom of repatriation are based on Soviet laws and guarantees of international law.

The Jewish people has undergone many persecutions and sufferings, many malicious or well-intentioned assimilation campaigns, and has succeeded in maintaining its identity.

We believe that now also Jews will respond to the anti-Israel campaign not by abdicating, but that, on the contrary, their pride in their people will grow stronger and that they will declare "Next year in Jerusalem!"

Although the letter was signed by many well-known Jewish activists, such as David Drabkin, Vitaly Svechinsky, and Vladimir Slepak, the central portion was actually written by Valery Chalidze. Chalidze had written numerous appeals and letters on behalf of Jews, but working on the text of the "Letter of the 39" was, for him, the most personally involving. It was the one time in his life when he felt as if he, too, were Jewish.

The letter's effect was unprecedented. Except for Vladimir and Maria Slepak and the Moscow engineer Vladimir Prestin, all the signers were eventually allowed to leave, most of them within a year after the press conference. The letter also highlighted the complex relationship between the Zionists and the democrats. Not only had it been written by Valery Chalidze, but it was also signed by Julius Telesin, a Jewish mathematician long identified with the human rights movement. Just before the Zionists came to take the letter to foreign correspondents, Telesin stopped by Chalidze's apartment, read the letter, then added his name. (Telesin's was the fortieth signature.) When the Zionists learned of Telesin's inclusion, many were angry at Chalidze. A friend of Alexander Esenin-Volpin and Victor Krasin, Telesin was often referred to as the "king of *samizdat*." After the trial of Sinyavsky and Daniel in 1966, Telesin, like Alexander Ginzburg, also compiled material on the case. Later he made a *samizdat* anthology of thirteen final speeches by defendants in political trials. Telesin, however, was also a Zionist. His mother is a Yiddish writer who emigrated to Israel a few years after her son.

Telesin's signature did not reduce the effectiveness of the letter. To everyone's surprise, he received permission to leave before the other signers, within a month after the protest was circulated. Telesin's departure stunned both the Zionist and the dissident movements. For the Zionists, it showed that meek appeals and quiet struggle were not necessarily more effective means of protest. Telesin had signed numerous petitions. He had attended demonstrations and compiled transcripts of political trials. His home had been searched several times. *Izvestia* had also denounced him for signing the "Letter of the 39." Instead of arresting him, though, the regime let him go.

His dissident colleagues were also surprised. Telesin was the first active dissident to leave. They could not believe that the government would allow such an articulate witness to reach the West. Some feared that his plane would be shot down or diverted to Siberia, where Telesin could be removed to a labor camp. His friends made him promise to call from Vienna to assure them of his safe arrival.

Telesin's departure from Sheremetevo Airport in Moscow on May 6, 1970, was the occasion for a large gathering. For the first time a large number of Zionists and democrats met one another. A photograph taken at the airport shows Telesin in the center of a large group of friends, among them Iosif Kerler, a Yiddish poet; Alexander Esenin-Volpin; Andrei Grigorenko, whose father, General Pyotr Grigorenko, was in a psychiatric hospital; and Boris Tsukerman, an active participant in both movements.

Although the "Letter of the 39" focused attention on Soviet Jewry (the New York *Times* prominently carried the story, with an almost complete text of the letter), the movement was actually faltering. Barely two thousand people left in 1969, and under a thousand would receive permission in 1970. The regime seemed in complete control. It allowed some to leave, including Jews who organized *samizdat* operations in major cities. It arrested others, like Boris Kochubievsky in Kiev, in order to intimidate and thereby forestall the impulse to emigrate within a community. The vast majority of applicants were harassed or simply ignored.

The frustration of waiting became unbearable for many Jews. Determined to leave or at least create a scandal that neither Soviet officials nor the West could ignore, a group of activists based primarily in Riga planned to hijack an airplane to Sweden. Their friends in other cities urged them to reconsider. Contact was made with Israeli officials to learn their reaction to the scheme.* They objected emphatically. Still, a small group was determined to make the attempt.

On June 15, 1970, twelve people were arrested at Smolny Airport in Leningrad. At the same time, the KGB carried out scores of searches in Riga, Kharkov, and Leningrad, confiscating material on Israel and Jewish history. The timing of the arrests and the subsequent trials made clear that the regime had learned of the plot well in advance of its attempt. With the conspirators in hand, the authorities hoped to crush the Zionist movement before it gained momentum.

One of the principal conspirators was Edward Kuznetsov. A decade earlier he had helped to organize the poetry readings in Mayakovsky Square, for which he spent seven years in the labor camps. Until that time Kuznetsov did not regard himself as a Jew. Born to a Jewish father and a Russian mother, he was given his mother's name, Kuznetsov, after his father died. At the age of sixteen, when, like all Soviet

---

*The attitude of the Israeli government to the renaissance of Jewish national feeling in the Soviet Union cannot easily be summarized or explained. For years, Israeli diplomats avoided direct contact with Soviet Jews, not wishing to provoke Soviet authorities. After the Six Day War, when diplomatic relations were severed by the Kremlin, the Israelis continued to maintain a publicly aloof role. But as more and more activists reached Israel, they prevailed on the government to support more openly the emigration movement. For a detailed study of the evolution of Israeli policy, see *The Last Exodus* by Leonard Schroeter (Universe, New York, 1974).

citizens, he registered for an internal passport, Kuznetsov had to choose the nationality of one of his parents; at his mother's urging he chose Russian. But in prison his outlook changed. He developed intense feelings about his Jewish origins and tried to change the entry on his passport. The prison director refused his request. Two years later, during his trial for the attempted hijacking, Kuznetsov described in a diary his transformation from a dissident to a Zionist.*

I long ago grew out of active dislike of the existing regime. I think that the essential characteristics of the structure of the regime are to all intents and purposes immutable, and that the particular political culture of the Russian people may be classed as despotic. There are not many variations in this type of power-structure, the framework of which was erected by Ivan the Terrible and by Peter the Great. I think that the Soviet regime is the lawful heir of these widely differing Russian rulers. A Jew with neither any inclination towards the wielding of power, nor with any love for meek resignation, nor nourishing any hope of seeing a radical democratization of an essentially repressive regime in

---

*Kuznetsov managed to write *Prison Diaries* in a Leningrad prison and then in a labor camp. It is not known how he concealed the material from his guards or how he smuggled it to his friends in Moscow. The diary was first published in Russian in 1973. Near the end of the year, the KGB interrogated Elena Bonner, the wife of Andrei Sakharov. They threatened her for helping to transmit the book to the West. In 1974, two young dissidents, Victor Khaustov and Gabriel Superfin, were convicted of smuggling *Prison Diaries* to the West and sentenced, respectively, to four and five years of labor camp. According to the prosecution, Khaustov had received the original manuscript from Elena Bonner. Unable to work on it himself, he turned to Superfin. Written on toilet paper, the manuscript was barely legible. Superfin typed it out completely and helped send it to the West.

At his trial in 1974, Superfin was convicted as well for his alleged role in editing the *Chronicle of Current Events*. A talented literary scholar, he had edited the memoirs of Anastas Mikoyan for *Novy Mir*. Superfin also helped Alexander Solzhenitsyn in his archival research; this may have aggravated his fate.

the foreseeable future, and considering myself responsible — however indirectly — as a citizen of this country,
for all of its abominations, I decided to leave the Soviet
Union. I consider it not only impossible but unnecessary
to fight against the Soviet regime. It fully answers the
heartfelt wishes of a significant — but alas not the
better — part of its population.

. . . Having observed the symptoms of anti-semitism
endemic among the people, and sometimes even fore-
seeing how these symptoms coincided with government
policy in certain respects, I grew mature enough to form
my own opinions and felt it essential that I personally
join the ranks of the oppressed.

I grew up in a Russian family and had practically no
knowledge whatsoever of Jewish culture, nor did I
know anything of the influence it had had on nearly
every culture in the world. Therefore my choice to live
and be a Jew was dictated in the early stages by emotional considerations rather than by a conscious feeling
of physical identity. Tsvetaeva says something of this:
"Is it not a hundred times more worthy to be a wander-
ing Jew? For the pogrom is as life itself to any human
being who is worthy of the name."

In the months between the exposure of the plot and the
hijacking trial, the democratic activists reviewed their own
attitudes toward the emigration struggle. The attempted
hijacking, however misconceived, contradicted their own
determination to keep within the law. Many democrats
were also annoyed by the narrow allegiance of some of the
Zionists, their excessive rhetoric that bordered on Jewish
chauvinism, and the frequent disdain many exhibited toward
the democrats. Several activists had also begun to fear that if
the Zionists were successful, the departure of many Jewish
intellectuals would weaken their own movement. But Vladimir Bukovsky, among others, insisted that the Jewish struggle

for national dignity was an integral part of the struggle for human freedom and that the right to emigrate had to be defended. His arguments prevailed.

The Leningrad hijacking trial began on December 15, 1970. Immediate relatives of the accused were permitted to attend after their passports were checked against special lists. No foreign newsmen were allowed into the courtroom. Technically, no provision of Soviet law explicitly covered air hijacking; other statutes were invoked. At the trial the defendants faced charges of treason, which carried a possible death penalty, responsibility for preparing a crime, anti-Soviet agitation and propaganda, and theft of state property on an especially large scale.

As the *Chronicle of Current Events* reported, "At the trial all the accused, without hesitation, related all the circumstances and all the factual aspects of the case." Several had also been involved in Jewish *samizdat* activity. The defendants, however, denied that they had intended to inflict harm on the U.S.S.R., thereby rejecting the charge of treason. They also denied intending to steal the airplane; upon reaching the West, they would have relinquished the airplane to officials in Sweden.

The charge of treason, under article 64 of the criminal code, gave the trial disturbing significance. The hijacking itself had not been attempted because the conspirators were arrested as they approached the airplane. Their only weapons were sixteen truncheons and one pistol. The pistol could not be fired, as expert testimony disclosed. The defendants had brought the weapons to frighten the crew.

The trial lasted eight days. To keep the outside world informed of the proceedings, the dissidents, under Vladimir Bukovsky's direction, devised means to transmit information from Leningrad to Moscow, where it could be translated and passed to Western journalists. Bukovsky was an old

friend of Kuznetsov's — they were both veterans of the
Mayakovsky Square poetry readings — and understood that
only publicity could restrain the regime. Bukovsky arranged
for English translations of the trial's major exchanges and of
the defendants' final statements. When Kuznetsov and Mark
Dymshits, who was to pilot the airplane, received the death
sentence on Christmas Eve, Bukovsky quickly relayed the
verdicts to Western newsmen.

In Europe, the United States, and Israel, demonstrators
urged clemency for the defendants. Twenty-four governments and the Vatican intervened officially on their behalf.
Even Western Communist parties objected. The French
Communist newspaper *L'Humanité* was especially blunt:
"We don't believe that an abortive attempt should be penal-
ized by a death sentence which we hope — and we say it
again — will not be applied. It is almost unnecessary to say
that French Communists, who respect a German Jew named
Karl Marx, are resolutely against anti-Semitism which is a
stupidity and a degradation." The day before the Leningrad
judgments were announced, a Spanish court-martial had
sentenced six Basque nationalists to death. Protests soon
linked the two trials, increasing pressure on the Kremlin.

Inside the Soviet Union, too, the regime received letters
and telegrams from Zionist as well as democratic activists.
Valery Chalidze, Alexander Esenin-Volpin, Andrei Tverdokhlebov, Boris Tsukerman, and Leonid Rigerman wrote to
President Podgorny:

> Do not permit the murder of Kuznetsov and Dymshits!
> You must understand that their attempt to break the
> law was motivated by extreme necessity — no state is
> safe from similar attempts as long as it holds people
> in the country by force. Let all those go who want to.
> Recognize the Jews' right to *repatriation!* Execution
> and terror are no evidence of the strength of a state.

Under intense pressure, the regime reacted quickly. Although by law an appeal could not be heard before January 5, the Supreme Court of the Russian Republic met six days after the Leningrad verdict to review the case. Several relatives and Andrei Sakharov were allowed into the courtroom. Outside the courthouse dozens of dissidents and Jews gathered, trying in vain to enter the building. On the first day, December 30, a Jewish woman from Novosibirsk spoke to newsmen about anti-Semitism and her inability to reach her son in Israel. KGB agents led her away, but the newsmen, prompted by Bukovsky, intervened. She was released. That same day, General Franco set aside the death sentences given the Basques by a court-martial.

On the second day of the appeal hearings, a much larger crowd assembled, expecting to learn the judgment of the court. Again the KGB would not tolerate overt defiance. Lev Shenkar, a Moscow activist and Hebrew teacher, wore a cloth sign over his neck. It read in Hebrew, "Thou shalt not kill." The KGB accused him of hooliganism and gave him two weeks in jail.

Later that morning, Sakharov emerged from the building. In a calm, soft voice he announced that the death sentences for Dymshits and Kuznetsov had been commuted to fifteen years in a labor camp. The sentences for three other defendants were also reduced. "We have won. I congratulate you," he told the crowd. "If you need any help, call me or Chalidze."

The extent of their victory was not clear for a few months. The regime still planned other trials — in Leningrad again, then in Kishinev, Riga, and Odessa. In the aftermath of the hijacking trial, it hoped to stop the Jewish movement altogether. But the strategy collapsed. The Jews were not giving in. Thirty-one Moscow Jews asked the authorities to allow Vitaly Svechinsky and Boris Tsukerman to act as observers at the forthcoming trial in Leningrad. Tsukerman was famous for his legal acuity, and the regime preferred not having him in a courtroom. Both he and Svechinsky were allowed to leave for Israel in the beginning of 1971. Many other activists, too, including some who had waited for years, received visas to Israel.

In March the dam finally burst. With the Party about to hold its twenty-fourth congress in Moscow, the government grew nervous. It was anxious to avoid incidents, with foreign delegates and journalists assembling in the capital. Jews from Kiev, Riga, and Vilnius were refused train tickets to Moscow; others were physically removed from trains. Still, Jewish activists took unprecedented measures. There were public demonstrations, then a sit-down strike by twenty-four Moscow Jews in the reception room of the Supreme Soviet. The regime capitulated. In March alone, more Jews emigrated than in 1970. In all, more than fourteen thousand Jews would leave in 1971. In 1972 and again in 1973, more than thirty thousand would leave.

The Zionists were able to establish greater freedom of action than their colleagues in the human rights movement. They appealed more systematically to the West, having witnessed the lack of constructive response from Soviet officials to all the petitions by Crimean Tatars, Ukrainians, and Moscow dissidents. They received persistent attention through the efforts of Jewish organizations. They established personal contacts with foreign tourists, while the democrats had no natural constituency in the West to champion their cause. The Zionist appeals grew more rhetorical and inflammatory. Gradually, they retreated from allies like Valery Chalidze, whose prudent, judicial advice no longer seemed to them necessary or appropriate. They began to employ civil disobedience, a tactic that contradicted the philosophy of the human rights movement. In effect, the Zionists deliberately provoked the authorities, while the democrats remained committed to challenging the government to obey its own laws.

At the same time, the two movements shared important concerns. The Zionists, by insisting on proper judicial and administrative behavior from the government, on the right to communicate freely and the right to hold opinions contrary to those of the regime, were affirming principles the democrats also upheld. If defended successfully by the Zionists, these principles would provide important historical and psychological precedents.

Although more than sixty thousand Jews left the U.S.S.R. in 1972 and 1973, the regime did not dismantle all obstacles to emigration. It found new means to discourage people from applying. A growing number of Jews, many of whom held responsible positions in scientific work, were refused permission to emigrate and denied employment in their professions. Unable to leave and cut off from normal social contacts, the refuseniks, as they came to be called, form a small pariah caste in numerous Soviet cities. They never receive a written explanation, simply a phrase in an interview or over the telephone: "departure inexpedient," "state security," "army service ten years before," "your father's secret work," "not close enough relatives in Israel," "the reason itself is a state secret," "regime considerations." There is no pattern or logic to these refusals. One scientist may leave while his subordinate, who worked in the same laboratory on the same project, will be refused. OVIR has often invoked "security reasons" in cases of people whose professions, such as carpentry or meat cutting, do not remotely involve scientific or military research.

Even worse, the KGB occasionally chooses a Jew — a well-known activist or someone without obvious stature — and arranges a spurious charge. Alexander Feldman of Kiev was one such victim. Despite repeated rejections, he had persisted in his struggle to reach Israel. Feldman was also active among the dissidents, helping to circulate appeals and *samizdat*. He

was arrested in the fall of 1973, then convicted of hooliganism for knocking a cake out of a woman's hands and ad-
dressing her obscenely. His trial was equally contrived. All
the prosecution witnesses were connected with the Kiev
police department. When Feldman's attorney exposed inconsistencies in the alleged victim's testimony, he was not
allowed to examine her further. Feldman was forced to
spend three and a half years in a labor camp before reaching
Israel in 1977.

Among other fabricated cases, the most outlandish involved Isaac Shkolnik, a mechanic in an appliance factory
in the Ukrainian city of Vinnitsa. When he was arrested in
July 1972, he and his family were awaiting invitations
from Israel so they could apply for exit visas.

At first, Shkolnik was charged with circulating defamatory
statements about the regime, an offense that carries a possible three-year term. Then the accusation was changed to
anti-Soviet agitation and propaganda, punishable by up to
seven years. During the investigation, however, the KGB
found British magazines and letters and a visiting card of a
British engineer whom Shkolnik had met at the factory in
1968. After six months of pretrial detention, the KGB
changed the indictment to spying for the British government — treason — punishable by execution.

But after British authorities denied the charges, Shkolnik
was brought to trial as an Israeli spy. The regime did not
feel embarrassed by its own fabrications. No evidence was
presented of Shkolnik contacting an Israeli agent. The
prosecutor asserted that Shkolnik had been memorizing
technical details about his factory in order to sell them to
the Israeli government upon his arrival there. Tried in a
closed military court, Shkolnik was convicted and given a
ten-year sentence. On appeal the sentence was reduced to
seven years.

While the regime pursued a policy of selective repression,

it also sought means to profit from the growing urge to emigrate. On August 3, 1972, the authorities formally obliged specialists leaving for Israel to pay a large education tax, ranging from 4,000 to 25,000 rubles a person, depending on the level of higher education. For an engineer such a tax could equal five to seven years' salary. The decree was a cynical ploy by the regime, a pretext to compel Israeli and Western Jews to ransom their brethren by providing the Soviet government much-needed foreign currency. Soon after promulgation of the decree, an official in the Ministry of Finance told a group of Jews: "We are not so naïve as to think that you possess such large sums. But you know where you can get them, and I suppose that you will be able to do so."

The regime miscalculated. The emigration of thousands of Jews could not obscure arbitrary measures designed to discourage would-be applicants. Events in the summer of 1972 deepened suspicions of the Kremlin and transformed the issue of emigration from a Jewish concern to one of international diplomacy.

With the onset of détente, Richard Nixon visited Moscow in May 1972, the first visit of a U.S. President. In the weeks before his arrival, numerous activists were detained and telephones disconnected. A month after Nixon's departure, Pyotr Yakir was arrested, increasing pressure on the *Chronicle of Current Events*. In September, Israeli athletes were murdered at the Munich Olympics; in reaction, twenty-five Moscow Jews demonstrated peacefully before the Lebanese embassy. The group, including Andrei Sakharov, was broken up and briefly detained. A memorial service at Babi Yar in Kiev was disrupted by police, and eleven Jews received fifteen days in jail.

Soon after Nixon's visit, Moscow activists alerted their supporters in the U.S. Congress to the increased repression. By August, there was discussion of linking Nixon's proposals on trade and credits to the education tax specifically and to Soviet emigration policy in general. This was the origin of the Jackson-Vanik amendment to the trade bill, making extension of the lowest regular tariff rates — called most-favored-nation status — dependent on Soviet willingness to allow freer emigration.

With this development in Congress, the emigration movement achieved a level of publicity and support the human rights movement has never reached. Visiting senators and congressmen began calling on prominent refuseniks, often on the same day they met with high-ranking Soviet officials. Perhaps, as politicians, the visitors had ulterior motives for meeting Jewish refuseniks. Nonetheless, they sought advice and shared ideas with them, as if the activists constituted an opposition party whose problems and perceptions offered a necessary counterweight to discussions with government officials. While the Nixon administration and its supporters warned that the Jackson-Vanik amendment would harm prospects for emigration, the refuseniks made clear that only Western pressure and not merely "quiet diplomacy" or pious statements of concern could move Kremlin officials.

As the debate in Washington continued, the Soviet government tried to appease Western public opinion. The education tax was suspended in April 1973, although the decree formally remained in the statute books. Silva Zalmanson, the wife of Edward Kuznetsov and one of the convicted conspirators in the hijacking case, was released. After four years in detention her health had deteriorated; the regime commuted the remaining six years of her sentence and allowed her to reach Israel in September 1974.

At the same time, the government granted a pardon to Simas Kudirka, a radio operator on a Soviet trawler who had jumped to an American ship in November 1970. The captain had returned Kudirka to the Soviet ship. He was then convicted of treason and sentenced to ten years in the camps.

In the summer of 1974, the United States government recognized Simas Kudirka as an American citizen because his mother had retained her U.S. citizenship. At the end of August he was pardoned, and in November, with his mother, his wife, and two children, Kudirka left the Soviet Union.

In the midst of the congressional debate, Andrei Sakharov assumed a startling and dangerous role. For several years Sakharov had restricted his activity to written appeals and careful analyses of judicial abuses. He defended a broad range of human rights, not fearing to act on behalf of Jews, Ukrainians, Volga Germans, fellow dissidents, and Crimean Tatars, among others. Yet the right to emigrate carried particular importance for him. As a liberal, he regarded the right to leave one's country as an "essential condition of spiritual freedom. A free country cannot resemble a cage, even if it is gilded and supplied with material things." As a scientist, he knew many colleagues whose applications for visas led to their dismissal—to lack of professional work without any guarantee of when or whether they would be permitted to leave. And as a humanist, he regarded anti-Semitism as particularly loathsome.

In the summer of 1973, with the human rights movement under intense pressure (the Yakir-Krasin trial would take place in August) and the issue of Soviet emigration before the U.S. Congress, Sakharov held his first interviews with Western correspondents. While he outlined his own ideas on a variety of topics, he spoke specifically about emigration and urged the West not to make détente "some kind of capitulation, a game involving the internal interests of the people of the West in which we merely play a role of small change." In September he appealed directly to Congress on the emigration issue. Unlike many Americans, Sakharov would not allow Soviet abuse of human rights to be reduced to a question of Jewish emigration. He specifically urged the Congress to support the Jackson-Vanik amendment to the trade bill.

> The abandonment of a policy of principle would be a betrayal of the thousands of Jews and non-Jews who want to emigrate, of the hundreds in camps and mental hospitals, of the victims of the Berlin wall.

> Such a denial would lead to stronger repressions on ideological grounds. It would be tantamount to total capitulation of democratic principles in the face of blackmail, deceit, and violence. The consequences of such a capitulation for international confidence, détente, and the entire future of mankind are difficult to predict.

No method can adequately gauge the effect of Sakharov's intervention: the inventor of the Soviet hydrogen bomb, the country's most decorated scientist, was advising a foreign government on how to conduct diplomacy with the Soviet regime. The move infuriated Soviet authorities. In the fall of 1973, they launched a harrowing campaign against Andrei Sakharov and Alexander Solzhenitsyn in the country's press. The headlines of these articles, particularly against Sakharov, reflect the nature and tone of the denunciations: "A Foul Endeavor," "At One with the Enemy," "A Rebuff to the Slanderer," "The Limit of Degradation."

The refuseniks could not remain aloof. Ten prominent Jewish scientists who had been refused visas for Israel, among them Benjamin Levich, Mark Azbel, and Alexander Lunts, distributed an open letter proclaiming,

> We decided to leave Russia because we feel that our place is not here; but we cannot be indifferent to Russia, her people, and her culture. If there were an enemy who hated everything Russian and who would

like to destroy everything that is beautiful about Russia, he would begin with Solzhenitsyn and Sakharov. Any great country would be proud of these people, but only Russia, continuing her ancient tradition, devours her best sons.

This was not the first time that refuseniks felt compelled to act in defense of their democratic allies. In January 1972, a group of activists appealed to President Podgorny on behalf of Vladimir Bukovsky. Bukovsky had attracted international attention for exposing the regime's penchant for sending political nonconformists to psychiatric hospitals, but the Jews remembered as well his persistent support of their cause. In their letter they protested his closed trial and reminded the regime that for Jews "who want to go to Israel, it is far from being a matter of indifference that there is injustice in any corner of the globe, including the U.S.S.R."

And in the spring of 1975, Vitaly Rubin, Vladimir Slepak, and Alexander Lunts urged support for Andrei Tverdokhlebov, a founder of the Moscow Committee for Human Rights and a member of the Moscow chapter of Amnesty International. Tverdokhlebov had been arrested in April, when the regime tried to suppress the Amnesty group; these Jewish activists, who had long awaited visas, did not allow his arrest to pass unnoticed. Later that year, before Sergei Kovalyov was placed on trial in Vilnius, officials warned refuseniks to stay away from the courthouse. One refusenik, Alexander Drot, came on the first day nonetheless. He received his exit visa that night with the condition that he not try to attend further sessions.

As Soviet authorities realized that emigration was the easiest right they could grant, they came to understand the advantages of expelling their most persistent critics. Protests in the West tended to focus on well-known prisoners whose writing or activity earned them international support. By allowing or compelling dissidents to leave, the regime hoped to reduce their influence and the unwelcome publicity that attended awkward trials and imprisonment. In many cases, dissidents applied for visas after the KGB made clear that expulsion was the only alternative to prison. By 1974, numerous dissidents and independent intellectuals — Jews and non-Jews — had left the country: the cellist Mstislav Rostropovich, the poet Joseph Brodsky, writers such as Victor Nekrasov, Vladimir Maximov, and Andrei Sinyavsky, and leading dissidents Pavel Litvinov, Anatoly Yakobson, and Alexander Esenin-Volpin.

Gradually, the regime's intentions became clear. While prominent dissenters were forced to leave, others less famous or otherwise more vulnerable were sent to labor camps, prisons, and mental hospitals. The emigration of well-known figures, the government hoped, would camouflage increased repression inside the country. At the same time, by insisting that all the emigrants carry a visa for Israel, the authorities used emigration as a means to humiliate political noncon-formists and discredit the Zionist movement.

The regime has its own motives for insisting on Israel. For years it has tried to discredit the human rights move-ment by identifying its non-Jewish supporters as Jews in dis-guise. Even Solzhenitsyn has been dubbed "Solzhenitsker" in some of the Party's propaganda. In addition, the regime is anxious to use the issue of emigration to Israel as a means of increasing the resentment of Ukrainians, Russians, and other nationalities against Jews and dissidents alike. Many Ukrai-nians, after all, would like to emigrate or at least visit rela-tives in the West, but only Jews and some dissidents appear to have this privilege.

As a matter of principle, several non-Jewish dissidents have resisted the regime's efforts to force them to emigrate. In 1975, Anatoly Marchenko, Andrei Amalrik (whose wife,

Gyusel, is a Moslem), and Valentin Turchin, the head of the Moscow group of Amnesty International, were harassed and pressured to leave the country on Israeli visas; at first, all three refused to cooperate. But Amalrik had just served a difficult term in a labor camp and in exile and could not risk another sentence. In the summer of 1976, under threat of further arrest, he and his wife departed with Israeli visas. Turchin also refused to accept a visa for Israel until 1977, when the regime made clear that his activity, and in particular his book *The Inertia of Fear*, made his arrest imminent. Marchenko faced the harshest reprisal. As already noted, he insisted on his right to go to the United States. As a result, he was arrested and exiled to Siberia on a fabricated charge.

Since the Helsinki Accords were signed in August 1975, cooperation between democrats and the emigration movement has increased. From the outset, prominent refuseniks like Vitaly Rubin and Vladimir Slepak, who had always maintained personal contact with dissidents, were active in the Helsinki Watch Group in Moscow. Younger refuseniks like Anatoly Shcharansky in Moscow, Isai and Grigory Goldshtein in Tbilisi, and Eitan Finkelshtein in Vilnius joined Helsinki groups in their own cities, reinforcing contact not only with dissidents but with nationalist groups of Georgians or Lithuanians who share their concern for human rights and see the Helsinki Accords as a useful means to embarrass the regime.

Faced with a common antagonist, if not united by a common goal, it is only natural for dissenting groups in the Soviet Union to cooperate. Even though the emigration movement has achieved astonishing success, Jewish activists know the struggle is not nearly over. Regardless of how many Jews eventually emigrate, a majority of Russia's three million Jews will remain, either because they prefer to stay or because the regime prefers to keep them. In any case, life for Soviet Jews will not become any easier. For decades, Jews have been denied their own religious and cultural institutions. Yiddish is a dying language. Hebrew books are unavailable. But even as the regime enforces assimilation, it does not allow a Jew to forget that he is a stranger, that he cannot be trusted. So discrimination increases and Jews, in reaction, remember who they are. And though the right to emigrate will remain a paramount demand, those left behind may want to defend their rights as Jews and as citizens. If they do, the human rights movement will be as important as pressure from abroad for Soviet Jews. For without allies in the human rights movement, it would be impossible for Soviet Jews to sustain a struggle for their own national dignity.

6

DÉTENTE AND THE DISSIDENTS

THE PROCESS of East-West détente has bewildered Soviet dissidents. They have always understood Russia's isolation — her reluctance to trade with the West, her feverish competition in space and military research — as complementary to the regime's internal controls. They never imagined a policy of détente, whether it was called convergence or rapprochement, that did not include adjustments in the internal situation. By 1973, however, Andrei Sakharov already wondered what kind of détente the West desired, for as governments emphasized outward and often empty demonstrations of friendship, the Kremlin intensified repression of dissident activity.

The crackdown on dissidents was highlighted by the trial and public confessions of Pyotr Yakir and Victor Krasin. Innumerable others, like Bukovsky, Plyushch, Gluzman, Chornovil, and Superfin, were shipped to labor camps, prisons, or the confines of mental hospitals. The KGB managed to prevent publication of the *Chronicle of Current Events* from October 1972 until May 1974. According to Andrei Sakharov, the regime let it be known that for every new appearance of the *Chronicle,* "appropriate persons would be arrested and those already under arrest would be sentenced to long terms." While the government allowed many leading dissident figures to leave the country, the emigration of Soviet Jews, which had reached a peak of 34,000 in 1973, was severely reduced in subsequent years. Sakharov believes that these events were related to the onset of détente. "The authorities seem more impudent," he told Western reporters, "because they feel that with détente they can now ignore Western public opinion."

Under the guidance of Richard Nixon and Henry Kissinger, the United States developed a policy of détente that ignored fundamental Western values. Contrary to Kissinger's suggestions, a defense of Andrei Sakharov or Alexander Solzhenitsyn would not have increased chances for nuclear war. Since the early 1960s, the massive arsenals of both countries have been the principal deterrent to a nuclear exchange. Détente was supposed to increase mutual understanding and cooperation so that both sides could restrain a dangerous and costly competition. The Soviet Union, however, did not abandon its ideological struggle and did not expect the West to relinquish its values and ideas. In February 1974, Henry Kissinger stated before the Senate Foreign Relations Committee that among the guiding principles of our détente policy would be our willingness "to use our influence to the maximum to alleviate suffering and to respond to humane appeals."

When it was announced in the spring of 1972 that Richard Nixon would visit Moscow, many Soviet Jews appealed for his help. They asked for individual and collective audiences. They sent letters describing recent arrests and attacks on synagogues. A group of prominent Moscow Jews offered to serve as an information committee, to advise the President and supply him with objective data on the situation of Soviet Jewry.

The KGB, too, was making preparations. Telephones were disconnected; activists faced sudden calls for military retraining or two-week jail terms for "hooliganism." Members of the information committee were kept in prisons far from Moscow until the President departed. A full report of these measures was made to the American embassy, yet there was never an indication, even after his departure, that Nixon raised objections with his hosts.

The following year, refuseniks accused Steven Lazarus, deputy assistant secretary of commerce for East-West trade, of pressing Moscow Jews to stop public protests lest they jeopardize adoption of the pending trade bill. Lazarus was said to have urged them to appeal to Jewish organizations in the West to drop their support for the Jackson-Vanik trade amendment.

The dissidents believe that, in the fall of 1973, the United States changed the content of news programs on the Voice of America as a further gesture to the Kremlin. Soviet citizens rely on foreign radio broadcasts to help them learn of events in their own country. Stations such as the Voice of America, Radio Liberty, and Radio Free Europe, regardless of their cold war origins, provide an important service in countries where the government controls the means of mass communication. American authorities conceded that the Voice of America began to present more music and less news beginning on September 11, 1973, when the Kremlin ceased to jam the station's broadcasts. With the end of jamming, they explained, there was no need to repeat the news; besides, they added, young listeners had asked for more music. Still, without the Voice of America regularly broadcasting news of arrests and trials, the activity of the dissidents grew more disheartening.

Finally, one small incident involving Alexander Solzhenitsyn confirmed for the dissidents the cynical nature of American politics. Despite his controversial ideas, the dissidents understand that Solzhenitsyn has become a symbol of their defiance. So when President Gerald Ford avoided meeting Solzhenitsyn during the author's visit to Washington in 1975, his decision demonstrated that the West relegated issues of human rights to a position of near irrelevance.

While actions of the U.S. government disappointed the dissidents, the process of détente led the Soviet regime to tighten its control of internal affairs. Soviet leaders are aware of the attitude in the West and among some of the dissidents that as the Soviet Union develops, achieves a higher standard of living, and maintains an ever-larger class of sophisticated workers — a class roughly corresponding to our middle class — the regime will gradually relax ideological controls and adopt a more open and more democratic political system. Undoubtedly, at least some in the Kremlin regard détente as a catalyst to such a development. In turn, Soviet dissidents and their supporters have hoped that the opening of the regime toward the West, even if it means only expanded trade and infusions of technology, would signal a beginning, however small, of genuine liberalization. Everyone, it seems, needed reassurance to the contrary. From the point of view of the Kremlin, it was useful to show both its own hard-liners and the dissidents themselves, if not the entire country, that détente would not foreshadow another "thaw."

For years, as journalists filed stories on trials and demonstrations, as men like Alexander Solzhenitsyn, Andrei Sakharov, Andrei Amalrik, and Roy Medvedev published works abroad in defiance of the Soviet government's ability to retaliate, the West gained an impression that all the dissidents share a certain program or at least a number of principles. Although they do share an abhorrence for certain practices of the regime, especially those involving judicial and administrative abuses, censorship, and the general atmosphere of contrived hypocrisy, there exist vast differences among the dissidents over questions of methods, goals, and the future their country ought to desire.

Solzhenitsyn recognizes the significance of this debate for a country that has long been accustomed to silence. "For many decades now," he tells us in *From Under the Rubble*, a collection of essays he compiled in 1974, "not a single question, not a single major event in our life has been freely and comprehensively discussed, so that a true appreciation of it could be arrived at and solutions found." East-West détente, however, has not helped to unite the dissidents but has actually reinforced the vigor of their debate.

Among the dissidents, Andrei Sakharov, Roy Medvedev, and Alexander Solzhenitsyn have long embodied three divergent attitudes representing substantial segments of those in the country who desire some kind of change. While the ideas of these men revolve around questions of political institutions, national development, and the role of religion, their differences over the process of détente have come to embody almost all their concerns, for détente raises the tortuous dilemma of Russia's relationship with the West. This dilemma has provoked widespread controversy throughout modern Russian history and has always served to crystallize arguments over the character and the destiny of the Russian people. Indeed, the present debate over détente has its origins in the nineteenth century, when the polemic over Russia's relationship with the West affected all discussions of political and social reform.

Traveling in Russia in 1839, the Marquis de Custine wrote his impressions in a journal that has since become the most famous and most quoted report of a foreigner's encounter with Russia. (His book, *Journey for Our Time*, is often compared to Alexis de Tocqueville's *Democracy in America*.) At the time, his comparison of Russia with the rest of Europe drew particular attention, and even today his comments reflect a dispiriting amount of truth. "The more I see of Russia," he wrote, "the more I agree with the Emperor when he forbids Russians to travel and makes access to his own country difficult for foreigners. The political system of Russia could not withstand twenty years of free communication with Western Europe."

Czar Nicholas I had good reason to confirm de Custine's judgment. In 1814, after the defeat of Napoleon, young Russian officers had returned from Western Europe ashamed at the backwardness of their country. On Nicholas's accession to the throne in 1825, a group of these officers — called the Decembrists — attempted to take power. Their revolt failed miserably. Five leaders were executed, while more than a hundred conspirators were exiled to Siberia. By severely punishing the group, Nicholas magnified their importance and gave an example of martyrdom to future Russian radicals. Although the Decembrists' desire to see Russia emulate political progress in the West was frustrated, the example of western Europe remained alluring for many people, in particular for a young aristocrat named Pyotr Chaadaev.

Chaadaev had been among the triumphant Russian troops who entered Paris in 1814. Seven years later he quit his military career and soon after left Russia for western Europe. When he returned in 1826, officials detained him at the border; his name had been linked to members of the Decembrist conspiracy. Although Chaadaev had known several of them, he was not connected to the plot; his absence from the country during the revolt saved him. During the next four years Chaadaev retreated completely from society, except for a series of discussions he maintained with a young noblewoman who shared her religious and philosophical anxieties with him. In reply to a letter asking for his advice, Chaadaev began to record his ideas on Russian culture and society; within a few years, these "Philosophical Letters" caused a literary sensation.

Only the first was actually published in Russia, in 1836.

The government immediately ordered confiscation of the journal in which it had appeared. The editor was sent to Siberia, the censor dismissed, and the daily press forbidden to mention the author's name. Anticipating his latter-day successors, Nicholas I proclaimed Chaadaev officially insane. He was ordered to remain at home and, for a time, made to endure the periodic visits of a doctor. Naturally, a copy of the first philosophical letter became the valued possession of every Russian intellectual. Book dealers sold copies secretly, while hundreds of manuscript copies passed from hand to hand in the salons of Moscow and St. Petersburg.

Alexander Herzen provides a vivid account of the essay's effect: it was "a shot that rang out in the dark night; whether it was something foundering that proclaimed its own wreck, whether it was a signal, a cry for help, whether it was news of the dawn or news that there would not be one — it was all the same: one had to wake up."

Chaadaev's notoriety and the details of his treatment by the czar only confirmed the pessimism and shame his essay expressed over the backward condition of Russian life. "One of the most deplorable things in our unique civilization," he wrote, "is that we are still just beginning to discover truths which are trite elsewhere. . . . What has long since constituted the very basis of social life in other lands is still only theory and speculation for us." In particular, Chaadaev abhorred the obscurantist influence of Russian Orthodoxy, deriving much of his anxiety from the history of this branch of Christianity.

Chaadaev, however, did not attempt to devise a consistent philosophy. Instead, he was the first to raise fundamental problems that others would then pursue. One of the curious aspects of his work is that he combined tendencies that soon after formed the contending extremes of the polemic between the westernizers and the Slavophiles. Like the former, he admired and envied western Europe and refused to idealize the history of his country. He was a Francophile (the "Philosophical Letters" originally were written in French), and he deplored the cultural isolation the autocracy imposed. But Chaadaev also posed a dilemma for his liberal admirers. After his characterization of Russian backwardness, Russia's future as a European nation was no longer so obvious. Like the Slavophiles, Chaadaev placed an enormous emphasis on religion. Because of his antipathy toward Russian Orthodoxy, he embraced a form of mystical Christianity that leaned to Roman Catholicism. Although he looked to the West for ideas — not finding in Russia values he considered universal and absolute — Chaadaev shared with the Slavophiles a messianic belief in the mission of the Russian people. "We are one of those nations," he remarked, "which does not seem to form an integral part of humanity, but which exists only to provide some great lesson for the world." For Chaadaev, this lesson was a distinctly pessimistic one.

The Slavophiles, on the other hand, saw advantages in Russia's backwardness and hoped to influence Russia's development away from the evils of western European materialism. In line with their idealized view of Russian history, the Slavophiles deplored the reforms of Peter the Great more than a century before, blaming him for the introduction of coercion into Russian political life — as if Ivan the Terrible had never existed — and for undermining Russian traditions out of fascination for western European customs. (Peter had even decreed European habits of dress and shaving.) Of great importance for the Slavophiles, the West meant capitalism and inequality and, worst of all, politics. They opposed suggestions of political reform, preferring to rely on moral restraint rather than whatever legal structures might be wrung from the czar. The extreme Slavophile writer Konstantin Aksakov even admonished his countrymen not to "strive after state power," for it would "undermine the freedom of the inner spirit."

The Slavophiles opposed any form of coercive government for Russia. In accord with their view of history, they proposed an "open autocracy," one where the czar did not force his will on his subjects but made his wishes coincide with those of his people. They believed that Russia had once been ruled by consensus, and in order to return the country to its most natural condition they viewed freedom of the press as a necessary means to bring the czar closer to his people. Otherwise, they reasoned, how would he know what the people desired?

They demanded freedom of speech but wanted the czar to retain complete freedom of decision. As might be expected, their peculiar view of autocracy did not spare them repression. The czar understood, if they did not, that a people endowed with civil freedom would not long leave the government free to govern. But while they endured constant conflict with the autocracy, the Slavophiles never relinquished their loyalty to an autocratic form of rule or recognized the necessity for its fundamental reform. Others, however, did.

In the nineteenth century, numerous political thinkers — even advisers to various czars — encouraged proposals for reform, hoping to plant seeds for some kind of political institution removed from the direct control of the autocracy. Unlike the Slavophiles, a prominent statesman like Mikhail Speransky, and later Timofei Granovsky and Boris Chicherin, regarded western European political development as a necessary and beneficial process for all societies. In the context of czarist society, however, their efforts achieved only marginal success. In 1832, Speransky accomplished the first codification of Russian law. In 1861, Czar Alexander II abolished serfdom, and three years later an independent judiciary was established. But none of these reforms, however hopefully they were greeted by the westernizers, began to resolve the dilemma of Russia's political future. In the decade before his tragic death in 1837, Alexander Pushkin noted in several letters and unpublished essays that freedom could be insured only by an institutional framework defined by law. He was not oblivious to Russia's own traditions; he did not advocate constitutionalist schemes in the naïve hope that they would alter Russia's destiny. He simply longed to see reform of the autocracy and deplored every appearance of cultural backwardness in Russian society.

At times, this shame for Russia's backwardness gave rise to absurd expressions of self-loathing, even among the country's most acute observers. Chaadaev himself wrote that "we have given nothing to the world, taken nothing from the world, bestowed not even a single idea upon the fund of human ideas, contributed nothing to the progress of the human spirit." The Marquis de Custine repeated the same gloomy account of Russian culture for his European readers, including the story of Chaadaev's own punishment as an example of Russian despotism. Both men, however, exaggerated the condition of Russian society and allowed the morass of her political life to obscure the vitality of her culture. De Custine, in particular, had no idea of the moral earnestness, the intense idealism, or the devotion to one's country that spurred numerous Russians to deplore the conditions he described. De Custine could not recognize the beauty of Russian poetry, which in the 1820s enjoyed a famous golden age; he even denied the originality of Pushkin's verse. As a Frenchman, the silence of Russian life overwhelmed his senses — the fact that "nothing is said, but everything is known." To his credit, however, de Custine realized what would occur if the need to be silent abated, "for as soon as speech is restored, one will hear so much dispute that an astonished world will think it has returned to the confusion of Babel."

The debate among Soviet dissidents confirms the truth

of his prophecy. Although it echoes themes from a century ago, often in words that recall identical warnings and arguments, we cannot forget that neither Russia nor the world is the same as it was. Today it is impossible to dismiss Russia's power or charge her with backwardness. Andrei Sakharov has spoken of Russia as a primary resource for the world, as one of the principal societies from which solutions to man's age-old dilemmas can be found. As a staunch patriot, Alexander Solzhenitsyn also writes with pride of Russian power, of his country's considerable role in the defeat of nazism. Still, much like the young officers who returned to Russia after the defeat of Napoleon, Solzhenitsyn and Sakharov retain a sense of shame and disappointment that so much power can come to so little good.

Since the outset of détente, their anxiety over the future of Russia has increased. For years Solzhenitsyn, Sakharov, and Roy Medvedev have articulated dissimilar opinions on the course Russian society ought to adopt. Based on his idealized view of Russian history, Solzhenitsyn longs for a return to Russia's own traditions, including a spiritual renaissance and a rejection of "the murky whirlwind of progressive ideology [that] swept in on us from the West." A genuine reactionary, he mistrusts political activity and prefers the establishment of a benevolent, authoritarian order for Russia. In contrast to Solzhenitsyn, Andrei Sakharov admires Western institutions and sees no alternative to the development of democracy. Roy Medvedev, however, advocates Soviet communism's return to what he considers its original Marxist-Leninist principles. In a manner reminiscent of the polemic a century ago, these divergent attitudes have been further complicated by the process of détente and the dilemma of Russia's relationship with the West.

Sakharov in particular has hardened his beliefs. In his first manifesto, "Progress, Coexistence, and Intellectual Freedom," written in 1968, he was still a socialist, willing to use the conventional language of Soviet discourse: "The restoration of Leninist principles of public control over places of imprisonment would undoubtedly be a healthy development." Now, however, Sakharov writes more directly of legal abuses and no longer couches his criticism in language the authorities prefer to hear. More important, Sakharov no longer considers himself a socialist. Since the end of the 1960s his life has changed considerably, and the development of his thought, especially his increasing disillusion over prospects for change in Soviet society, parallels his more intimate awareness of certain of that society's dimensions.

"Progress, Coexistence, and Intellectual Freedom" touched upon themes commonly referred to in present-day discussions of détente: the need for genuine coexistence and cooperation between the United States and the Soviet Union in order to relieve the arms race and enhance mankind's ability to resolve problems of disease and hunger. In addition, Sakharov encouraged his own government to adopt a more liberal internal policy, end censorship, respect human rights, and effect a general reform of the economic system. Without a relaxation of bureaucratic and ideological controls, Sakharov warned, the regime would only retard the country's economic and technological development and fall increasingly behind the United States in crucial areas of research. "Convergence," however, what Sakharov envisioned as the necessary and beneficial rapprochement of the United States and the Soviet Union, would diminish chances for nuclear war and improve the internal situation in both countries.

Coming from a Soviet scientist of the highest standing, the manifesto merited the intense interest it generated, both in the West and in the Soviet bloc. For underneath Sakharov's use of familiar language and optimistic proposals lay fundamental criticism of Soviet life. By stating that all industrial societies face common dilemmas, such as pollution, urban development, and diminishing supplies of natural sources of energy, Sakharov deflated the long-trumpeted Soviet contention that it had devised panaceas for the problems of modern industrial development. And by calling these problems by name and insisting that the conditions of Soviet life complicated the search for solutions, Sakharov challenged the regime either to respond or to expose once again its unwillingness to acknowledge the country's problems. In subsequent years he has not raised such questions so politely.

Since 1970, Sakharov has taken a leading role in the dissident movement, signing petitions, standing outside courthouses during "open" trials of political nonconformists, and lending his prestige and intelligence to the cause of freedom in his country. This activity has influenced his political thinking. Now he wonders whether the Soviet Union has that much to contribute and whether the socialist system, as he knows it, is really an alternative to capitalism. "This socialism contains nothing new," he told an interviewer in 1973. "It is only an extreme form of that capitalist path of development found in the United States and other Western countries but in an extremely monopolized form." He remains concerned about international questions and still believes in the necessity of convergence. Only now Sakharov insists on democratization as the most genuine indication of the regime's willingness to cooperate with the West.

On the fifth anniversary of the invasion of Czechoslovakia, Sakharov explained his anxiety over the direction of détente to a group of Western correspondents.

I mean rapprochement without democratization, rapprochement in which the West in effect accepts the Soviet Union rules of the game. Such a rapprochement would be dangerous in the sense that it would not really solve any of the world's problems and would mean simply capitulation in the face of real or exaggerated Soviet power. . . . I think that if rapprochement were to proceed totally without qualifications, on Soviet terms, it would pose a serious threat to the world as a whole. . . . It would mean cultivation and encouragement of a closed country, where everything that happens may be shielded from outside eyes.

Sakharov recognizes few, if any, encouraging trends within Soviet society. Although he acknowledges that détente represents a move away from Russia's isolation, he believes the primary impetus for change must come from the West. His support of the Jackson-Vanik amendment was consistent with this evaluation, for by linking certain trade benefits with the level of Soviet emigration, the amendment attempted to instill respect for a fundamental human right. But the Soviet government rejected this condition, claiming that the United States has no right to make internal Soviet affairs subject to international negotiations.

Like many of his colleagues in the human rights movement, Sakharov insists on the need to raise the legal consciousness in the country at large and within the regime itself. The Soviet Union has ratified numerous agreements on human rights, including the Universal Declaration of Human Rights adopted by the United Nations in 1948. Yet, as Valery Chalidze has written, "a state makes commitments to guarantee human rights on its own territory, while it tells those to whom the commitment was made that securing human rights is exclusively its internal affair." Sakharov argues that if the Soviet Union sincerely desires relaxation of international tension, it should begin with adherence to its own pledge to uphold recognized standards of behavior.

A century ago, the westernizers understood the need for Russia to overcome her isolation, not merely in order to adopt western European institutions but to overcome the belief that Russia's problems were too unique to be resolved along lines familiar to other societies. Among the dissidents today, Andrei Sakharov and Roy Medvedev are the most articulate defenders of this point of view. Furthermore, Sakharov and Medvedev agree, as the latter writes in his book *On Socialist Democracy*, that "without the growth of economic, cultural, and scientific links abroad, no country can count on rapid economic or cultural progress." Despite these points of agreement, however, the two men understand the role of the West in this process quite differently.

In contrast to Sakharov, Roy Medvedev is a Marxist-Leninist who was dismissed from the Communist party over his dissident activity. For the past several years he has published scathing accounts of Soviet life, including a massive study of the Stalin era and a detailed report of his twin brother Zhores's forced confinement in a mental hospital. In addition, he has written numerous memoranda, including a denunciation of official anti-Semitism and several responses to the work of Alexander Solzhenitsyn.

Unlike Sakharov, Medvedev believes, as he wrote in his essay "Problems of Democratization and Détente," that "the fundamental problems of any country, and especially of large powers such as the USSR, can only be resolved by the government of that country." In line with this belief, Medvedev has devoted enormous attention, in the essay and in his book *On Socialist Democracy*, to exploring various groups and tendencies within Soviet society that give him cause for optimism. As a result, Medvedev is much less sanguine than Sakharov over the influence Western governments can exert on internal Soviet affairs. He believes that if the United States makes concessions from the regime a condition for the further progress of détente, it would only strengthen those elements in the Kremlin who already oppose détente. According to Medvedev, this faction of the Party wants to preserve the country's isolation and "revive acrimonious polemics with the West." In addition, pressure from Western governments for internal reform is said to undermine Party members who support détente and democratization. And again, unlike Sakharov, Medvedev has no illusions about the willingness of Western governments to exert pressure on behalf of human rights "at a time when the development of trade relations with the Soviet Union promises no small advantages to the West."

Medvedev, however, does encourage continued pressure from Western public opinion. He recognizes that demonstrations in the West, including pressure from the American Congress, overthrew the education tax on emigrants and that protests from Western scientists saved Andrei Sakharov from severe repression in the fall of 1973. For Medvedev, "it is precisely in periods of détente that the efficacy of public opinion grows considerably in shaping the internal affairs of each major power. By contrast, a country which is isolated and cut off from the outside world by various Cold War barriers becomes insensitive to protests and views beyond its frontiers. . . . In this sense, it must be said that the relaxation of international tension is in itself a very important pre-condition, though not the only one, for the development of democracy in Soviet society."

In turn, Medvedev subscribes to a Marxist conception of how a society matures. According to classical Marxist theory, changes in the country's fundamental economic arrangements provoke changes in its political structure. Although Medvedev concedes in his book that the "struggle for democratization must be a political one," his belief in Marxist theories leads him to place enormous emphasis on the development of modern technology and the "objective demands" a modern economy makes on an outmoded, bureaucratic, authoritarian regime. At this point in Soviet history, Medvedev argues, a basic contradiction exists between the impulses inherent in a modern industrial economy and the factors resisting democratization. In time, he contends, this contradiction can only be resolved in favor of democratization.

Medvedev believes that the regime must initiate reforms in order to develop the country properly. And then, as the economy matures, there will be further pressure for democratization. But since the government cannot invigorate the economy because of its unwillingness to relax bureaucratic controls, "objective demands" for democratization may never appear unless another manner can be found to hasten the introduction of necessary innovations. Medvedev believes that détente will play this catalyzing role.

While Medvedev and Sakharov hope that détente will serve to liberalize Russian society, Alexander Solzhenitsyn's opposition to détente complements his mistrust of democracy. As far back as 1969, when he first replied to Sakharov's call for convergence (in the essay "As Breathing and Consciousness Return," included in *From Under the Rubble*), Solzhenitsyn expressed his aversion to parliamentary democracy and other Western-inspired solutions. As for convergence itself, he had nothing but contempt. "If we are concerned with solving mankind's moral problems," he argued, "the prospect of convergence is a somewhat dismal one: if two societies, each afflicted with its own vices, gradually draw together and merge into one, what will they produce? A society immoral in the warp and the woof?"

Like the Slavophiles, Solzhenitsyn developed his philosophy from a deeply flawed, idealized view of Russian history. "For a thousand years," he proclaims in his *Letter to the Soviet Leaders*, "Russia lived with an authoritarian order and at the beginning of the twentieth century both the physical and spiritual health of her people were still intact." In line with this singular conception of history, Solzhenitsyn rejects the need for Russia to adopt democratic habits or end her isolation, convinced that "Russia, with all its spiritual peculiarities and folk traditions, [can] find its own particular path."

Although he is famous for his opposition to an arbitrary government, Solzhenitsyn has adopted the peculiar view of autocracy held by the Slavophiles. He derides elections, political parties, the entire range of endeavors we associate with politics, in favor of an authoritarian order that reflects the notions and will of the population." In his *Letter to the Soviet Leaders,* which Solzhenitsyn sent secretly to the Kremlin in September 1973, and which he only divulged after his forced exile in 1974, he declares: "Let it be an authoritarian order, but one founded not on an inexhaustible 'class hatred' but on love of your fellow men — not of your immediate entourage but sincere love for your whole people." In turn, the contradictions of the Slavophiles, too, have become his own. Demanding civil freedom, he denies the benefits of political democracy; a fierce opponent of censorship, he equivocates over the right to publish political tracts; believing in the goodness of his people, he remains convinced they had best not govern themselves.

At times, even Solzhenitsyn's language recalls the reactionary statements of some of the Slavophiles. A century ago, Konstantin Aksakov wrote:

Every striving of the people after state power deflects it from its inner moral path, and, by means of political external freedom, undermines the freedom of the inner spirit. To exercise political power becomes, as it were, an aim for the people, and the highest aim disappears — inner truth, inner freedom, the spiritual act of life. If the people is sovereign, if the people is government, then there is no people.

In the postscript to his reply to Sakharov, "As Breathing and Consciousness Return," Solzhenitsyn poses a similar dilemma:

Can external freedom for its own sake be the goal of conscious living beings? Or is it only a framework within which other and higher aims can be realized? We are creatures born with inner freedom of will, freedom of choice—the most important part of freedom is a gift to us at birth. External, or social, freedom is very desirable for the sake of undistorted growth, but it is no more than a condition, a medium, and to regard it as the object of our existence is nonsense. We can firmly assert our inner freedom even in external conditions of unfreedom.

During his first tour of the United States in 1975, Solzhenitsyn restrained this aspect of his opposition to détente and emphasized instead his distaste for its commercial arrangements. In Solzhenitsyn's view, the regime is becoming increasingly incompetent and incapable of handling the country's economic difficulties. Furthermore, according to Solzhenitsyn, the government cannot continue to support a gigantic military budget and hope, simultaneously, to improve the country's standard of living. By trading with Russia, though, the West gives indirect (and sometimes direct) support to the Kremlin's ability to control and pacify the population. But if the West refused to trade, the economic difficulties that would result—like shortages of bread and meat and fewer consumer goods—might provoke widespread disaffection, perhaps even food riots similar to those that occurred in Poland in 1970. At that point, Solzhenitsyn believes, the regime would be willing to relax controls.

But this seems unlikely to happen. In 1971, a year after the riots in Poland, the newly unveiled Soviet five-year plan emphasized the growth of consumer goods and not heavy industry. But by 1974, these goals "proved unreachable," as the regime explained it, and the next plan reverted to the usual priorities.

Détente, as Solzhenitsyn knows, also concerns the relaxation of international tension and the need to diminish prospects for nuclear war. On this issue, he again invokes a disquieting idea, warning mankind not to accept a fraudulent peace as the alternative to armed conflict. In fact, Solzhenitsyn's speeches — expressing his belief that the West has already lost World War III — reflect his mistrust of the entire process of East-West détente. For him, détente signifies "complaisance" and "concession," the "cowardly self-deception of comfortable societies and people who have lost the will to live a life of deprivation, sacrifice, and firmness." Détente merely confirms his suspicion of our society: a people overwhelmed with external freedom and unable to develop the moral and spiritual resources to resist its own demise.

Both Sakharov and Medvedev articulate political positions that bear strong resemblance to a conventional Western philosophy of government; namely, a fundamental commitment to civil freedom, political democracy, and independent judicial institutions. But neither man can point to a single, viable institution — in Russia's past or at the present time — that could assert legitimate and effective power against the power of the regime. It is an old and tragic Russian dilemma. Sakharov says he does not "recognize the arguments of those Westerners who consider the failure of socialism in Russia to be a result of its so-called lack of democratic traditions." But he can only recall the reforms of Alexander II and other "democratic achievements," none of which ever exercised effective power or offered a viable alternative to the only genuine institution the country had — the autocracy. Medvedev, in turn, places his hopes in a weak and isolated faction of the Communist party and in the inevitable pressures for democracy generated by the need for economic reform. Like the westernizers of a century ago, they can only invoke a "scientific, rational approach to social and national phenomena" (according to Sakharov) and seemingly disregard the national realities of Russia, as their critics contend.

In particular, Sakharov's reliance on the West seems overly optimistic. Since the outset of détente, the United States has been anxious to reduce tensions and negotiate arms control, while issues of human rights, until the administration of Jimmy Carter, have only been raised as a result of constant prodding by the Congress and various interest groups, especially the American Jewish community. During negotiations associated with the Conference on Security and Cooperation in Europe in the early 1970s — which led to the Helsinki Accords — the Western Europeans, more than the Americans, were unwilling to agree on the recognition of borders unless the Soviet Union yielded concessions with regard to information and cultural exchange.

Furthermore, given the realities of international politics, it is naïve to expect the Soviet Union or any other powerful country to make a major adjustment in its internal policy in reaction to pressure from other governments. This does not imply that such efforts are worthless; often, together with the force of international opinion, pressure from Western governments has evoked a positive response from the Soviet regime. The Kremlin, after all, is sensitive to its image abroad, but it is rarely willing to give the impression of weakness in the face of Western complaints.

Although Roy Medvedev seems to have a more realistic understanding of international relations than Sakharov, his optimism over the future of Soviet society presents numerous difficulties. In his book *On Socialist Democracy*, Medvedev argues that the demands of a modern industrial economy will lead inevitably to liberalization of the regime. But Russian and Soviet history testify against Medvedev's argument. For centuries Russia has imported Western technology but resisted the social and political influence of the West. Since the Revolution, vast economic and social changes have already occurred without provoking increased political democracy. What seems "irresistible" for Medvedev may

seem worth preventing or retarding by developing the economy in such a manner and in such an atmosphere that
democratization becomes unnecessary. In fact, this may be
what the regime is attempting to do. Rather than introduce
democratization as a means to invigorate the economy,
the government may prefer to import the technological
expertise it cannot afford — for political reasons — to develop
itself. (For example, the regime cannot allow photocopying
machines to proliferate because they would make it too
easy to reproduce *samizdat.*) Medvedev understands this,
and while at first it seems to undermine his argument, it
may be the unstated reason for his support of détente.

In Medvedev's favor is the fact that present economic
imperatives are extremely different from those that existed
when the country developed heavy industry under Stalin.
Although the Soviet Union rivals the United States in coal
and steel production, these industries are no longer the
primary symbols of economic vitality. Today the Soviet
Union needs to develop its chemical industries and integrate
computers into its economy. These innovations, because
they demand greater intellectual expertise and coordination,
may also require greater contacts with the West; détente, as it
now stands, is one indication that the regime recognizes
this. But what we cannot know right now — Marxist deter-
minism notwithstanding — is whether technological innova-
tion inevitably leads to democratization. Presently, Soviet
scientists find it easier to obtain foreign journals. Can this
minor adjustment, a crack in the self-defeating wall of the
regime's control, really portend significant change to come?
It is too early to tell.

Medvedev, however, bases his opinion on several weak
presumptions. While he undoubtedly knows numerous
Party members who share his liberal views, they can hardly
constitute a significant faction within the Communist party.
Medvedev himself acknowledges several times in *On Socialist*

Democracy that important positions in the Party are awarded only to the most obsequious candidates, while anyone with the least amount of talent or ability to discern truth from falsehood views a professional Party career as unworthy of respect. Under these conditions, it is unlikely that the few liberals who remain in the Party could exert much pressure toward democratization.

Furthermore, Medvedev presupposes the growth of a technocratic elite who will resist ideological and bureaucratic controls and encourage democratization through demands for greater technological efficiency. This hope, too, seems overly optimistic. Technological acumen does not necessarily lead to democratic beliefs. Although Sakharov and Medvedev developed their ideas in the liberal atmosphere of the "scientific-technical intelligentsia" (in the words of Sakharov), there is little evidence to suggest that this ever-increasing group of workers will demand liberal reform. Although *some* have demonstrated their desire for the rule of law — at great risk to themselves — there are several reasons to doubt that a large "class of specialists" will exert irresistible pressure on the government.

The regime has always been willing to deprive the most talented, most highly trained people of any responsible position once such people expressed oppositionist beliefs. At a high point of the human rights movement, between 1966 and 1972, hundreds of distinguished people in mathematics and physics, in cybernetics and various fields of the humanities were dismissed from their positions at leading institutes and universities. By the end of the 1970s, untold numbers of specialists in mathematics, physics, and biology — Jews and non-Jews alike — were leaving the country. Medvedev is undoubtedly correct to believe that "the prime impulses towards democratization in the U.S.S.R. must necessarily come from within Soviet society itself." But he provides few, if any, convincing indications of where these impulses will arise.

Neither Sakharov nor Medvedev desires or anticipates a serious economic crisis in the Soviet Union. While the regime may not be capable of fully modernizing the economy, they recognize that it has sufficient control of the economy to provide basic necessities and continued, if awkward, advances in the standard of living. Furthermore, they know, as Solzhenitsyn himself has emphasized, that the regime retains the means of control that Stalin employed and that while it is reluctant to introduce these methods again, it may resort to them in order to reverse a deteriorating situation. For this reason, Sakharov and Medvedev have explored patterns of gradual political evolution, however unlikely they may appear, hoping to save Russia from the violent solutions it usually endures. Solzhenitsyn, however, is unmindful of the implications of his ideas. He expects an economic boycott of the Soviet Union to cause a severe breakdown of the regime. It is more likely that economic difficulties, regardless of their origin, would aggravate the internal situation and compel the authorities to go on the offensive against the population once again.

Moreover, Solzhenitsyn's plea that the West effect change in Soviet life contains perilous and inconsistent assumptions. Several times, in his Nobel lecture and in his letter to the Swedish Academy proposing Sakharov for the Nobel Peace Prize, Solzhenitsyn has emphasized the unity of the world. "Meanwhile," he declares, "no such thing as Internal Affairs remains on our crowded Earth. Mankind's salvation lies exclusively in everyone's making everything his business." The implications of this argument reflect his complaint that Western society fosters "complaisance" and "concession" while Solzhenitsyn himself has long accepted "deprivation" and "sacrifice" as necessary and not altogether adverse conditions for a worthy life.

However, Solzhenitsyn's insistence that the West pursue an active and deliberate policy of intervention in Soviet affairs contains the implicit threat of increased tension and even war. In a speech to the AFL-CIO in 1975, he reproached the Western powers for entering a military alliance with Stalin in 1941 because "world democracy could have defeated one totalitarian regime after another, the German, then the Soviet." Aside from the historical unreality of this statement, Solzhenitsyn presumes a moral duty on the part of the West that cannot be justified. The West was not responsible for the horrors of Stalin's regime. And though Solzhenitsyn, to be consistent with the view of history he shares with the Slavophiles, cannot recognize the origins of Soviet communism within the contours of Russian history, he cannot expect the West to bear both the blame for the Bolshevik Revolution and the burden of overthrowing it.

In addition, although Solzhenitsyn proclaims the end of internal affairs, he has often criticized Sakharov for paying too much attention to political repression in Europe and Latin America. And in his *Letter to the Soviet Leaders*, he expresses his belief that Russia needs political, commercial, and ideological isolation in order to facilitate its development. Even Solzhenitsyn's opposition to the commercial aspects of détente touches upon his ethnocentric concerns, for although he dislikes the economic benefits the regime may receive, he is also unhappy over the export of Russia's supplies of natural gas and timber; these are needed for Russia's development. While all the dissidents want the West to take a greater interest in Russia's internal affairs and not allow the regime to carry out its policies in secret, only Solzhenitsyn believes that increased isolation would help the country resolve its difficulties.

For several years, within the Soviet Union and the United States, the debate over détente was unwelcome and perhaps even irrelevant. Since debate was carried out primarily in Western publications, the Soviet public remained completely unaware of its complex dimensions, while the intelligentsia could only follow it with sympathetic curiosity. Western governments seemed unable or at least unwilling to respond to the dissidents' concerns, while the Kremlin posed similar questions about democracy and Russia's relationship with the West and then enforced answers of its own.

Nonetheless, the process of détente generated unexpected results. After years of negotiation, the Conference on Security and Cooperation in Europe concluded its negotiations; the agreements were signed in Helsinki in August 1975. For many dissidents, and particularly for their supporters in the West, the Helsinki Accords — with their provisions on family reunification and freer contacts and exchange of ideas — were seen as simply another group of principles the regime could, at once, proudly sign and blithely ignore.

Events soon disproved this initial judgment. By 1976, the Accords were providing a useful framework in which the dissidents could criticize the government, while a new American administration, professing sympathy for human rights, was about to take office. Détente would take an unexpected shift and put the Soviet regime under a scrutiny it thought it had managed to avoid. No one foresaw this turn of events.

For a time, the human rights movement seemed defeated, its most effective activists in prison or abroad. The debate over détente, in spite of its intellectual appeal, reflected the dissidents' confusion in the face of Soviet pressure and Western indifference. The regime tolerated the debate, recognizing that it was a harmless method for several dissidents to articulate their ideas while not actually effecting a serious challenge to Soviet policy.

The debate, however, may have been more useful than it first appeared to be. By focusing attention on Russia's relationship to the West, the debate reflected a fundamental disadvantage the dissidents needed to overcome — their isolation. The Helsinki Accords provided a vehicle by which they could revive their struggle and regain the attention of the West. The regime still sought financial aid and technical assistance for its lagging economy. It still exercised control over its dissidents, which Western protests could only hope to restrain. But it could no longer use détente to obscure repression. At the outset, détente had confused the dissidents; now it would bewilder the regime.

7

THE HELSINKI WATCH GROUPS

FEW OF THE dissidents who had initiated aspects of the human rights movement were still active by the middle of the 1970s. Many were in Europe, Israel, or the United States, among them Pavel Litvinov, Natalya Gorbanevskaya, Alexander Esenin-Volpin, Valery Chalidze, and Anatoly Yakobson. Others, like Sergei Kovalyov and Vladimir Bukovsky, faced long years in prison. Anatoly Marchenko was in exile. Yuri Galanskov was dead. Pyotr Yakir and Victor Krasin were discredited.

While the fate of individual dissidents was being decided, events in Europe unexpectedly provided the groundwork for the next stage in the human rights movement. For years the Soviet government had pressed for the convening of a Conference on Security and Cooperation in Europe. The West regarded the conference primarily as a means for the Kremlin to gain official recognition of territorial changes in Eastern Europe that it had imposed at the close of World War II. In order to secure the agreements, however, the Soviet regime had been obliged to accept a group of humanitarian provisions at the insistence of the Western Europeans. They concerned the reunification of families, greater freedom of communication and contact, and a commitment to respect "freedom of thought, conscience, religion or belief"; to "promote and encourage the effective exercise of civil, political . . . cultural and other rights," to accord ethnic minorities "equality before the law," and to "act in conformity" with international commitments on human rights.

Despite these high-sounding principles, most observers in the West saw little reason to applaud the agreements. The West had long relinquished any hope of reversing Soviet gains in Eastern Europe. As part of détente, there were provisions involving troop movements and visas for journalists that were designed to reduce suspicion and encourage confidence. As for the humanitarian provisions, or Basket Three as they were dubbed, they were regarded by official and nonofficial observers in the West as simply another declaration the Soviets could ratify and then disregard.

To everyone's surprise, not least of all for the Soviet government itself, the Helsinki Accords became an unprecedented means to defend human rights. Within weeks of their ratification, on August 1, 1975, a handful of dissidents in Moscow was already discussing their importance. A delegation of congressional representatives was in Moscow at the time and met with several activists, among them physicist Yuri Orlov, Valentin Turchin, the head of the Moscow chapter of Amnesty International, and Benjamin Levich, a distinguished scientist and longtime refusenik. They argued that the accords could put pressure on the Kremlin if other signatory governments, and especially the United States, openly monitored Soviet compliance. (Representative Millicent Fenwick of New Jersey was particularly impressed by their reasoning. A month later she introduced legislation creating the United States Helsinki Commission, made up of senators, congressmen, and representatives from the executive branch.)

More important, within Moscow itself dissidents were considering means to exploit the Helsinki Accords. Already that fall and winter a number of appeals — by prisoners on a hunger strike in Mordovia, by Jewish refuseniks, and by Andrei Sakharov — contrasted political trials and ongoing violations of human rights with the Kremlin's solemn pledge at Helsinki. But these individual appeals had limited resonance. References to the Helsinki Accords carried as little weight as the usual references to the Universal Declaration of Human Rights or the Soviet constitution. If the Helsinki Accords were to become a greater embarrassment, they would have to be approached in a new and more startling manner.

The most important strength of the human rights movement has been its ability to attract activists who can revitalize and extend well-established techniques. At times the movement has been curtailed, particularly in 1973 during the Yakir-Krasin case and the initial period of détente, when the multitude of arrests, the emigration of numerous figures, and the suppression of the *Chronicle of Current Events* overwhelmed the dissidents. At each crisis, though, new dissidents took the initiative and revived the cause. The *Chronicle* resumed publication in 1974; three dissidents publicly took responsibility for its distribution. In 1975, prisoners in labor camps began organized efforts to resist forced labor and gain status as political prisoners. And in 1976, under the leadership of physicist Yuri Orlov, the Public Group to Promote Observance of the Helsinki Accords in the USSR was begun.

Yuri Orlov was not completely new to the dissidents' cause. He was an old friend of Valentin Turchin; they had attended Moscow State University together in the early 1950s. By then Orlov was a member of the Communist party. After graduation he began to work at the Institute of Theoretical and Experimental Physics. He completed his thesis in 1956 and published his first scientific article; several of his papers were presented at a conference in Geneva.

Orlov's career took an abrupt and decisive turn in 1956. At a meeting held to discuss the Twentieth Party Congress, where Khrushchev had denounced Stalin, Orlov (in his own words) "spoke of the general loss of honesty and morality and of the need for democratic changes. The meeting tumultuously supported this and other speeches made in the same spirit." But his talk did not go unchallenged for long. "A few days later," he recalled in an autobiographical note, "a devastating, slanderous special article was published in *Pravda*, then came a secret letter from the Central Committee to the Party members in which a Party assessment was given of our speeches. I was immediately dismissed by an order from 'the very top' and expelled from the CPSU. My name was struck out from scientific reports and reviews since 'my name brings disgrace to Soviet science,' as I was officially told. I was forbidden to defend my thesis."

Orlov did not work for six months. Colleagues in Moscow collected money to support him and others who had been dismissed. He could not find a research or teaching position in Moscow. The brother of his former director headed a similar institute in Yerevan; he invited Orlov to work there, and in Soviet Armenia Orlov successfully resumed his career. He was permitted to defend his doctoral thesis. He received access to "secret work," which allowed him entry once more to special library reserves. Orlov became a distinguished authority on particle acceleration and was elected a corresponding member of the Armenian Academy of Sciences.

Orlov returned to Moscow in 1972 but did not take up political activity right away. In 1973, though, during the press campaign against Andrei Sakharov, Orlov felt obliged to respond. In September he wrote a long letter to Brezhnev himself, posing questions about life and ideology in the country. In October he helped establish the Moscow group of Amnesty International. By January he was dismissed from his job during "a staff reduction," then excluded from the list of persons being considered for a state prize. When Nixon visited Moscow in June 1974, Orlov was kept under house arrest and members of his family were tailed by the KGB.

After the signing of the Helsinki Accords in the summer of 1975, Orlov began considering how the dissidents could act. He talked with many people, in particular with Andrei Amalrik, who had returned from a long period of imprisonment and exile, and with Anatoly Shcharansky, a young refusenik who impressed everyone with his energy and intelligence.

Orlov wanted to form some kind of group, but he proceeded cautiously, knowing the regime feared organized activity most of all. With hindsight, Orlov's ideas for the group seem altogether natural and inevitable, but at the time his proposals required keen political judgment.

The group would act openly. Unlike the *Chronicle*, its members would sign their reports. The group would send its appeals directly to all the signatory governments of the Helsinki Accords, and not only to Soviet leaders or international organizations. (Orlov himself had made appeals to Soviet authorities and knew of myriad others. Not once had the regime replied.) The group would represent the views of more than its individual members. Orlov understood the opportunity the Helsinki Accords offered for coordinated activity among a variety of nonconformist groups.

Orlov chose the members carefully. He had formed the group, hoping that Andrei Sakharov would accept its leadership. By temperament, though, Sakharov was not an organizer. He would help the group (its first press conference was held in Sakharov's apartment) while his wife, Elena

Bonner, and his secretary, Alexander Ginzburg, would become members. In 1974, after the exile of Alexander Solzhenitsyn, Ginzburg began to administer the Russian Prisoners' Aid Fund that Solzhenitsyn subsidized through the sale of his books in the West. Ginzburg distributed money and other material assistance to families of political prisoners. He himself was still subject to administrative surveillance. Under its terms Ginzburg could only stay in Moscow for two days before returning to his home in Tarusa.

Other original members of the Helsinki Watch Group included General Pyotr Grigorenko, Lyuda Alexeeva, and Malva Landa. Grigorenko was one of the most highly revered figures among the dissidents. In June 1974, he was released from his second term in a psychiatric hospital after more than five years of incarceration. Lyuda Alexeeva had been involved in the movement since the arrest, nearly ten years before, of Andrei Sinyavsky and Yuli Daniel. She had signed numerous appeals, administered a fund for prisoners and their families, and was well acquainted with all the editors of the *Chronicle*. It would be her responsibility to reproduce the group's reports. Malva Landa, a geologist by training, was especially knowledgeable about prisoners and maintained correspondence with many of them.

Orlov also recruited Vitaly Rubin and Anatoly Shcharansky to represent the Jewish emigration movement. Rubin was an expert on ancient Chinese philosophy and an old friend of many of the dissidents; Shcharansky's knowledge of English and rapport with journalists would be invaluable. Even from exile in Chuna, Anatoly Marchenko added his name to the group's original membership, if only to demonstrate his solidarity and his legal right to participate.

The authorities knew of Orlov's plans. On May 12, 1976, he was invited for questioning by the KGB. Orlov understood that the regime wanted to prevent the group from announcing its formation. Undeterred, Orlov went to Sakharov's apartment, where they invited Western journalists by telephone. At a hastily prepared press conference, Sakharov introduced Orlov to them as the chairman of the Public Group to Promote Observance of the Helsinki Accords in the USSR. Then Orlov read the group's statement of purpose.

Three days later, on May 15, Orlov was picked up by the KGB and warned that his proposed group was "illegal and unconstitutional"; its very name was a provocation. They warned Orlov that he would be held responsible if the group did not disband. That same day, while Orlov was still under questioning, Tass, the official news agency, reported (in its foreign service) the warning issued to Orlov and described the formation of the group as an attempt to disrupt détente and to cast doubt on the U.S.S.R.'s fulfillment of international obligations.

The warning did not stop Orlov or his colleagues. The KGB had detained him as he was about to attend the group's final meeting before what was to be its formal announcement. Orlov came late. The others waited for him, not knowing if he would be released at all. In earlier years, they would have argued about whether to disband the group. They knew it would not be too long before arrests would begin. But that afternoon no one even raised the issue; they were determined to proceed.

On May 18, the Helsinki Watch Group held another press conference at Sakharov's apartment. Orlov read the group's first document to assembled journalists. It concerned Mustafa Dzhemiliev, a Crimean Tatar activist who had been convicted of "anti-Soviet slander" a month before. In the report the group noted that Dzhemiliev's conviction "for expressing his views on the abnormal situation of the Crimean Tatar people" violated the Helsinki agreement that calls for freedom of thought and conscience.

In the next eight months, before Orlov and Ginzburg were arrested in the beginning of 1977, the Moscow Helsinki

Watch Group issued seventeen more numbered documents and much supplementary material. As formulated by Orlov, the group's primary strategy was to raise an echo in the West, to use the Helsinki Accords as a bridge to Western governments and public opinion. The first problem involved reproduction and distribution of the reports. There were no machines available to photocopy or mimeograph their material. If a typist made five copies at a time, he would still have to type each document seven times before producing one copy for each of the thirty-five signers. (Orlov intended each report to be a page and a half long, but they almost immediately assumed more ambitious lengths.) Lyuda Alexeeva had supervised typists before, but the scale of this operation was too large for her to organize by herself. In Moscow she knew a man who had established a typing service for *samizdat*, which employed ten full-time typists. Alexeeva knew him pretty well, but he was unknown to the authorities because he never signed appeals. Occasionally, he would reproduce important *samizdat* documents for free, then cover his costs by charging a bit extra for popular literary work. In solidarity with the group, he copied the Helsinki documents without charge, while someone else donated stationery with the group's letterhead to give their reports an established, official look.*

The first six reports were sent by mail, return receipt

---

*The use of letterhead stationery by activists always produces a curious effect on recipients in the Soviet Union. For example, when the Moscow chapter of Amnesty International began its work, it had stationery printed for the members' use, a standard procedure for groups in every country. Valentin Turchin, the group's chairman, wrote to the ambassador from Sri Lanka, asking about a prisoner there. (No Amnesty group works for release of prisoners in its own country.) Soon after, the ambassador called to assure Turchin that he would personally look into the case. Turchin was astonished by the call but realized that the ambassador mistook the Amnesty chapter for an official Soviet organization, one he would be obliged to respond to. Apparently, the ambassador later grasped the truth, because Turchin never heard from him again.

requested, to the Moscow embassies of all the signatory countries. But the only receipts the group received were from
Brezhnev's office. The other two hundred copies disappeared.
So the group changed its tactics. It continued to send Brezhnev all its reports by mail — they regarded their activity as
legal, and the Soviet Union, after all, had signed the Helsinki Accords — but other copies were handed to reporters
and sent by roundabout means to governments that had
expressed interest in them: the United States, England,
often Canada, and occasionally West Germany. Copies of
all the documents were also sent to Amnesty International
in London. Reports on the abuse of religious believers were
sent to Keston College in England, a recognized research
center in the field, while documents on Jews went to Jewish
organizations in the West.

The unique nature of the Helsinki Accords reinforced the
work of Orlov's group. For the first time in an agreement
between governments, the question of human rights was
connected to issues of cooperation and security, and compliance would be subject to periodic review. The Helsinki
Accords were published in their entirety in *Pravda* and
Izvestia, so people knew what they contained. (The Soviet
government likes to boast that it published enough copies
to reach the country's entire population, while Western
newspapers carried only excerpts.) In contrast, when the
Universal Declaration of Human Rights was adopted by the
United Nations General Assembly in 1948, the Soviet Union
abstained from the vote. The document is known to few
people inside the country and is hard to locate in libraries.
Copies have been confiscated during police searches and
included among items listed as "anti-Soviet propaganda."*

---

*In the labor camps, prisoners are treated to a more candid expression
of the regime's attitude to the Universal Declaration of Human Rights.
In his book *A Voice from the Chorus*, Andrei Sinyavsky quotes a
guard in charge of a work party: "You don't understand. It's not for
you. It's for negroes."

But the Helsinki Accords had an altogether different status. It was an agreement between Western governments, including the United States, and the Soviet bloc. Because the text was published in the official press throughout Eastern Europe, people naïvely expected the human rights provisions to be honored. As Orlov made clear in the group's opening statement, it would be working in a framework the government itself had erected.

When the formation of the Helsinki Watch Group was announced over Western radio broadcasts, people descended on the group's members. They came from all over the Soviet Union, much in the way petitioners visited Pavel Litvinov in 1968 and Valery Chalidze in 1971. The *Chronicle of Current Events* also reported abuses of human rights, but its editors were anonymous. Now individuals were accessible who, by the group's definition, were there to collect information.

The group dubbed its visitors *khodoki,* an old Russian word for walkers, which once denoted messengers who delivered petitions from the peasants to the authorities. Some came with personal complaints or reported violations of the rights of friends or relatives. Others represented groups such as the Pentecostals, who number about half a million people in the Soviet Union.

Listening to their stories was tiring work. It would take hours and sometimes all day. Group members had to separate emotional exaggerations and inaccuracies from the facts of the case. For their final reports, they often attached official documents — court verdicts, for example — to verify stories they originally gathered from total strangers.

One visitor, a taxi driver named Vladimir Pavlov, came from Maikop, an industrial city in the North Caucasus. In 1971, he was convicted of "anti-Soviet slander" on the basis of remarks he made to passengers; he spent three years in a labor camp. A year after his release, in 1975, he read the Helsinki Accords. The regime was promising to respect the exchange of information, so he asked the Supreme Court to be rehabilitated. The court rejected his appeal. Hearing about the Orlov committee on the radio, he decided to carry his complaint to Moscow.

In the capital, though, he did not know where Orlov or Sakharov lived. So he stood on Gorki Street, not far from Red Square, and asked certain passers-by — "those who looked intelligent," he later explained — if they knew Professor Orlov's or Academician Sakharov's address.

Most people ignored or shunned him altogether. But one man asked him why. Pavlov replied that his rights had been violated and that he wanted to complain either to Sakharov or to the Helsinki Watch Group. The fellow in the street did not know Orlov or Sakharov, but he had an artist friend who could reach the committee.

The group took Pavlov's testimony and included it in document 13, entitled "The Necessity of Emigration for Economic-Political Reasons from the Standpoint of the Workers." In it, they described the families of four workers who wanted to emigrate. They did not belong to any ethnic minorities. They did not have relatives abroad, so they could not base their applications on the right to be reunited with their families. As they had explained to the Helsinki Watch Group members, they wanted to leave the Soviet Union for economic and political reasons. By the end of 1979, two of the four workers, including Vladimir Pavlov, had emigrated.

Whenever possible, the group sought on-the-spot testimony. In the fall of 1976, Lyuda Alexeeva visited Lithuania to check information she received from Lithuanian Catholics about religious persecution. One incident concerned seven boys who had been expelled from a high school in Vilnius, the capital of Lithuania. Alexeeva was told the boys had been thrown out because they attended church services and visited the home of Viktoras Petkus, a Catholic activist and longtime prisoner who would become a founding member of the Lithuanian Helsinki Watch Group.

Secondary education is obligatory in the Soviet Union. It is difficult to officially remove even those students who have actually dropped out or who continually disrupt classes. But in this case seven boys, all seniors, had been expelled from a single school.

In her testimony to the U.S. Helsinki Commission in Washington, D.C., on June 3, 1977, Lyuda Alexeeva, who had been forced to leave the Soviet Union in February, described what happened in Vilnius.

Taking a list of the expelled students, I visited the office of the Lithuanian SSR Minister of Education, A. Rimkus. I was accompanied by Tomas Venclova, a poet and well-known Lithuanian dissident, who later became a founding member of the Lithuanian Helsinki Group.

I explained to the minister that I was a member of the Moscow Group to Promote Observance of the Helsinki Agreements in the USSR, and that I was interested in the reasons for the exclusion of seven students from the Vilnius school.

Apparently, the minister does not listen to foreign broadcasts, and so had not heard about our group. He probably assumed that some sort of official group had been formed for windowdressing and asked: "To what agency is your group attached?" I answered: "It is a public group." "Who directs it?" "Dr. Yuri Orlov, a corresponding member of the Armenian Academy of Sciences."

The minister decided that with a man of such academic rank heading the group, it deserved his confidence and he agreed to provide an explanation. He stated that the expelled students were hooligans. But he could not tell us the precise actions which had led to the exclusion of each of the seven boys. "I only know the general outlines of the case," he told us.

"Probably the school's directors could answer my question," I suggested, and the minister agreed, emphasizing that everything was "strictly legal" in this case. He meant that minutes existed of a session of the school's faculty council which has the right to petition the local board of education to exclude students from the school. The minutes should describe the students' actions which prompted the petition and record the vote of the faculty council.

We left for the school in order to study the minutes.

The academic principal of the school, Dobinas, met us. I explained: "I am from Moscow. We just visited the Minister of Education at his office concerning the exclusion of seven boys from your school. He recommended that we visit the school to find out the facts." I then asked to see the minutes of the faculty council meeting, but the principal said the minutes were not at the school. "The secretary took them home to rewrite them," the principal told me, even though more than a month had elapsed since the students' expulsion. "Couldn't you send someone for the minutes?" "No. I know that no one is home now at the secretary's house."

The principal summoned four teachers and I asked each of them to explain the reasons for the expulsions. They gave confused and contradictory explanations. It was impossible to clarify the real facts of the case from their statements.

After an hour and a half the telephone rang and the principal was called out of the room. When he returned he was as "white as a sheet." Apparently, he had just been informed who his visitors really were. But it was too late. The meeting needless to say, came to an abrupt end.

Afterward, I met with the boys who had been expelled and with several of their classmates. They told me

that during the previous school year these seven stu-
ents had been summoned from their classes by the
principal, sometimes at the request of KGB Senior
Lieutenant Verbitsky and sometimes at the request of
Police Captain Semyonov. Verbitsky or Semyonov
took them away for interrogations where they were all
asked similar questions: "Do you go to church?" "Do
you listen to Radio Vatican broadcasts?" The boys
were also asked to explain why they visited Viktoras
Petkus.

In the police station, Captain Semyonov shouted at
the boys, lacing his speech with obscenities. In the
KGB, Senior Lieutenant Verbitsky was polite. But
both Semyonov and Verbitsky threatened that the boys
would not be admitted to college unless they gave
compromising depositions against Petkus. They even
frightened one boy, Bogushes, by threatening to send
him to a labor camp for teenagers.

The boys declined to give false testimony and declared that they would not stop going to church.

When the boys declined and then showed up at
school after the summer holidays, they were told that
they had been expelled, but neither they nor their
parents could get anyone to show them the decision
of the faculty council.

Orlov's committee also sent a representative, Lidia
Voronina, to Pentecostal communities in the Far East.
For years, Moscow dissidents had heard about the persecution of religious believers. Baptists who refused to recognize the government's authority over religion had organized
themselves and circulated a bulletin defending their own
prisoners of conscience. The Pentecostals faced even harsher
reprisals. They were fundamentalist Christians and abhorred
any political activity, even contact with people like the
dissidents, who would have tried to help them. As their
misery increased, though, they gradually understood the need

to publicize their situation, appeal to the West, and seek to emigrate.

In December 1976, Lidia Voronina, a twenty-nine-year-old former student of philosophy, spent two weeks among Pentecostals in Starotitorovka, in the North Caucasus, and Nakhodka, near Vladivostok, nearly seven thousand miles from Moscow. The communities awaited her visit. Beginning at 6 A.M., people stood in line to speak with her. Each family had a tragic story. Under Stalin, the communities had fled by stages across the breadth of the country. They had first lived in Odessa where the sect was founded, then in central Asia and Siberia, before reaching the Far East. They faced persecution, even execution, in every city. One woman had seen her grandparents shot. Her parents escaped to a forest, where they and their children lived in caves.

The young men refused to bear arms. Though they agreed to serve in construction battalions, the regime insisted they take conventional oaths, which the boys refused to do. Many were sent to labor camps, often after military trials that were plainly illegal because the boys never actually entered the armed forces.

The everyday life of the community was also difficult. The families were large because parents did not use artificial birth control methods or resort to abortions. Yet the mothers were not granted medals or small cash subsidies which, by law, they were entitled to receive for bearing many children. The government did not leave them undisturbed. Their prayer meetings were disrupted and the participants fined. During searches, Bibles and religious objects were confiscated.

The regime knew the Pentecostals were no longer passively accepting their fate. Voronina herself saw how they devotedly listened to Western radio broadcasts, a sure sign of social resistance. When she visited Nakhodka, the regime dispatched two "official" Pentecostal priests to caution the community. With Voronina in one house, lecturing the villagers about the Helsinki group, the priests were nearby, telling people to rely on God's help and shun contact with "left political forces."

By the beginning of 1977, Orlov's committee was challenging the regime as no dissident group had done before. Its documents were comprehensive and well chosen. The group did not try to report all the violations it learned of — that was the work of the *Chronicle* — but instead chose those that best represented the regime's failure to observe the Helsinki Accords: unjust trials, interference with postal and telephone communications, treatment of prisoners of conscience, separation of families and the right to emigrate, persecution of believers, of small ethnic minorities, and of Jews.

The Helsinki Accords also provided a means to unite disparate groups. Suddenly, nationalists in different republics, religious believers, Zionists, and Moscow dissidents could use a common vocabulary and recognize their common antagonist. The Moscow group physically could not handle all the information directed its way. But within a year of its birth, other Helsinki groups were formed in the Ukraine (November 1976), Lithuania (November 1976), Georgia (January 1977), and Armenia (April 1977). Each had a similar focus: the defense of cultural, ethnic, and religious values against efforts by the regime to impose Russian cultural and linguistic dominance. By choosing to act within the framework of the Helsinki Accords, these nationalists found it easier to cooperate with other dissidents whose particular concerns differed from their own. The Lithuanian group, which was formed primarily by Lithuanian Catholics, included the refusenik Eitan Finkelshtein. In Tbilisi, the refusenik brothers Grigory and Isai Goldshtein joined the Georgian Helsinki group. Each of these groups kept in close touch with Orlov's committee in Moscow. Their members brought reports to the capital, where press conferences were arranged. They helped with distribution too. The first report from Kiev was in Ukrainian, so Lyuda Alexeeva and Anatoly Shcharansky translated it into Russian before it was typed and distributed to reporters.

Among the many issues the dissidents confronted, none threatened them more than psychiatric confinement. For more than a decade, since Vladimir Bukovsky and Pyotr Grigorenko first served time in mental hospitals, activists knew first-hand how widespread the practice was and how liable they were, at any moment, to be incarcerated.

The human rights movement responded as best it could. For years the *Chronicle* had documented the practice, even publishing accounts of compulsory treatment by General Grigorenko and the bricklayer, Vladimir Gershuni, which they managed to send out to friends in Moscow. In 1971, Vladimir Bukovsky collected official diagnoses of several activists and sent them to the West, hoping that psychiatrists there would study the documents, then condemn Soviet psychiatric practice.

Bukovsky was arrested, but in labor camp he did not relinquish the struggle. At his camp in Perm he met Semyon Gluzman, the young Jewish psychiatrist from Kiev who had written a counterdiagnosis of General Grigorenko based on Bukovsky's material. They became good friends and participated in a secret seminar among the political prisoners: a Jewish inmate lectured on Zionist history, in Russia and the world at large; a Ukrainian spoke about his national struggle. Bukovsky and Gluzman prepared a lecture on psychiatric abuse. The other prisoners understood how vulnerable all their colleagues were to this reprisal and urged Bukovsky and Gluzman to record their lecture on paper. They then wrote *A Manual on Psychiatry for Dissidents* in 1974. Dedicated to Leonid Plyushch, who was then being held in Dnepropetrovsk Special Hospital, the manual describes the techniques of prison psychiatrists and suggests in some detail how to behave under interrogation. The manual was sent from Perm through secret channels to Moscow, where it circulated in *samizdat*.

Faced with publicity, the regime occasionally backed down. In January 1976, Leonid Plyushch was taken from his hospital, put on a train, and sent to Vienna with his family. His release came after a long and bitter struggle. Until his last day in the hospital, doctors administered neuroleptic drugs, including triftazin. In December of that year, Vladimir Bukovsky would also be freed, in exchange for the Chilean Communist leader Luis Corvalan. As Bukovsky would remark, "It had happened in the past that two hostile countries had exchanged foreign spies they caught or prisoners of war. But to exchange your own citizens — I had never heard of that before." It was a spectacular release. But psychiatric abuse continued, even though its most famous opponent and one of its most prominent victims were in the West. Once again the dissidents took up the challenge.

Issue 43 of the *Chronicle of Current Events,* dated December 31, 1976, mentioned a certain Alexander Podrabinek. According to the report, Podrabinek traveled to Mogilev, a town in Byelorussia (White Russia) more than eight hours by train from Moscow, to inquire about Mikhail Kukobaka, a worker who had been put in a psychiatric hospital for distributing copies of the Universal Declaration of Human Rights. His diagnosis stated that he suffered from "a mania for the reconstruction of society." Podrabinek talked with doctors and objected to Kukobaka's hospitalization, citing legal and medical requirements for compulsory confinement. The doctors insisted they "could not decide anything," although, as Podrabinek reminded them, the hospital has the right to review all cases. He also told them that Kukobaka's case was known in Moscow and that activists intended to complain publicly. The next day Kukobaka was unexpectedly let go. The doctors assured Podrabinek that his visit had nothing to do with the patient's release. "His treatment," they claimed, "was simply over."

At first glance, Alexander Podrabinek hardly appeared a likely candidate for the role he fashioned for himself. Slightly built and young (he was born in 1953), he enrolled in 1970 in the Department of Pharmacology in a medical institute. But he left after a year and went to work as an assistant in a biology laboratory at Moscow State University. During this time he failed to gain admission to medical school, perhaps because he had refused to join the Komsomol as a student and therefore graduated from high school with a poor character reference. From 1971 to 1974 he studied at a school for medical assistants and received certification as a *feldsher*, or paramedic. Podrabinek then worked for more than three years in the Moscow ambulance service, which, he found out, has been used as an inconspicuous means of taking dissidents to mental hospitals.

His interest in psychiatric abuse began in 1971 when he read Vladimir Gershuni's memoir of his treatment in Oryol Special Psychiatric Hospital. Within two years he began compiling his own book, *Punitive Medicine*, where he intended to examine in detail the political abuse of psychiatry in the Soviet Union.

He worked quietly on his own, and only after his visit to Mogilev, in November 1976, did he become a conspicuous figure, helping to organize the Working Commission to Investigate the Use of Psychiatry for Political Purposes. Attached to the Moscow Helsinki Watch Group, its members adopted the forthright style Podrabinek exhibited in Mogilev. They visited psychiatric hospitals, introduced themselves as members of the Working Commission, and inquired about individual prisoners. They wrote appeals on group stationery to hospital doctors, alerting them to their concern. Some-times the doctors thought they represented an official organization and hastily released patients.

Soon after its formation, the group began to issue an *Information Bulletin.* Copies circulated in *samizdat* and were read over Western radio broadcasts. People seeking help responded to the reports and brought commission members new information. The commission included an experienced lawyer, Sophie Kallistratova, who offered legal advice. Two psychiatrists, whose names were not publicized, also were members. They examined people who were threatened with confinement in hospitals or who had just been released. Simply by visiting the commission, people exposed them-selves to further reprisals. KGB agents photographed visitors to Podrabinek's apartment; some were interrogated. Still, people wanted commission psychiatrists to examine them in order to gain independent evidence of their sanity.

So many people contacted Podrabinek's group that within a few months the commission could respond almost imme-diately to the confinement of a "client." Often the regime abandoned plans to confine an individual. In its first year of work, out of twenty-two cases of political incarceration the commission reported, fourteen people were released within two months. Using the Helsinki Accords, dissidents were able to marshal grassroots resistance to the "cops in white coats," compelling the regime to adjust its tactics.

The success of the Helsinki Watch Groups, their formation in several republics, their contacts with religious believers, and their focus on psychiatric abuse could not continue with impunity. The groups had earned too much attention and credibility in the West. The dissidents expected harass-ment, even arrests, but no one anticipated the bewildering series of events that began near the end of 1976 and con-tinued into 1977.

December 18: Vladimir Bukovsky was exchanged for Luis Corvalan.

December 24: The KGB searched the homes of Ukrainian Helsinki monitors. At Mikola Rudenko's, dollars were said to be found; pornographic postcards allegedly were confiscated from Oles Berdnyk; an old German rifle was taken from Oleksy Tikhy.

January 4: The apartments of Moscow Helsinki monitors Alexander Ginzburg, Yuri Orlov, Lyuda Alexeeva, their colleague Lidia Voronina, and the mother of Alexander Ginzburg were searched. Tass linked the Helsinki Watch Groups to NTS, a Russian émigré organization based in Frankfurt.

January 5: The Working Commission to Investigate the Use of Psychiatry for Political Purposes was founded. Yuri Orlov was interrogated.

January 10: Tass reported an explosion in the Moscow subway two days before. Many people were said to have been killed or injured. Victor Louis, a Soviet journalist with links to the KGB, wrote an article in the London *Evening News*, suggesting that the explosion was a terrorist bomb planted by a dissident group and that the Soviet public demanded retribution.

January 14: Andrei Sakharov met with Western correspondents. He feared the explosion might have been a provocation by the KGB to persecute dissidents. He asked for a public investigation with the participation of foreign experts.

January 18: Sakharov issued a statement that a friend of Efrem Yankelevich's, his son-in-law, had been interrogated about the explosion.

January 19: Vladimir Albrecht, acting secretary of the Moscow Amnesty International group, also was interrogated about the blast.

January 20: Jimmy Carter became President of the United States. In his inaugural address he declared: "Because we are free we can never be indifferent to the fate of freedom elsewhere."

January 21: Sakharov wrote Carter, urging him to appeal publicly on behalf of persecuted political and religious activists in the U.S.S.R. and Eastern Europe.

January 22: "Traders of Souls," an hour-long film, was shown on Moscow television. It depicted Jewish refuseniks and activists as "soldiers of Zion inside the Soviet Union" and accused them of being part of an anti-Soviet conspiracy. Individual refuseniks, such as Vladimir Slepak, were shown and identified.

January 26: The U.S. State Department charged that Czechoslovakia violated the Helsinki Accords by harassing dissident activists.

January 28: The State Department warned the Soviet Union not to try to silence Andrei Sakharov.

February 1: Yuri Orlov was interrogated again.

February 2: An article in Moscow's *Literaturnaya Gazeta* accused Alexander Ginzburg of currency speculation.

February 3: Ginzburg was arrested while making a call from a telephone booth. His wife was not informed, and she spent the evening going from one police station to another, looking for him.

February 4: Mikola Rudenko and Oleksy Tikhy, Ukrainian Helsinki monitors, were arrested. George Krimsky, Moscow correspondent for the Associated Press, was ordered to leave the country. Other Western newsmen were also harassed. (The last American journalist to be expelled had been John Dornberg of *Newsweek* in 1970.)

February 7: The State Department issued a statement of concern for Alexander Ginzburg.

February 10: The arrest of Yuri Orlov.

February 11: The State Department voiced concern over Orlov's arrest.

February 17: Sakharov received a reply from President Carter, written on February 5. Carter assured him of his concern for human rights.

February 22: Lyuda Alexeeva was forced to leave the Soviet Union.

March 1: President Carter received Vladimir Bukovsky at the White House.

March 5: An article by the refusenik Sanya Lipavsky appeared in *Izvestia*. He accused other refuseniks, among them Anatoly Shcharansky and Alexander Lerner, of working for the Central Intelligence Agency.

March 14: Dr. Mikhail Shtern, a Jewish physician framed on charges of demanding bribes from patients, was released early from his labor camp term. Alexander Podrabinek's home was searched. The manuscript of *Punitive Medicine* and Podrabinek's file on more than two hundred political inmates of mental hospitals were confiscated.

March 15: The arrest of Anatoly Shcharansky.

Not since Alexander Solzhenitsyn's banishment in February 1974 had repression in the Soviet Union received so much attention. President Carter's pronouncements on human rights and State Department responses to the arrests in Moscow made headlines around the world. It is impossible to assess with certainty how Carter's gestures affected the Kremlin and whether they made matters worse for the dissidents. The dissidents themselves were heartened by the President's appeals and saw no connection between his statements and the actions of the regime. In a country where the government has never been inhibited about arresting its citizens — and where millions have perished in labor camps — it seems illogical to blame arrests on a President's public support for prominent activists.

Furthermore, the regime had other, more pressing reasons to act. Events in Eastern Europe also troubled the Kremlin. In June 1976, Polish workers rioted to protest a sudden rise in food prices. Railroad tracks were torn up outside of Warsaw, and Communist party headquarters were set afire in Radom. Hundreds of workers were beaten and arrested. The Polish government rescinded the increase in food prices but could not calm hard feelings in the country. A Workers' Defense Committee was established by leading intellectuals. The Roman Catholic church also supported the workers and pressed for their release.

In Czechoslovakia, the Kremlin witnessed a revival of protest. The Czech government had signed the International Covenants on Human Rights, and in October 1976 they were published discreetly in the law code, thereby becoming a formal part of the legal system. It was easy to see the discrepancy between obligations the government accepted and the behavior of government agencies such as the judiciary and the police. On January 1, more than 250 writers, intellectuals, and ousted leaders of the liberal regime of Alexander Dubček signed Charter 77. Addressed to their own government, the appeal contrasted provisions of the Covenants on Human Rights with routine practices of Czech authorities, making explicit reference to the Helsinki Accords and the Universal Declaration of Human Rights. In subsequent months, despite the arrest of some of its leading figures, hundreds more signed the appeal, posing a serious challenge to the government's authority.

There were even signs of discontent in Rumania and East Germany. On February 8, 1977, the Rumanian novelist Paul Goma wrote to the signers of Charter 77, declaring his full support. Other people learned of his letter and wrote to him, expressing admiration for his initiative.

It is estimated that 200,000 East Germans applied for emigration, citing the Helsinki Accords as a guarantee of their right to leave. The popular balladeer Wolf Biermann was exiled to the West, while others who protested his banishment were imprisoned.

The Helsinki Accords became a universal point of reference throughout Eastern Europe. In East Germany, people crowded into government offices, clutching copies their own government had printed. In Czechoslovakia, Poland, and Rumania nonconformist writers, students, and workers cited the Accords in appeals to authorities.

Among Western European Communist parties trying to demonstrate their loyalty to democracy and independence from Moscow, news of protest and repression in the "socialist bloc" could not pass unnoticed. The Spanish, French, and Italian Communist party leaders spoke openly about the dissidents and their right to express their opinions.

All these developments made Kremlin leaders uneasy. They did not expect the Helsinki Accords to be taken so seriously. But given the reaction throughout Eastern Europe, they had to both set an example for their satraps and make clear to Western European Communists, too, that regardless of their electoral problems, only the Soviet leaders could define the essential nature of Soviet communism.

Despite the arrest of Yuri Orlov and others, the Helsinki groups did not turn into mere defense committees, only issuing appeals for their colleagues' release. Contacts throughout the country broadened and intensified. New members came forward in Moscow, and especially in the wake of Shcharansky's arrest, there was considerable contact between dissidents and Jewish refuseniks. Other activists took over responsibility, publicly, for administering the Prisoners' Aid Fund, among them Kronid Lyubarsky, a distinguished astronomer who had just finished a five-year term for distributing "anti-Soviet literature."

The Working Commission on psychiatric abuse, having begun only in January, became one of the most effective and audacious examples of Soviet dissent. Until Podrabinek's own arrest in May 1978, the group issued more than a hundred statements and appeals. Its *Information Bulletin* provided extensive material on individual cases, much of it gathered through visits to hospitals in remote areas and interviews with doctors. Podrabinek did not allow the arrest of his friends to interfere with his work, and he soon became one of the most visible dissidents in Moscow. In April 1977, he was detained by the police at a meeting of Baptists who were discussing the confinement of a coreligionist. At the behest of the Moscow Helsinki Watch Group, Podrabinek traveled to Siberia to gather information about prisoners in exile. In the fall, after a visit to Lithuania, he reported on a large nationalist demonstration near Vilnius.

Sixteen members of Helsinki Watch Groups had been arrested by the end of 1977, but Alexander Podrabinek persisted. As his group's *Information Bulletins* reached the West, he became a well-known figure abroad, and the regime hesitated to arrest him. But on October 10, 1977, the KGB carried out searches at the homes of Working Commission members and also searched the apartment of Kiril Podrabinek, Alexander's older brother. Soon after, it became clear how the authorities intended to pursue Alexander Podrabinek.

His brother Kiril was not a prominent figure. His name did not appear in *samizdat* material until May 1977, when he and his father Pinkhas Podrabinek visited Kronid Lyubarsky in Kaluga, a hundred miles southwest of Moscow. At the time, Lyubarsky was administering the Prisoners' Aid Fund, but Pinkhas Podrabinek wanted to talk with him about starting an independent science journal. (Before his arrest in 1972, Lyubarsky had been part of a research project, studying Mars with the aid of automated space laboratories. Pinkhas Podrabinek has a medical degree and pursued research

in theoretical biophysics and molecular biology.) On the train back to Moscow, the Podrabineks were stopped by police, questioned, and searched on "suspicion of concealing narcotics." Kiril continued his activity, traveling to the Ukraine in June to attend the trial of Oleksy Tikhy and Mikola Rudenko. Like other friends of the defendants, he was not admitted to the courtroom. Instead he was detained by the police and not released until the trial ended three days later. Then in September Kiril circulated an essay of his own. Entitled "The Unhappy Ones," it criticized conditions in the Soviet army and especially the treatment of conscripts. He charged that young soldiers were systematically subjected to cruel treatment by senior officers, exhausting and unhealthy work, inadequate nourishment, and poor medical treatment.

It is impossible to determine if Kiril Podrabinek's own activity led to his arrest, but there is no doubt that the regime initiated and increased pressure on him as a means to blackmail his brother Alexander. On October 10, the KGB searched Kiril's place of work (he was employed as a watchman at a railway crossing) and confiscated a harpoon gun for underwater fishing and 127 small-caliber cartridges.

Four days later, the KGB came to Kiril's apartment. During the search, an officer opened a closet, reached into a jacket hanging there, and pulled out two more small-caliber bullets. Kiril denied owning these bullets and accused the KGB officer of planting them.

Two weeks later, on a night Kiril was scheduled to be on duty at the railway crossing, two men attacked the sentry. Kiril, however, was sick at home; his colleague was knocked unconscious.

On December 1, Pinkhas Podrabinek and his two sons were advised by the KGB to leave the country within twenty days or else Alexander and Kiril would be imprisoned. They understood that Alexander, in particular, would have to leave to prevent his brother's arrest. Alexander refused to submit to blackmail, telling KGB agents who urged him to emigrate that the country would be better off if they left. And at a press conference at the home of Andrei Sakharov he made the following statement:

> I do not want to sit in prison. I value even the image of freedom, which I have now. I know that in the West I could live freely and receive, finally, a genuine education. I know that there I would not be followed by four or five agents, threatening to beat me or push me under a train. I know that there I would not be placed in a concentration camp or a psychiatric hospital for trying to defend the rightless and the oppressed. I know that there I could breathe freely, whereas here — heavily. They stop up your mouth and smother you if you speak too loudly. I know that our country is unhappily doomed to suffering. And therefore I will stay.
>
> I do not want to sit behind bars, but I am not afraid of prison camp. I value my freedom, as I do the freedom of my brother, but I will not sell it. I will not yield to any blackmail. For me a clean conscience is more valuable than everyday well-being. I was born in Russia. It is my country and I must remain in it even if it is difficult here and easy in the West. As much as I can I will try henceforth to defend those whose rights are so crudely trampled in our country. That is my answer. I will stay.

Other activists pressured Alexander to relent, but Kiril asked them not to criticize Alexander for his decision. Soon after, Kiril submitted his own visa application. The KGB, however, insisted that Alexander, too, would have to go. Alexander stood firm and, on December 29, Kiril was arrested.

He maintained a hunger strike, despite force feedings, from the day of his arrest until his one-day trial on March 14, 1978. Convicted of illegal possession of firearms, Kiril received two and a half years in a labor camp. Because he was charged with an ordinary crime, he was placed among common criminals and not with other political prisoners. His friends feared that, as a dissident and a Jew, Kiril would face officially inspired harassment from other prisoners.

From the time of the initial arrests of Helsinki monitors in 1977 until the spring of 1978, the Soviet government was under constant scrutiny. In the fall, signatories of the Helsinki Accords met in Belgrade to review compliance. The conference lasted for several months, and the United States embarrassed the Kremlin with persistent questions about Orlov and his colleagues. That winter, the nine-month limit for pretrial detention passed for Orlov, Ginzburg, and then Shcharansky, but still there was no word about plans for their trials.

The Belgrade conference came to a close in March 1978 with an innocuous communiqué failing to mention human rights violations. Within a few days, the regime announced that the cellist Mstislav Rostropovich, his wife, the soprano Galina Vishnevskaya, and General Pyotr Grigorenko, who were all in the West (Rostropovich and Vishnevskaya were allowed to leave on an extended concert tour in 1974; Grigorenko came to New York in November 1977 on a temporary visa for medical treatment and to see his son), were stripped of their Soviet citizenship.

This was the first move by the Kremlin following the Belgrade conference to indicate its indifference to criticism at home and abroad. In subsequent months, harsher events soon took place.

March 14: The trial of Kiril Podrabinek.

May 14: The arrest of Alexander Podrabinek.

May 15–18: The trial of Yuri Orlov. No defense witnesses were called. His wife was stripped naked and searched by male attendants before being allowed to enter the court. During the proceedings, while the prosecutor used documents prepared by Orlov's committee as evidence of "anti-Soviet propaganda," the Helsinki Watch Groups were never mentioned by name. During Orlov's final speech, a custom reserved for all defendants, the judge left the courtroom. Outside the courthouse on the day the verdict was read, police grabbed Andrei Sakharov and Elena Bonner and took them to a police station. Orlov was convicted and sentenced to seven years in a labor camp and five years of exile.

May 17: On the third day of Orlov's trial, Iosif Begun was arrested outside the court. A refusenik and Hebrew teacher, Begun had recently completed a two-year term of exile for "parasitism." He was charged with "infringement of residence regulations."

May 15–19: The trial of Zviad Gamsakhurdia and Merab Kostava in Tbilisi, Georgia. Kostava did not renounce his activity. Gamsakhurdia defended his position on all Georgian national, religious, and cultural questions, but he expressed regret for distributing works by Solzhenitsyn and other "anti-Soviet" books. He admitted that his actions were incompatible with patriotism. After the trial the central television network showed Gamsakhurdia's "repentance" speech. On May 25, the New York *Times* reported that friends of Gamsakhurdia suspected the "nationally televised confession had been fabricated by the authorities."

May 23: Women refuseniks in Moscow began a series of demonstrations by standing near the Kremlin wall with placards saying: "Visas for Israel."

June 1: Many of the women were barricaded in a single apartment to prevent their holding another demonstration. The apartment of Vladimir and Maria Slepak also was blockaded by the police, and in reaction, the Slepaks hung placards from their balcony. (They were living on the eighth floor of a building near Red Square. Were it not for the police activity — throwing scalding water from another balcony, striking the Slepaks with long poles — pedestrians would never have noticed the placards.) After breaking down the apartment door, the police arrested the Slepaks.

June 2: Ida Nudel, a longtime refusenik who was beloved for her concern and support for prisoners, was arrested during a women's demonstration against the arrest of the Slepaks.

June 3: An inscription, "Death to the Jews!" appeared on the pavement in front of the apartment of refuseniks Grigory and Natalya Rozenshtein. Grigory, an observant Jew, donned a prayer shawl and recited Psalms while standing over the inscription. Police and plainclothesmen taunted him.

June 9: A small group of women refuseniks and Boris and Natalya Katz, with their nine-month-old daughter Jessica (who had been severely ill; the family had sought permission for Jessica to join her grandmother in America for medical treatment), displayed placards across from KGB headquarters. They were immediately surrounded by plainclothesmen shouting "stinking yids," "Hitler didn't kill enough of you," and the like. The demonstrators, including Boris Katz clutching his daughter, were shoved into a police van and taken away. They were released in the evening, several hours later.

June 12: An American businessman, Francis J. Crawford, was dragged from his car and accused of buying 20,000 rubles on the black market.

June 21: The trial of Ida Nudel. She was convicted of malicious hooliganism and given four years of Siberian exile. She had been awaiting a visa for seven years. Vladimir Slepak also was convicted of malicious hooliganism and given five years of exile. Slepak had been a leader in the Jewish emigration movement since April 1970, when he was first refused a visa. He joined the Moscow Helsinki Watch Group in June 1976, after the emigration of Vitaly Rubin.

June 28: The trial of Iosif Begun, who had been on a hunger strike since May 17. Begun was semiconscious during court proceedings. He was convicted of violating residence regulations and given three years of exile. He has been a refusenik since 1971. Craig Whitney of the New York *Times* and Harold Piper of the Baltimore *Sun* were formally accused in a Moscow court of libeling television employees by suggesting in their articles that the televised confession of Zviad Gamsakhurdia may have been fabricated.

July 10–13: The trial of Viktoras Petkus, a Lithuanian Helsinki monitor. During the trial there were crude attacks on Petkus's morality. He was convicted of "anti-Soviet agitation" and homosexual corruption of minors. His sentence was three years of prison, seven years of labor camp, and five years of exile.

July 10–13: The trial of Alexander Ginzburg. For the record, he stated that his nationality was "prisoner." Inmates testified that conditions in labor camps and prisons were satisfactory. Other prosecution witnesses related how Ginzburg "bought information" from alcoholics with money from the Prisoners' Aid Fund. Ginzburg, who was known as a quiet, shy, and generous man, was portrayed as a lecherous drunkard who lived off money from abroad. The chief witness against him had spent more than twelve years in prison for theft, forgery, and pornography. No defense witnesses were allowed. On the second day, Ginzburg's wife was forcibly removed from the courtroom after protesting the testimony of one witness and was not permitted to return on subsequent days. Friends of Ginzburg's who traveled to Kaluga were not able to find rooms in hotels. They slept in cars or packed into friends' homes. None was allowed into the courtroom. "Bystanders" taunted them outside the building. Ginzburg was convicted of "anti-Soviet agitation," declared an especially dangerous recidivist, and given eight years in the camps. He was also required to pay 1,500 rubles in legal costs.

July 10–14: The trial of Anatoly Shcharansky.

Although still a young man (he was born in 1948), Shcharansky found himself at the center of much dissident activity in Moscow because of his energy and talents. Sakharov used to insist that Shcharansky translate into English for him during press conferences. Shcharansky's talent for chess was legendary. One time, while he was being held in a police station for ten hours because the authorities suspected he was planning a protest for that day, the KGB agents started to talk with him. They, too, were bored and wanted something to do. One of them suggested a chess game. Shcharansky agreed to play but proposed that the loser would have to crawl under the table. The agents agreed, and within a short time they both found themselves on the floor.

Shcharansky's case aroused greater anxiety than the others. It marked the first time since the death of Stalin that a charge of treason was used for such a blatant political purpose, with overtones of anti-Semitism and against so prominent a figure. In June 1977, President Carter publicly declared that Shcharansky had no connection to the CIA. His prosecution, therefore, would also be a direct rebuke of the President. Still, the KGB proceeded to interrogate more than a hundred people, asking primarily about the emigration movement.

On Friday, July 7, 1978, Tass announced to foreign journalists that the trials of Ginzburg and Shcharansky would begin on Monday. Ida Milgrom, Shcharansky's mother, was never officially notified; she learned about the trial from David Shipler of the New York *Times*. Although incarcerated for sixteen months and facing a capital offense, Shcharansky was not able to prepare a defense with the assistance of a lawyer. His mother had wanted Dina Kaminskaya to defend him. Kaminskaya was well known among the dissidents for her spirited defense of Bukovsky, Litvinov, and others. But by 1977 she no longer had a *dopusk*, or special clearance from the Collegium of Lawyers to accept cases involving KGB investigations. (All political cases and many cases of currency violations are handled by the KGB.) Such a regulation does not appear in the criminal code, but the practice is well known and well documented nonetheless. Dina Kaminskaya was forced to emigrate in November 1977.

The prosecution accused Shcharansky of disrupting Soviet-American trade. It held him responsible for the Jackson-Vanik amendment, although as Shcharansky pointed out, it was first proposed in 1972, before he had applied to emigrate.

The primary charge against Shcharansky involved his work among the refuseniks. In February 1977, activists began keeping a list of those denied visas for reasons of state security. Many such refuseniks worked in officially unrestricted, open institutes that received complex technical equipment from abroad. If the institute or factory were conducting secret work, foreign governments would not have authorized the sale of advanced technology. On the other hand, if the institutes were genuinely open, the grounds for refusal to grant visas would be nonexistent.

Shcharansky himself was not involved in preparing lists of those refused for reasons of state security. Like many activists, he would sometimes wait around OVIR offices to meet new refuseniks. Shcharansky did discuss with Robert Toth of the Los Angeles *Times* many topics of mutual concern, including the regime's emigration policies. They never concealed their close association. Toth had a special interest in Soviet science and parapsychology. Shcharansky helped him collect information and served as Toth's interpreter when Toth was doing research on the Soviet space program. In June 1977, Toth was detained after meeting a biologist named Valery Petukhov on the street.

Toth was then interrogated on four separate occasions, enduring more than twelve hours of questioning. In response to KGB pressure, he signed a long statement in Russian — which he could not completely understand — before he left the country. The statement has never been made public, and it is not known if the KGB found it useful to produce during the closed sessions of Shcharansky's trial. Nonetheless, two months after Toth's departure, Tass announced that he was a spy.

The regime did not appreciate Shcharansky's contact with newsmen, his work in the Helsinki group, or his help to fellow refuseniks. Still, the government relied on Lipavsky's betrayal of his refusenik colleagues and the charade of espionage surrounding Toth to manufacture its case against Shcharansky.*

His trial held no surprises. Among all his friends and relatives who waited outside the court, only his older brother Leonid was allowed into the trial. His mother, Ida Milgrom, was forced to stand on the street, hoping in vain to be

---

*On December 16, 1979, David Shipler of the New York *Times* reported on Lipavsky's motivation. Shipler, who was the *Times* Moscow bureau chief during the Shcharansky trial, later took an assignment in Jerusalem. There he interviewed Boris Kamenetsky, formerly a senior aide to the chief prosecutor of Uzbekistan, where Lipavsky grew up. According to Kamenetsky, as far back as 1962 Sanya Lipavsky became an informer for the KGB in order to save his father from the death penalty. The elder Lipavsky was under arrest for stealing huge quantities of expensive fabric from a textile factory, where he was chief engineer. A law had been passed making capital punishment retroactively applicable to him. Sanya wanted his father to confess in order to save himself but his father refused. Whereupon, Sanya offered the KGB evidence about other thieves and currency speculators whom he claimed he knew from his father's house, but about whom the authorities knew nothing. In return, Sanya wanted a promise that his father would not be shot. The KGB apparently accepted the deal. Lipavsky's father was spared the death penalty and instead was sentenced to thirteen years, as Anatoly Shcharansky would be in 1978.

admitted. Shcharansky conducted his own defense but could not call witnesses in his own behalf or cross-examine prosecution witnesses without interference from the judge. At least during the officially "open" sessions, the prosecution avoided outright anti-Semitic and anti-American remarks. The CIA was not mentioned, only "foreign intelligence circles."

Shcharansky, of course, was convicted and sentenced to three years in prison and ten years in a labor camp. As his friend Lidia Voronina once said of him, "Shcharansky spoke the truth and what is worse, he spoke it in English."

Shcharansky's trial was the culmination but not the end of the summer's events. Other trials soon began, of Lev Lukyanenko, a Ukrainian Helsinki monitor, and of Alexander Podrabinek. A year before, the World Psychiatric Association voted in Honolulu to condemn the political abuse of Soviet psychiatry. Podrabinek's activity was well documented. Other dissidents, too, were equally well known but still faced long years in prison. By August, however, the authorities may have been prepared to subdue their harsh pattern of reprisal.

Podrabinek did not make it easier for them. At his trial, where he was accused of "anti-Soviet slander," he asked for extensive material evidence and numerous witnesses who could confirm his innocence. The court rejected all his appeals, whereupon Podrabinek demanded to be removed, declaring, "I have no artistic talent and therefore shall not take part in this show, even as an extra." The court tried to ignore his request, but Podrabinek smoked and whistled until the court was obliged to remove him. He was convicted in absentia and sentenced "only" to five years of exile. The verdict was predetermined, so what did Podrabinek's behavior or presence matter?

The reaction to this series of arrests and trials was overwhelming and unprecedented. For weeks at a time the repression of Soviet dissenters was front-page news. The nature of the trials was easily exposed because the defendants were not anonymous victims but people whose character and activity could be compared against the reprisals of the regime. Avital Shcharansky, who had been allowed to emigrate in 1974, traveled from continent to continent, meeting government leaders and urging the release of her husband. President Carter canceled trips to Moscow by various government delegations. Scientists pledged a boycott in defense of their imprisoned colleagues.

In Moscow, it soon became clear that activists were determined to continue their work. Numerous petitions circulated among diverse groups in defense of Orlov, Ginzburg, and Shcharansky, testifying to the range of people their activities had touched. The Working Commission to Investigate the Use of Psychiatry for Political Purposes came to Podrabinek's defense with a startling public announcement. Its previously anonymous consultant psychiatrist, Dr. Alexander Voloshanovich, met Western newsmen and reported on his examinations of former mental patients. He could find no grounds for compulsory hospitalization in any of the twenty-seven cases.

Orlov's sacrifice had not been in vain. Although the framers of the Helsinki Accords did not expect its provisions to be more effective than other, similar declarations, the work of the Soviet Helsinki groups and the activity of dissidents throughout Eastern Europe transformed the Accords from mere platitudes into a useful vehicle for monitoring all the signatory governments, and especially the Eastern European regimes.

Orlov's committee summarized its own attitude in one of its reports a half year after his arrest:

> For the first time respect for human rights was declared to be a necessary element of interstate relations designed to preserve peace and develop cooperation.

This idea lies at the very heart of the Helsinki Accords. No matter how successfully this idea may have been implemented or what its effect has been up till now, we believe that it has become a permanent issue in international politics. This represents a giant step forward for mankind on the road toward securing individual liberties and toward collective security.

The dissidents made it impossible for their own government to turn détente into a wordless commerce between vast, obedient bureaucracies. The need for arms control, reduction of tensions, increased cultural contacts — the dissidents shared these goals too. But they insisted that human liberty not be submerged in pursuit of human survival.

8

THE STRUGGLE AGAINST FEAR

TO APPRECIATE the change in Soviet life the dissidents have helped to effect, it is necessary to recall how arrests took place under Stalin. A person would not show up for work or return to his family in the evening. There were no protests, among his colleagues or from the West. In his autobiography, *Testimony*, Dmitri Shostakovich recalls the death of Vsevolod Meyerhold, a leading actor and Moscow theater director. Meyerhold had just begun working on a new opera, *Semyon Kotko*. It was Meyerhold's last project. "In fact," Shostakovich remembers, "he never finished it, he was arrested in the middle of it. . . . The director was arrested but the work went on as though nothing had happened. This was one of the terrible signs of the age, a man had disappeared but everyone pretended that nothing had happened. A man was in charge of the work, it had meaning only with him, under his direction. But he was no longer there, he had evaporated, and no one said a word. The name Meyerhold immediately disappeared from conversations. That was all."

In the early 1970s, Andrei Amalrik commented that "even now the regime exists, perhaps not only, but mainly, on the interest from the capital of fear amassed in those times." Stalin's successors have only partially disowned his methods. In 1961, Stalin's corpse was removed from the Lenin Mausoleum in Red Square, but the purge of his earthly remains could not expunge his legacy of fear. The apparatus of control he bequeathed — the secret police, the labor camp system, the strict censorship — has not been dismantled. Even forced collectivization, which ranks among the most disastrous crimes of our century — having left millions dead and Soviet agriculture at a level of inefficiency and waste it has yet to overcome — has not been repudiated.

The achievements of the human rights movement deserve to be assessed against this enforced silence. In 1968, following a series of trials, three dissidents, Ilya Gabai, Yuli Kim, and Pyotr Yakir, wrote a letter to Soviet cultural and scientific figures, warning against the rebirth of Stalinism. They understood that the regime relied "on our own passivity, our short memory, and the bitter fact that we are accustomed to an absence of freedom." Only exposure, it seemed, could restrain the authorities. Recalling the country's isolation under Stalin, when it seemed as if the West had no knowledge of his crimes, Pyotr Yakir described the movement's principal goal: "They tried to make public every illegal act committed in our country so that all the world may know. . . . This is a great stride forward by comparison with Stalinism. Under Stalin there was always an iron curtain and no one knew what was going on here. Millions of people were destroyed and nobody knew anything about it. Now we try to publicize every arrest, every dismissal. . . . We consider this the main task today."

Yakir's generation was determined not to submit once again, in silence, to acts of repression. Younger activists who had matured after Stalin's death defiantly refused to accept the omnipotence of the KGB and even appealed to the West for help. As Vladimir Bukovsky once explained, "The essence

of the struggle, in my view, is the struggle against fear —
the fear which has gripped the people since the time of
Stalin and which has still not left people and thanks to
which this system continues to exist, the system of dictatorship, of pressure, of oppression. It is into the struggle
against fear that we put our greatest efforts, and in that
struggle great importance attaches to personal example —
the example which we give people."

The human rights movement reflects and reinforces
a breakdown in the cultural and political isolation of the
Soviet Union. As unsanctioned poetry circulated, then
novels, and finally detailed information about political
trials and conditions in labor camps, the regime's control of
information grew less effective. Through correspondents,
diplomats, and tourists the West also learned about Soviet
life in greater and more vivid detail. The regime could not
ignore this development. For the most part, the authorities
responded with arrests and imprisonment, but the repression
inflicted on the dissidents should not obscure for us in the
West the tangible changes in Soviet life they accomplished.

The growth of independent public opinion and a more
natural social and cultural life began to emerge. Intellectuals
signed petitions and called upon leading figures in science and
culture to shed their silence. The dissidents did not think
differently from everyone else, as the word *dissent* implies.
Rather, they decided to say what everyone else knows. For
the first time, individuals did not have to submit, through
inertia, to the regime's lawlessness but could decide for themselves how to respond. In his book *The Challenge of the
Spirit*, Boris Shragin describes their predicament:

> In Russia at the present time such questions are not
> a matter of social and political speculation but of
> pressing personal reality. Instead of having to decide
> between parties and political program, the choice is

between two ways of life. One consists of obeying one's own conscience with all the suffering that is bound to ensue; the other, of avoiding anxiety by renouncing one's freedom.

No moral dilemma existed under Stalin because the consequences of open dissent were so certain and often so final. There was also a complete lack of information about the scale of repression. People who might have been willing to protest, despite the risks, had no means to communicate their ideas. Once the regime relented, though, it was only natural that at least some people would test the limits of free expression and by their example encourage others to do the same.

By the late 1960s, within fifteen years of Stalin's death, this makeshift collection of individual activists — liberal Marxists, Orthodox believers, democrats, writers, and scientists — could be said to constitute a movement because they shared certain fundamental beliefs and possessed sufficient moral and political solidarity. They did not operate within a broadly political or social framework; they were not interested in creating political parties or mobilizing masses of people. But they had learned, as Shragin again commented, that "moral and legal demands are a force in themselves" that can drive the physically omnipotent but spiritually bankrupt authorities into a corner.

No aspect of the Soviet human rights movement is more crucial than its insistence on legality. At times, numerous activists reacted harshly to the work of "legalists" such as Valery Chalidze. Among Russian intellectuals, legal standards of justice have long been regarded as too formal, cold, and unconstructive. Alexander Solzhenitsyn shares this attitude. In his essay "As Breathing and Consciousness Return," he comments that "the state system which exists in our country is terrible not because it is undemocratic, authoritarian, based on physical constraint — a man can live in such conditions without harm to his spiritual essence."

In the face of such a widespread belief, the rise of legal consciousness is all the more remarkable. The demonstration on behalf of Sinyavsky and Daniel in December 1965 was the first demonstration in Soviet history in defense of individual rights. Since that time, an entire range of appeals — by the Moscow Committee for Human Rights, by Helsinki Watch Groups, by committees in defense of various religious communities — all refer to Soviet laws and international agreements the regime has signed but continues to ignore.

The demand for legality is important for reasons of principle and strategy. By emphasizing legal norms, the dissidents hope to nurture a sense of personal responsibility and self-discipline and thereby weaken aspects of Russian culture that glorify moral certainty and absolute values. Yuri Orlov's role in the Helsinki Watch Groups exemplifies the crucial nature of this approach. Using the Helsinki agreements as their framework, dissidents of various origins were able to work on one another's behalf, creating unlikely alliances of Ukrainian nationalists and Orthodox believers, Zionist activists and Crimean Tatars.

The demand for legality is not the only response to the ideological bankruptcy of the regime. The crude social atmosphere, economic shortages, widespread drunkenness, the general dedication to material pursuits, provoke longing for a less cynical, more idealistic approach to life. Among many people, a devotion to Russian nationalism, to religion, or even a superficial nostalgia for Stalin reflects growing disaffection. The Communist party appears dedicated solely to maintaining the status quo. Brezhnev and his associates are regarded as weak and ineffectual leaders with no particular plan for the country's evolution. Under Stalin, the regime was on the offensive, forcing collectivization, annihilating nationality groups, transplanting large segments of the population. At the same time, paradoxically, there was genuine enthusiasm for the utopian goal of building communism. But now Soviet rulers no longer seek to alter the society in any particular way and have gone on the defensive against an increasingly politically mature population.

Many dissidents are concerned over the growing revival of Russian nationalism. Great Russians still form the dominant ethnic group in the country. Russian language is a required subject where the native language — Uzbek or Georgian, for example — is the one used in schools. In the government and Party bureaucracies, at the national level and in non-Russian republics, Russians are placed in positions of control.

Nonetheless, there is an emerging pattern of independent expression in Russian national feeling. The work of Alexander Solzhenitsyn exemplifies resentment against elements of Communist ideology that conflict with Russian nationalism. For Solzhenitsyn, Marxism is "a dark un-Russian whirlwind that descended on us from the West." For his colleague, the Moscow mathematician Igor Shafarevich, Marx and Engels "always displayed a special hatred for Russia and Russians." Solzhenitsyn emphasizes the suffering of the Russian people under Communist rule, while other intellectuals claim that Russian culture suffered the most drastic assault of all. Editions of Marx and Lenin crowd bookstore shelves, but the works of classical Russian literature are difficult to find. The destruction of historic architecture in old city neighborhoods and especially the demolition of churches are seen as attacks on Russian history. Industrialization, as dictated by Communist ideology, disrupted the more simple, stable, and moral life of the countryside that is said to have existed.

The dissidents understand that elements of Russian nationalism reinforce aspects of the present regime: resentment and suspicion of ethnic groups, fear of Western influence and values, anti-Semitism, intellectual intolerance. The human rights movement, with its emphasis on ideological tolerance, the rule of law, and contact with the West, may not have secured as broad a following as the conservative, authoritarian appeal of Russian nationalism. But the dissidents have achieved contacts and influence that cannot be discounted in assessing the country's future.

Numerous other groups have adopted the vocabulary and methods of the human rights movement. In Lithuania, Roman Catholic activists fashioned their own journal directly on the *Chronicle of Current Events*. One priest told Lyuda Alexeeva, when she visited Lithuania as a representative of the Helsinki Watch Group, that in the past Lithuanians regarded all Russians as enemies. But the appearance of the Moscow *Chronicle* convinced them that other types of Russians also exist.

As the reports of the Helsinki groups make clear, legal consciousness has spread to far-flung areas of the country: among nationalists in Armenia and Georgia, the Ukraine and Lithuania, and among harassed religious communities in the Far East and the Caucasus. Since the outset of the human rights movement, there have always been independent religious figures — Anatoly Levitin-Krasnov, Sergei Zheludkov, Gleb Yakunin — who signed petitions with the democratic activists and circulated information on the plight of the churches under Communist rule. These religious activists have been Russian Orthodox believers who feel alienated from the officially recognized church and share the dissidents' concern for political as well as religious freedom.

Other religious activists, who represent large communities of believers, have also adopted open methods of struggle. Inspired by the civic courage of the Moscow dissidents, Initiative Baptists, Pentecostals, and Seventh-Day Adventists have begun systematically to publicize the regime's harassment. Whole sections of the *Chronicle*, as well as reports by Helsinki group members, carry details of church services being disrupted and prayer facilities destroyed.

Such efforts have not been without some tangible success. In Lithuania, the Catholic church has achieved a greater measure of freedom. By 1979, twelve unofficial *samizdat* journals were circulating, defending the integrity of the church and of Lithuanian culture. By Soviet standards, Lithuanian activists have created a virtually free press.

Georgians and Armenians have successfully defended the official status of their native languages after a proposed draft of the new Soviet constitution, which circulated for comment in 1977, attempted to remove the special status of the two languages.

The Crimean Tatars, too, have drawn concessions from the regime. They were officially cleared of treason in 1967, almost certainly in response to their open, legal, and large-scale struggle. (The Crimean Tatars had collected more than three million signatures on appeals directed to the Soviet government. This means, in effect, that each adult Tatar had signed his name at least ten times.) But efforts to reestablish a community in the Crimea have been frustrated; only a relative handful of families have been permitted to return.

The Helsinki Watch Group has reported on the attempt by a group of disabled individuals to petition the government for better social services, facilities, and financial support. The regime could only respond with threats and interrogations. But the efforts of these people, who live in cities separated by thousands of miles, reflect the power of the dissidents' example. Suffering from war injuries, occupational accidents, and congenital diseases, they have tried to establish an All-Union Society for the Handicapped. Their goals have no explicit political content, but they have adopted the measured, open stance of the dissidents and insisted on the legal status of their concerns.

Among the various forms of dissent, no group has captured as much attention in the West as the Jewish emigration movement. Within the context of Soviet history, the emigration of more than 200,000 individuals marks the most significant humanitarian concession the regime has made since the release of millions of political prisoners after Stalin's death. As was discussed earlier, the Zionist activists accepted the contacts and techniques of the human rights movement. And though they were able to generate tremendous publicity and solidarity within Western Jewish communities — a crucial factor in the effectiveness of their movement — the inspiration and support of their democratic allies has been a fundamental reason for their success.

It serves the interest of the regime to allow troublesome activists to leave. No doubt the government assumed that emigration would help defuse ferment in Soviet society, first among Jews and then among their colleagues in the human rights movement. For the regime the strategy has proved useful, depriving both movements of effective and potentially active protesters. When it allows Jews "to be reunited with relatives abroad" — the only motivation Soviet officials publicly accept — the regime appears to be acting in a compassionate manner. And when it compels democratic activists to emigrate or face imprisonment, the authorities can be credited with implementing a humane alternative to repression.

What is only beginning to be appreciated, however, is the effect of large-scale emigration on the internal atmosphere of the country. The possibility of leaving encourages all citizens to regard the regime more independently. Boris Khazanov, the pseudonym for a writer who still resides in Moscow, has remarked that for at least three years, already, I see myself in an un-believable situation. A dream which for years has drained me has become real: to leave. To leave — to escape, without looking around, without saying adieu, without wasting time on arguments and separations, to leave, and the farther the better. . . . You can sit at home all you want, not feeling the need to go out onto the street, but as soon as it reaches your con-sciousness that the door is locked and you don't have the key, your maternal home, for you, turns into a jail. . . . Even if only one hundred families left . . . the situation would not cease to appear incredible and wonderful; and such is the way it will forever remain for a generation who matured in the conviction that to leave the Soviet Union was impossible, as it is im-possible to throw a rock so high that it will not fall back to earth.

A fundamental component of the regime's control has been the inability of Soviet citizens to live elsewhere. Re-garding their own country as an enormous jail from which there is no escape, they develop a psychological dependency on the government that keeps them. Education, health care, and employment are provided by the regime, but these bene-fits can be withdrawn and no private institutions exist to employ or take care of outcasts. The individual is totally subservient to the whim of the regime. Consequently, for Soviet citizens it is both a physical and a psychological act of courage to declare oneself openly opposed to the government. Though Soviet officials have learned that emigration is the easiest right they can grant, for an ordinary citizen to demand an exit visa was, until recently, the most outlandish request imaginable.

The Kremlin cannot satisfy the principal demand of the human rights movement — to obey the Soviet constitution — without changing the nature of the regime itself. Emigration, too, may not be as uncomplicated as the government presumed. The urge to leave can be infectious. As emigration continues, increasing numbers of citizens may reach the same conclusion as the émigrés: that it is hopeless to try to effect internal reform and that emigration is a necessary path of escape. By the late 1970s, the large-scale emigration of Jews was already provoking this reaction. Citizens of German origin — those stranded on Soviet territory after the war or who lived in the Baltic states when they were annexed or who are descendants of the Volga Germans who settled in Russia during the eighteenth century — began a movement to leave. In 1972, the West German government secured an agreement from the Kremlin that has permitted between six and eight thousand people to reach West Germany every year. Armenians have also achieved a small emigration, particularly among those from Western countries who had joined their families in Soviet Armenia after World War II (when Soviet propaganda urged them "to return"). By 1980, more than ten thousand Armenians had emigrated.

Within the religious communities, too, there is a growing awareness that the authorities will not reduce their hostility toward believers. Fundamentalist Christians, most notably Pentecostals, have begun demanding the right to leave in order to practice their religion without harassment. As yet, only a handful out of the thirty thousand who have applied have received permission, but one family, the Vashchenkos, along with two of their friends, have managed to generate enormous publicity. In June 1978, three adults and four children slipped by Soviet guards and entered the American embassy in Moscow. They demanded exit visas. The Americans could not satisfy their demand, so the family, who had suffered repression in the past and feared reprisals if they left the embassy, took up residence in the lobby of the consular section. They lived there for two months until the ambassador allowed them the use of a one-room apartment in the basement. As of this writing, the Vashchenkos are still holding out in the embassy.

While the struggle to leave has involved a broad range of people within the Soviet Union, large-scale emigration is also affecting the country's isolation. Emigrants have emerged from all professions and social classes: scientists, engineers, blue-collar workers, doctors, judges, prosecutors, lawyers, teachers, even Party and government bureaucrats. Renowned cultural figures, some of whom like Mstislav Rostropovich and Victor Nekrasov had established official reputations, have also departed.

The presence of these former Soviet citizens in Europe, America, and Israel counteracts the closed nature of the regime. As sources of information, these people are an endless repository of historical and anecdotal testimony. Their memoirs and stories, their descriptions of everyday Soviet life, present a system of repression so extensive and thorough that Western observers can hardly appreciate the life they describe.

While still in prison, Vladimir Bukovsky anticipated this difficulty. He used to dream of explaining "something very important in English" to people gathered in a brilliantly lit room: "Every now and then they would politely and sympathetically nod and exclaim 'Aha!' as if they had just grasped the meaning of what I was saying. But from their faces I could see that they hadn't understood a thing." Nonetheless, as first-hand evidence accumulates, the regime will find it increasingly difficult to find articulate apologists in the West. Already there are no longer intellectuals of genuine stature — as there were in the 1930s, when Stalin destroyed millions of people — who defend the regime's internal policies.

At the same time, the establishment in the West of large communities of former Soviet citizens has an effect inside the Soviet Union. Since the Revolution, people have been taught to believe, through a mixture of propaganda and fear, that life in the West does not offer an attractive alternative to life under "triumphant socialism." Moreover, for many years contact with foreigners was severely discouraged, often by imprisonment. Now, however, former Soviet citizens live abroad. They work and raise children. They call their relatives in the Soviet Union and send letters and packages. Suddenly, the West is no longer a forbidden and alien place, only a different and unfamiliar one.

In the context of Soviet history, the goals of the human rights movement are revolutionary. But the dissidents, at least the most mature and experienced among them, have no illusions that they can overturn the government or change the course of Russian history. They regard their work more realistically. Simply put, they hope that breaches in the country's isolation and exposure of the regime's abuses will encourage the government to evolve in a more flexible, more humane manner.

The regime has reacted harshly to dissent. In 1965, Andrei Sinyavsky and Yuli Daniel were arrested for publishing their work abroad. But the publicity surrounding their case compelled the regime to reconsider. Since that time the authorities have not arrested writers solely for publishing unauthorized work abroad. Vladimir Voinovich, Alexander Zinoviev, Georgi Vladimov, and others have published novels in the West to great acclaim without facing arrest in Moscow. Roy Medvedev pursues historical research on Stalinism. Andrei Sakharov has been a primary source of information for journalists. For several years, until his forced exile in 1974, Alexander Solzhenitsyn openly defied the regime. These men could not have continued their work without the support of a wide network of *samizdat* readers who privately circulate manuscripts and who, by their interest, alert the regime that the arrest of a writer for his creative work would provoke widespread protest.

As in any political struggle, however, there have been

casualties. The government could increase repression, for reasons of its own, and by taking prisoners hope to disrupt the movement as a whole. Despite publicity and protest, the dissidents have been unable to save their arrested colleagues. But again, in the context of Soviet history, the regime has been forced to grant extraordinary concessions.

The prisoners do not simply disappear. Details of their trials or their compulsory confinement in mental hospitals reach the West. They are not forgotten or cut off completely from the outside world. Word of their protests, hunger strikes, and living conditions reaches their supporters. And when an activist dies while under detention, as happened to Yuri Galanskov, the regime is powerless to cover up its own responsibility.

Fortunately, there have also been extraordinary releases. From the regime's point of view, it was humiliating to free Leonid Plyushch directly from a psychiatric hospital or to exchange Vladimir Bukovsky for an imprisoned Chilean Communist leader. However indirectly, the government was compelled to acknowledge they were political prisoners. Three years later, in 1979, the Kremlin released five well-known prisoners — the Ukrainian Valentyn Moroz, Mark Dymshits, and Edward Kuznetsov, leaders of the aborted 1970 air hijacking, the veteran dissident Alexander Ginzburg, and the Baptist minister Georgi Vins — in exchange for two convicted Soviet spies. The releases underscored the nature of the repressive regime. Why was a Baptist minister in Siberian exile? What crime had Valentyn Moroz committed to have spent fourteen of the previous fifteen years in prison and labor camps?

The regime has learned to use imprisoned dissidents and Zionist activists for its own purposes. In some ways they have become pawns in the strategic considerations of the Soviet and Western governments. Issues like emigration and dissident trials affect the progress of arms limitation talks and trade agreements. It is an achievement of the human rights movement that dissidents who want reform or Jews who wish to emigrate or believers who want to worship freely can no longer be disregarded. They have made themselves an issue and compelled the Kremlin not to ignore them, on the one hand, or harass them, on the other, without at least incurring further exposure.

Although the human rights movement has influenced broad sectors of Soviet society, a principal weakness of its activity has been its inability to foster contact with workers. The dissidents have not been indifferent to the economic circumstances of the country's blue-collar labor force. Andrei Sakharov has written about their inadequate salaries and poor working conditions. News of strikes — over lack of bread, for example — reach journalists through dissidents who try to follow such events. And there have been many individual workers who have been imprisoned for their human rights activities.

Many factors contribute to the lack of contact between Soviet dissidents and the working class. The society is highly stratified, with a broad range of privileges separating groups by educational background and professional status. Geography also influences the isolation of many workers. Living conditions are much worse in areas far removed from the principal cities; food is frequently rationed and consumer goods are hard to find. Most dissidents are well educated, and only if they make deliberate trips to the provinces or are forced to live in Siberian exile can they see first-hand how a great portion of the country lives.

Workers, on the other hand, have no means to publicize their concerns. The existing trade unions are controlled by the authorities. Their responsibility is to maintain labor discipline and help fulfill productivity goals set by the regime. The trade unions do not make a genuine attempt to protect workers' rights. Even the traditional means of defending workers' interests, the right to strike, is not recognized by Soviet labor legislation.

The activity of the Helsinki Watch Group improved contacts with workers. Learning of the group's existence, many workers came long distances to complain to Orlov and ask for help. The Helsinki group reported on individual workers who wanted to emigrate because they could not support their families. Vladimir Klebanov, a coal miner from Donetsk, a Ukrainian city north of the Black Sea, also found Orlov in Moscow, and their discussions influenced Klebanov's future activity.

By the beginning of 1978, Klebanov and other workers, most of whom were unemployed because, they claimed, they had protested illegal or corrupt management practices, announced the formation of the Free Trade Union Association of Workers in the Soviet Union. Its forty-three founders offered membership and help to "any blue- or white-collar worker whose rights and interests are being unlawfully infringed by administrative, Soviet, Party, or juridical organs." News of the group was broadcast over the Voice of America, and other workers, looking for help, contacted Klebanov in Donetsk.

Conditions exist in the Soviet Union that, in any other country, would lead to massive labor strife. The majority of workers live in poverty. "Mass dissatisfaction with their economic situation," Valery Chalidze writes, "a feeling that their human dignity has been degraded, a feeling which is reinforced by Soviet newspaper articles representing the workers as the masters of the country" fuels the workers' unhappiness.

The regime is aware of the explosive potential of a workers' movement and has always been willing to react with force to any such development. In 1962, soldiers fired on striking workers in Novocherkassk, leaving scores dead in the street. Against Klebanov and his colleagues, however, more subtle means of repression seemed appropriate. Klebanov was picked up, declared insane, and sent to Dnepropetrovsk Special Psychiatric Hospital. Other founders of the trade union also found themselves in hospitals, prisons, and Siberian exile.

When Klebanov first met Western reporters, he commented, "How this will end we don't know." Within a few weeks he was arrested, but his efforts cannot be termed useless. Klebanov was determined to expose conditions workers face under Communist rule. His initiative encouraged others to act, and in Moscow, the dissidents began receiving new information. From the Caucasus, the Ukraine, and from workers around Moscow itself, reports of meager salaries, arbitrary dismissals, and lack of political freedom reached the Helsinki group and editors of the *Chronicle of Current Events*.

It is hard to say how far a workers' movement could develop. Unlike the dissidents, many workers, as well as activists in various non-Russian republics, do not share a philosophical or pragmatic commitment to nonviolent protest. In the provinces, harsh living conditions nurture desperate emotions. Exiled dissidents like Pavel Litvinov have been approached by workers who offer to use violence against the government. In response, dissidents must patiently explain how unsuitable violence would be against a regime immune to moral inhibitions. In addition, if for the foreseeable future the Soviet government has no need to fear violent rebellion, it is not only because the regime maintains a monopoly on arms and communication. For nearly thirty years Stalin taught the country a lesson no one will easily forget. The same fear that inhibits open dissent also keeps workers and angry minorities in line.

In Eastern Europe, the various dissident movements in Czechoslovakia in 1968 and in Poland in the 1970s relied on strong personal and organizational solidarity among workers, students, and intellectuals. These societies are more ethnically homogeneous than Soviet society; such disparate groups, although separated by levels of income and education, share a fundamental patriotism, as Poles or Czechs, and recognize the need to unite against the occupying power and its local satraps. East European dissidents have more explicitly political goals, and the activity that emerges — from attempts at direct reform, as in the Prague Spring, to attacks on Communist party headquarters in Poland — reflects the depth of their strength.

Since the crackdown and trials of 1977–1978, the Soviet human rights movement has expanded its activity, particularly in the provinces. Helsinki groups still function in Moscow and Kiev, but the Western press is preoccupied with other events, within and outside the Soviet Union, making the dissidents' struggle all the more disheartening.

The regime also began a new wave of arrests. In 1979, six members of the Ukrainian Helsinki group were arrested, including one of its founders, the science-fiction writer Oles Berdnyk. One reprisal ended in tragedy. On March 6, after a prolonged nighttime search by the KGB, the writer Mykhaylo Melnyk, a Ukrainian historian with close ties to the Helsinki group in Kiev, committed suicide. The KGB had seized his life's work — twelve volumes of scholarly research and poetry.

In Moscow, too, the dissident community was shaken by the arrest of Tatyana Velikanova, Father Gleb Yakunin, and Victor Nekipelov. A mathematician by training, Velikanova was a founding member of the Action Group for the Defense of Civil Rights. In 1974, along with Sergei Kovalyov and Tatyana Khodorovich, she publicly distributed copies of the *Chronicle of Current Events* at a press conference, announcing its resumption after an eighteen-month suspension. Among the dissidents, only Andrei Sakharov had greater moral authority than Tatyana Velikanova, but her quiet work and modest demeanor prevented her from gaining much attention in the West. By the end of 1979, she had passed two months in jail without word of her condition or the charges against her reaching her friends.

Like the human rights movement, the regime itself is in a period of transition. Brezhnev is unlikely to remain in power much longer. The average age of the ruling Politburo is now close to seventy. The country's problems at home and abroad, particularly economic stagnation, the continuing arms race, and an increasing willingness to intervene militarily, make the forthcoming period, for the dissidents especially, one of depressing uncertainty. No one expects the regime to change its policies, regardless of who assumes Brezhnev's responsibilities. But as in every dictatorship, a period of transition makes everyone a bit more wary and cautious. What may seem permissible today could lead to arrest tomorrow.

Activity among the dissidents reflects this cautious mood. Their established methods of work — exposure of abuses, protests, occasional demonstrations, meetings with Western reporters, circulation of the *Chronicle* — all continue, but in a more restrained manner than before. Many veterans of the movement are in the West or under detention. But a new generation, including the children of previous activists, is now joining the fray.

For several years, the regime has felt compelled to refer to the dissidents in official publications. Knowledge of their work has spread too far for the Kremlin publicly to ignore. In *Pravda*, after the arrest of Yuri Orlov in 1977, the authorities branded the dissidents "unconcealed enemies of socialism" who "exist only because they are supported, paid, and praised by the West." The dissidents' activity was said to confirm that "remnants of the morals and prejudices of the old society have not been completely eradicated from our life and that individual Soviet citizens still take the bait of bourgeois propaganda." After sixty years of Soviet rule, including the purges of Stalin, the forced industrialization of the country, and the isolation of its society, the regime's explanation for dissent underscores its own ideological exhaustion. The dissidents have tried, in vain, to initiate a dialogue. But the government has been unable to respond constructively or acknowledge that what irks the dissidents ought to concern them as well.

Perhaps in preparation for the Olympic games in 1980, or perhaps out of sheer impatience, the regime once again seems intent on destroying the human rights movement. It is easy to understand why. The dissidents may not have nurtured a sense of embarrassment in the Kremlin, but they have educated the world at large. It was Soviet dissidents who first relied on international agreements to explain and advance their cause. It was the dissidents who first made human rights an international issue and added such words as *samizdat, gulag,* and *dissident* to the world's vocabulary.

For the past fifteen years, the dissidents have provided a consistent and reliable means for the West to see and understand the reality of Soviet life. No other manifestation of open dissent would have been possible — by ethnic minorities or religious believers, by Zionists or Russian nationalists, by liberal writers or Soviet workers — without the example of the human rights movement. The dissidents created the first channels to the West, the phenomenon of political *samizdat,* and the example of courage in the struggle against fear. They proved that one could challenge the regime and survive, that truth provided its own strength, that law was worth defending. Their setbacks do not mark the triumph of a heartless, arrogant regime over an oppressed, intimidated people but rather a courageous struggle, however quixotic or doomed to failure, between two Russias: the Russia of violence and deceit and the Russia of justice and humanity.

POSTSCRIPT

ON JANUARY 22, 1980, Andrei Sakharov was arrested. The operation was efficiently planned and carried out. Each Tuesday afternoon an official limousine brought him to a seminar at the Physical Institute of the Academy of Sciences. But this time the car was stopped by policemen. Sakharov was placed in another vehicle and taken to the prosecutor's office.

There Alexander Rekunkov, the First Deputy Prosecutor, read Sakharov a decree of the Presidium of the Supreme Soviet, stripping him of all his state honors. Brezhnev's name appeared at the bottom of the order. (Sakharov remained a member of the Academy of Sciences, at least for a time. Under its rules, only a two-thirds majority of the members, in a secret ballot, could remove him. As an Academician, Sakharov will continue to receive a monthly stipend.) Then he was told of his banishment to Gorki, a major industrial city 250 miles east of Moscow. Because of the presence of military factories, the town is officially closed to foreigners. Elena Bonner could accompany him. He was allowed to call and tell her to be ready in two hours. Later that afternoon the couple was flown to Gorki.

The next day *Izvestia* accused Sakharov of divulging state secrets to foreign diplomats and journalists. "Sakharov had embarked on the path of direct betrayal of the interests of our motherland and the Soviet people, turned into a sworn enemy of the Socialist system and crossed over to the camp of militant anti-Communists." In conversations with journalists, the paper charged, "Sakharov repeatedly blabbed about things that any state protects as important secrets." It described his exile to Gorki as an administrative order by "competent organs," a euphemism for the KGB.

By sending Sakharov to Gorki without a trial, the regime broke its own laws that guarantee "such punishments may be imposed only by a court, after a criminal trial." But a judicial charade similar to those involving Yuri Orlov or Anatoly Shcharansky would be too inconvenient to impose on Sakharov, especially in Moscow. Administrative kidnapping was easier to arrange.

Sakharov's arrest occurred in the midst of a general crackdown on dissent. The detention of Tatyana Velikanova has already been mentioned. More than forty other activists, including religious believers, would-be emigrants, workers, and nationalists were also arrested in the final months of 1979. Some Jews who had received permission to leave have been deprived of their visas.

The regime has long wanted to arrest Sakharov or at least isolate him from dissidents and journalists. The invasion of Afghanistan provided a useful cover. Barely a week after it began, Sakharov called on the United Nations to persuade the Soviet Union to withdraw its forces. Already faced with condemnation in the General Assembly, growing resentment in the Islamic world, and a severe deterioration in relations with the United States, the regime may well have concluded that Sakharov's arrest could not make matters worse.

Once in Gorki, Sakharov learned of further restrictions. He and Elena Bonner would share a four-room apartment with a middle-aged woman whose function was not hard to guess. He was forbidden all contacts with foreigners, including correspondence and telephone conversations, as well as contacts with "criminal elements," a favored term for dissidents. Sakharov was also forbidden to leave the city limits and placed under official supervision, requiring him to report every ten days to the police.

Sakharov did not meekly accept these conditions. The day after his exile, he and Elena Bonner joined eight other activists, including members of the Moscow Helsinki Watch Group, in condemning the regime for "suppressing the independence of Afghanistan." (They had signed the statement the day before his exile, but from Gorki he let it be known he wanted it issued.)

Five days later, Elena Bonner returned to Moscow. She met with Western newsmen and under the glare of television lights handed out a statement from her husband. In it, Sakharov described his arrest and the conditions of his life in Gorki. He then listed six areas of the world — southern Africa, Cuba, and Ethiopia, the Middle East, Europe, and Afghanistan — where Soviet activity was contributing to international crises. He reminded the world of colleagues whose arrest did not provoke headlines. "The actions of the authorities against me in this situation are aimed at making the continuation of my public activities completely impossible," he explained. "They are aimed at humiliating and discrediting me and at the same time making possible further repressive measures against all dissident groups in the country, with less possibility of the world's finding out about them, and further international adventures . . . But I am prepared to stand public and open trial. I do not need a gilded cage. I need the right to fulfill my public duty."

Sakharov's exile generated protest around the world. American and European scientists demonstrated their support, many of them reiterating an earlier pledge, taken after the trials of Orlov and Shcharansky, not to participate in exchanges with Soviet colleagues. Jacques Chaban-Delmas, the head of the French National Assembly, cut short a ten-day visit to the Soviet Union. "As a guest of the Soviet leaders, I cannot intercede in this case without interfering in the internal affairs of the U.S.S.R.," he declared. "Being unable either to speak or to keep silent, I consider myself personally obliged to return to France as soon as possible."

Nineteen Soviet writers and artists, including several who were not known as dissidents, issued an appeal the following week. "To accuse Andrei Dimitriyevich Sakharov of 'subversive activities' is a blasphemous lie," they announced. "The name Andrei Sakharov has become a synonym of nobility of spirit, heroism, and humanism."

Bella Akhmadulina, too, a member of the Union of Soviet Writers and regarded as one of the finest Russian poets of this century, wrote a uniquely personal appeal. Her statement on Sakharov, in free verse, said:

When a man intercedes for humanity, obvi-
    ously he is not afraid of anything. He is
    afraid for humanity.
But I am only a human being. And I am
    afraid, afraid for him.
And also for humanity.
What I write now is not disinterested. But
    how else could I survive.
Strange: there are not other academicians to
    intercede for Academician Sakharov.
Just me: Bella Akhmadulina, honorary
    member of the American Academy of
    Arts and Letters.

Despite these appeals, the regime did not relax its pressure. While Elena Bonner was in Moscow, two men pretending to be drunken workers came to Sakharov's apartment and drew a pistol. "They threatened to make an Afghanistan out of my apartment and wreak complete havoc," Sakharov wrote. "They said: 'Don't think you're going to be here for long. There's a place in a psychiatric hospital thirty kilometers from Gorki that's ready for you.'"

Two days later, a local prosecutor warned him not to make any more statements. In case of further violations, Sakharov was told, his place and conditions of exile could be changed and the sanctions could also be applied against his wife.

At a time of international crisis, with the invasion of Afghanistan, the upheaval in Iran, and the impending Olympic boycott, Soviet dissidents find themselves more vulnerable and isolated than at any time since their movement began. Perhaps inside the Kremlin the passing of power from Brezhnev to his successors has already begun and is reinforcing hard-line attitudes more strongly than anyone anticipated. It is too early to know for sure.

The human rights movement is a part of Soviet life and only complete reform of the system, which no one expects, or a return to outright Stalinist methods, which many fear, could put the movement to an end.

Joshua Rubenstein
February 12, 1980

NOTES ON SOURCES

I WOULD like to acknowledge and thank the following people for sharing their first-hand experience with me. This book could not have been written without their cooperation.

Mikhail Agursky
Lyuda Alexeeva
Andrei Amalrik
Anthony Astrachan
Irina Belogorodskaya
Vladimir Bukovsky
Valery Chalidze
Vadim Delone
Alexander Esenin-Volpin
Alexander Feldman
Galya Gabai
Igor Golomshtok
Natalya Gorbanevskaya
Pyotr Grigorenko
Zinaida Grigorenko
Dina Kaminskaya
Victor Krasin
Edward Kuznetsov
Maya Litvinov
Pavel Litvinov
Tatyana Litvinov
Kronid Lyubarsky

Zhores Medvedev
Victor Nekrasov
Boris Orlov
Alexander Piatigorsky
Tatyana Plyushch
Inez Rubin
Vitaly Rubin
Natalya Sadomskaya
Dmitry Segal
Boris Shragin
Marya Sinyavsky
Masha Slonim
Michael Steiglitz
Julius Telesin
Boris Tsukerman
Valentin Turchin
Tomas Venclova
Marina Voikhanskaya
Lidia Voronina
the late Anatoly Yakobson
Efrem Yankelevich
Silva Zalmanson

In addition to interviews, I relied on three sources of information for primary material: the *Chronicle of Current*

Events, A Chronicle of Human Rights in the U.S.S.R., and the *Samizdat Archive.*

The first eleven issues of the *Chronicle of Current Events* are contained in Peter Reddaway's compilation, *Uncensored Russia.* Subsequent issues have been translated and published by Amnesty International.

A Chronicle of Human Rights in the U.S.S.R. has been published since 1973 by Khronika Press in New York. Its editors include Valery Chalidze, Edward Kline, Pavel Litvinov, and Peter Reddaway. Khronika Press offers *A Chronicle of Human Rights* in English and in Russian. It also publishes the *Chronicle of Current Events* in Russian.

The *Samizdat Archive* is compiled by the staff of Radio Liberty in Munich. It is reproduced by the Center for Slavic and East European Studies at the Ohio State University in Columbus.

BIBLIOGRAPHY

Amalrik, Andrei. *Involuntary Journey to Siberia.* Translated by Manya Harari and Max Hayward. New York: Harcourt Brace Jovanovich, 1970.

———. *Will the Soviet Union Survive until 1984?* New York: Harper & Row, 1970.

Anderson, Thornton. *Russian Political Thought: An Introduction.* Ithaca, N.Y.: Cornell University Press, 1967.

Belotserkovsky, Vadim. "Soviet Dissenters." *Partisan Review* 42, no. 1 (1975), pp. 35–59.

Berman, Harold J., and Spindler, James W. *Soviet Criminal Law and Procedure: The RFSFR Codes.* 2d ed. Cambridge, Mass.: Harvard University Press, 1972.

Bosley, Keith; Pospielovsky, Dimitry; and Sapiets, Janis (editors and translators). *Russia's Underground Poets.* New York: Praeger, 1969.

Browne, Michael, ed. *Ferment in the Ukraine.* London: Macmillan, 1971.

Brumberg, Abraham, ed. *In Quest of Justice: Protest and Dissent in the Soviet Union Today.* New York: Praeger, 1970.

———. *Russia under Khrushchev.* New York: Praeger, 1962.

Bukovsky, Vladimir. *To Build a Castle: My Life as a Dissenter.* Translated by Michael Scammell. New York: Viking, 1978.

Carlisle, Olga. *Poets on Street Corners.* New York: Random House, 1968.

SOVIET DISSIDENTS

Chaadaev, Peter. *The Major Works of Peter Chaadaev.* Translated by Raymond T. McNally. Notre Dame, Ind.: Notre Dame Press, 1969.

Chalidze, Valery. *To Defend These Rights.* Translated by Guy Daniels. New York: Random House, 1974.

Chornovil, Vyacheslav. *The Chornovil Papers.* New York: McGraw-Hill, 1968.

Coates, Ken, ed. *Détente and Socialist Democracy: A Discussion with Roy Medvedev.* New York: Monad Press, 1976.

Cole, William. "Interviews with Andrei Amalrik, Vladimir Bukovsky, and Pyotr Yakir." Translated by David Floyd. *Survey* 77 (Autumn 1970): 128-145.

Conquest, Robert. *Kolyma: The Arctic Death Camps.* New York: Viking, 1978.

———. *The Nation Killers: The Soviet Deportation of Nationalities.* New York: Macmillan, 1970.

———. *The Pasternak Affair.* Philadelphia: Lippincott, 1962.

Crankshaw, Edward. *Khrushchev, A Career.* New York: Viking, 1966.

Custine, Adolphe, Marquis de. *Journey for Our Time.* Edited and translated by Phyllis Penn Kohler. New York: Pellegrini and Cudahy, 1951.

Dudintsev, Vladimir. *Not by Bread Alone.* Translated by E. Bone. New York: Dutton, 1957.

Ehrenburg, Ilya. *Memoirs: 1921-1941.* Translated by Tatania Shebunina and Yvonne Kapp. Cleveland: World, 1963.

———. *Men, Years, Life.* Translated by Tatania Shebunina and Yvonne Kapp. Cleveland: World, 1965.

———. *Post-War Years, 1945-1954.* Translated by Tatania Shebunina and Yvonne Kapp. Cleveland: World, 1965.

Esenin-Volpin, Alexander. *A Leaf of Spring.* Translated by George Reavey. New York: Praeger, 1961.

Etkind, Efim. *Notes of a Non-Conspirator.* Translated by Peter France. New York: Oxford University Press, 1978.

Fireside, Harvey. *Soviet Psychoprisons.* New York: Norton, 1979.

Gerstenmaier, Cornelia. *The Voices of the Silent.* Translated by Susan Hecker. New York: Hart, 1972.

Gorbanevskaya, Natalia. *Red Square at Noon.* Translated by Alexander Lieven. New York: Holt, Rinehart and Winston, 1972.

Grigorenko, Pyotr. *The Grigorenko Papers*. Boulder, Colo.: Westview Press, 1976.

Hayward, Max, and Blake, Patricia, eds. *Halfway to the Moon: New Writing from Russia*. New York: Holt, Rinehart and Winston, 1964.

Hayward, Max, ed. *On Trial: The Soviet State Versus "Abram Tertz" and "Nikolai Arzhak."* New York: Harper & Row, 1966.

Herzen, Alexander. *My Past and Thoughts* (abridged). Translated by Constance Garnett. New York: Vintage Books, 1974.

Johnson, Priscilla, and Labedz, Leopold, eds. *Khrushchev and the Arts: The Politics of Soviet Culture 1962–1964*. Cambridge, Mass.: MIT Press, 1965.

Kaiser, Robert G. *Russia: The People and the Power*. New York: Atheneum, 1976.

Kennan, George F. *The Marquis de Custine and His "Russia in 1839."* Princeton, N.J.: Princeton University Press, 1971.

Khazanov, Boris [pseud.]. "Novaya Rossiya." *Vremya i My*, June 1976, pp. 135–146.

Kirk, Irina. *Profiles in Russian Resistance*. New York: Quadrangle, 1975.

Kuznetsov, Edward. *Prison Diaries*. Translated by Howard Spier. New York: Stein and Day, 1975.

Laber, Jeri. "The Real Solzhenitsyn." *Commentary*, May 1974, pp. 32–35.

Litvinov, Pavel. *The Demonstration in Pushkin Square*. Translated by Manya Harari. Boston: Gambit, 1969.

Litvinov, Pavel, ed. *The Trial of the Four*. English text edited by Peter Reddaway. Translated by Janis Sapiets, Hilary Sternberg, and Daniel Weissbort. New York: Viking, 1972.

Lowenthal, Richard. "East-West Détente and the Future of Soviet Jewry." *Soviet Jewish Affairs* 3, no. 1, pp. 20–25.

Mandelstam, Nadezhda. *Hope Against Hope*. Translated by Max Hayward. New York: Atheneum, 1970.

Marchenko, Anatoly. *From Tarusa to Siberia*. Edited by Joshua Rubenstein. Royal Oak, Mich.: Strathcona, 1980.

––––––. *My Testimony*. Translated by Michael Scammell. New York: Dutton, 1969.

Medvedev, Roy. "The Future of Soviet Dissent." *Index of Censorship* 8, no. 2 (March-April 1979), pp. 25–31.

———. *Let History Judge.* Translated by Collen Taylor. Edited by David Joravsky and Georges Haupt. New York: Knopf, 1971.

———. *On Socialist Democracy.* Translated and edited by Ellen de Kadt. New York: Knopf, 1975.

———. "Problems of Democratization and Détente." *New Left Review,* January-February 1974, pp. 27–40.

———. "What Lies Ahead for Us?" *New Left Review,* September-December 1974, pp. 61–74.

Medvedev, Roy, and Medvedev, Zhores. *A Question of Madness.* Translated by Ellen de Kadt. New York: Knopf, 1971.

———. *Khrushchev: The Years in Power.* Translated by Andrew R. Durkin. New York: Columbia University Press, 1976.

Medvedev, Zhores. *The Medvedev Papers.* Translated by Vera Rich. New York: St. Martin's, 1971.

———. *The Rise and Fall of T. D. Lysenko.* Translated by I. Michael Lerner. New York: Columbia University Press, 1969.

———. *Ten Years after Ivan Denisovich.* Translated by Hilary Sternberg. New York: Knopf, 1973.

Meerson-Aksenov, Michael. "The Jewish Exodus and Soviet Society." In *Essays on Human Rights: Contemporary Issues and Jewish Perspectives.* Edited by David Sidorsky. Philadelphia: Jewish Publication Society, 1979.

Moroz, Valentyn. *Boomerang: The Works of Valentyn Moroz.* Edited by Yaroslav Bihun. Baltimore: Smoloskyp, 1974.

Nekipelov, Victor. *Institute of Fools: Notes from Serbsky.* Translated by Marco Carynnyk and Marta Horban, New York: Farrar, Straus and Giroux, 1980.

Nekrich, Alexander. *June 22, 1941: Soviet Historians and the German Invasion.* Compiled by Vladimir Petrov. Columbia, S.C.: University of South Carolina Press, 1968.

———. *The Punished Peoples.* Translated by George Saunders. New York: Norton, 1978.

Pasternak, Boris. *Doctor Zhivago.* Translated by Max Hayward and Manya Harari. New York: Pantheon, 1958.

Plyushch, Leonid. *History's Carnival.* Translated by Marco Carynnyk. New York: Harcourt Brace Jovanovich, 1979.

Podrabinek, Alexander. *Punitive Medicine.* Translated by Alexander Lehrman. Ann Arbor, Mich.: Karoma, 1979.

Reddaway, Peter, and Bloch, Sidney. *Psychiatric Terror.* New York: Basic Books, 1977.

Reddaway, Peter, ed. *Uncensored Russia: Protest and Dissent in the Soviet Union.* New York: American Heritage, 1972.

Rosecrance, Richard. "Détente or Entente." *Foreign Affairs*, April 1975, pp. 464–481.

Rothberg, Abraham. *The Heirs of Stalin.* Ithaca, N.Y.: Cornell University Press, 1972.

Sakharov, Andrei. *Alarm and Hope.* Edited by Efrem Yankelevich and Alfred Friendly, Jr. New York: Knopf, 1978.

———. "In Answer to Solzhenitsyn." *New York Review of Books*, June 13, 1974, pp. 3–6.

———. *My Country and the World.* Translated by Guy Daniels. New York: Vintage, 1975.

———. *Sakharov Speaks.* Edited by Harrison Salisbury. New York: Vintage, 1974.

Saunders, George, ed. *Samizdat: Voices of the Soviet Opposition.* New York: Monad, 1974.

Schapiro, Leonard. *Rationalism and Nationalism in Russian Nineteenth Century Political Thought.* New Haven, Conn.: Yale University Press, 1967.

Schindler, Colin. *Exit Visa.* London: Bachman and Turner, 1978.

Schroeter, Leonard. *The Last Exodus.* New York: Universe, 1974.

Shcharansky, Avital, with Ben-Joseph, Ilana. *Next Year in Jerusalem.* Translated by Stefani Hoffman. New York: William Morrow, 1979.

Shostakovich, Dmitri. *Testimony: The Memoirs of Dmitri Shostakovich.* Edited by Solomon Volkov. Translated by Antonina W. Bouis. New York: Harper & Row, 1979.

Shragin, Boris. *The Challenge of the Spirit.* Translated by P. S. Falla. New York: Knopf, 1978.

Sinyavsky, Andrei [Abram Tertz]. *Fantastic Stories.* Translated by Max Hayward and Ronald Hingley. New York: Grosset & Dunlap, 1967.

——. *The Makepeace Experiment.* Translated by Manya Harari. New York: Pantheon, 1965.

——. *The Trial Begins* and *On Socialist Realism.* Translated by Max Hayward and George Dennis. New York: Vintage, 1965.

——. *A Voice from the Chorus.* Translated by Max Hayward and Kyril FitzLyon. New York: Farrar, Straus and Giroux, 1976.

Smith, Hedrick. *The Russians.* New York: Quadrangle, 1976.

Solzhenitsyn, Alexander. *Détente: Prospects for Democracy and Dictatorship.* New Brunswick, N.J.: Transaction Books, 1976.

——. *A World Split Apart.* Translated by Irina Alberti. New York: Harper & Row, 1978.

——. *The Gulag Archipelago, One.* Translated by Thomas Whitney. New York: Harper & Row, 1974.

——. *The Gulag Archipelago, Two.* Translated by Thomas Whitney. New York: Harper & Row, 1975.

——. *The Gulag Archipelago, Three.* Translated by Harry Willetts. New York: Harper & Row, 1978.

——. *Letter to Soviet Leaders.* Translated by Hilary Sternberg. London: Collins/Harvill, in association with Index on Censorship, 1974.

——. *One Day in the Life of Ivan Denisovich.* Translated by Max Hayward and Ronald Hingley. New York: Praeger, 1963.

——. "Peace and Violence." New York *Times,* October 15, 1973.

Solzhenitsyn, Alexander; Agursky, Mikhail; B., A. [pseud.]; Barabanov, Evgeny; Borisov, Vadim; Korsakov, F. [pseud.]; and Shafarevich, Igor. *From Under the Rubble.* Translated by A. M. Brock, Milada Haigh, Marita Sapiets, Hilary Sternberg, and Harry Willetts under the direction of Michael Scammell. Boston: Little, Brown, 1975.

Stern, August, ed. *The USSR vs. Dr. Mikhail Stern.* Translated by Marco Carynnyk. New York: Urizen, 1977.

Taylor, Telford; Dershowitz, Alan; Fletcher, George; Lipson, Leon; and Stein, Melvin. *Courts of Terror.* New York: Knopf, 1976.

Tőkés, Rudolf L., ed. *Dissent in the USSR.* Baltimore: Johns Hopkins, 1975.

Tőkés, Rudolf. "The Dissidents' Détente Debate." *The New Leader,* March 4, 1974, pp. 11-13.

Ulam, Adam B. *Stalin: The Man and His Era.* New York: Viking, 1973.

U.S., Congress, Senate, Committee on Foreign Relations, *Détente*, 93d Congress, 2d sess., August 15, 20, and 21, September 10, 12, 18, 19, 24, and 25, and October 1 and 8, 1974.

U.S., Congress, Commission on Security and Cooperation in Europe, *Implementation of the Helsinki Accords, The Right to Citizenship in the Soviet Union*, 95th Congress, 2d sess., May 4, 1978.

U.S., Congress, Commission on Security and Cooperation in Europe, *Implementation of the Helsinki Accords, Soviet Law and the Helsinki Monitors*, 95th Congress, 2d sess., June 6, 1978.

U.S., Congress, Commission on Security and Cooperation in Europe, *Implementation of the Helsinki Accords, Repercussions of the Trials of the Helsinki Monitors in the USSR*, 95th Congress, 2d sess., July 11, 1978.

U.S., Congress, Commission on Security and Cooperation in Europe, *Implementation of the Helsinki Accords, Aleksandr Ginzburg on the Human Rights Situation in the U.S.S.R.*, 96th Congress, 1st sess., May 11, 1979.

U.S., Congress, Commission on Security and Cooperation in Europe, *Reports of Helsinki-Accord Monitors in the Soviet Union.* Edited by the staff of the commission. February 24 and June 3, 1977, and November 7, 1978.

U.S., Congress, Commission on Security and Cooperation in Europe, *Reports of Helsinki-Accord Monitors in the Soviet Union, The Right To Know, The Right To Act*, May 1978.

U.S., Congress, Commission on Security and Cooperation in Europe, *Reports of Helsinki-Accord Monitors in the Soviet Union, Soviet Law and the Helsinki Monitors*, June 6, 1978.

Yakir, Pyotr. *A Childhood in Prison.* Edited by Robert Conquest. Coward, McCann & Geoghegan, 1973.

Vladimov, Georgi. *Faithful Ruslan.* Translated by Michael Glenny. New York: Simon and Schuster, 1979.

Voinovich, Vladimir. *In Plain Russian.* Translated by Richard Lourie. New York: Farrar, Straus and Giroux, 1979.

———. *The Ivankiad.* Translated by David Lapeza. New York: Farrar, Straus and Giroux, 1977.

———. *The Life and Extraordinary Adventures of Private Ivan Chonkin.* Translated by Richard Lourie, New York: Farrar, Straus and Giroux, 1977.

Voronel, Aleksander, and Yakhot, Viktor, eds. *I Am a Jew: Essays on Jewish Identity in the Soviet Union.* New York: Anti-Defamation League of B'nai B'rith, 1973.

Walicki, Andrzej. *The Slavophile Controversy.* Translated by Hilda Andrews-Rusiecka. Oxford: Clarendon Press, 1975.

Zinoviev, Alexander. *The Yawning Heights.* Translated by Gordon Clough. New York: Random House, 1979.

INDEX